Rethinking Interiority

SUNY series in Contemporary Continental Philosophy

Dennis J. Schmidt, editor

Rethinking Interiority
Phenomenological Approaches

Edited by
Elodie Boublil *and* Antonio Calcagno

Published by State University of New York Press, Albany

© 2023 State University of New York

All rights reserved

Printed in the United States of America

No part of this book may be used or reproduced in any manner whatsoever without written permission. No part of this book may be stored in a retrieval system or transmitted in any form or by any means including electronic, electrostatic, magnetic tape, mechanical, photocopying, recording, or otherwise without the prior permission in writing of the publisher.

For information, contact State University of New York Press, Albany, NY
www.sunypress.edu

Library of Congress Cataloging-in-Publication Data

Names: Boublil, Élodie, editor. | Calcagno, Antonio, 1969– editor.
Title: Rethinking interiority : phenomenological approaches / Elodie Boublil, Antonio Calcagno.
Description: Albany : State University of New York Press, 2023. | Series: SUNY series in contemporary continental philosophy | Includes bibliographical references and index.
Identifiers: LCCN 2022037712 | ISBN 9781438493138 (hardcover : alk. paper) | ISBN 9781438493145 (ebook) | ISBN 9781438493121 (pbk. : alk. paper)
Subjects: LCSH: Phenomenology. | Intentionality (Philosophy)
Classification: LCC B829.5 .R488 2023 | DDC 142/.7—dc23/eng/20230315
LC record available at https://lccn.loc.gov/2022037712

Contents

Acknowledgments — vii

Introduction — 1
   Elodie Boublil and Antonio Calcagno

Part One: Interiority and Subjectivity

Chapter 1
The Spatiality of Acosmic Interiority: A Phenomenological Attempt to Rethink "Lived Space" — 17
   Carla Canullo

Chapter 2
Interiority, Exteriority, Being-In: A Concise Analysis — 35
   Hans Rainer Sepp

Chapter 3
Self-Owning, Self-Transparency, and Inner Nudity: Hedwig Conrad-Martius on Interiority — 55
   Christina M. Gschwandtner

Part Two: Interiority, Alterity, and Transcendence

Chapter 4
"*In interiore homine*": The Presence and Absence of the Divine in the Human — 73
   Angela Ales Bello

Chapter 5
"It Is No Longer I Who Do It": Interiority and the Foreign-Body   85
   Brian W. Becker

Chapter 6
Inner Distance and Surreptitious Patience According to
Jean-Louis Chrétien   103
   Emmanuel Housset

Part Three: Interiority and World: Metaphysical and Ethical Applications

Chapter 7
The Self-Awakening (*jikaku* [自覚]) from the Citadel of the Self:
Everything is Interconnected with Everything   119
   Steve G. Lofts

Chapter 8
Ultima Ratio Decisions and Absolute Interiority: From Hegel to
Bonhoeffer   143
   Christian Lotz

Chapter 9
Critical Phenomenology and the Rehabilitation of Interiority   159
   Ann V. Murphy

Chapter 10
Joy, Interiority, and Individuation: A Steinian Account   175
   Elodie Boublil

Chapter 11
Gerda Walther's Phenomenology of Interiority and the Idea of a
Fundamental Essence   195
   Antonio Calcagno

Contributors   213

Index   217

Acknowledgments

This book developed during the pandemic, which caused many challenges. We are grateful to all the contributors for their hard work and patience. We also acknowledge the editors and staff at SUNY Press for their dedication and persistence, especially Dr. Michael A. Rinella.

We would like to thank the following granting institutions for their generous support during the various stages of this book project: the Alexander von Humboldt Foundation, the Social Sciences and Humanities Research Council of Canada, and the Academic Dean's Office at King's University College at UWO.

Introduction

ELODIE BOUBLIL AND ANTONIO CALCAGNO

In his liminal essay on existence and hermeneutics, Paul Ricoeur denounces the philosophical illusion that consists of either absolutizing the ego and the self—along the lines of Cartesian methodological doubt—or reducing all realities to their natural or historical evidence. The polarization of the "for-itself" and the "in-itself," the reflexive subject and the outer world of objects and matter found throughout the history of Western thought, has led philosophy to be forgetful of its paradoxical function: to bring to light and to language the complexity of lived experiences whose precise articulations cannot be exhausted by speech or symbols. In this original state of wonder before the world's and the other's concrete reality, we are often led back to question the status of our interpretations and reflections. In delineating the hermeneutics of such trajectories, Ricoeur reminds us of the necessity of digging further, always, into the layers of interpretation through which we apprehend and live our interactions:

> The *cogito* is not only a truth as vain as it is invincible; we must add, as well, that it is like an empty place which has, from all time, been occupied by a false *cogito*. We have indeed learned, from all the exegetic disciplines and from psychoanalysis, that so-called immediate consciousness is first of all "false consciousness." Marx, Nietzsche, and Freud have taught us to unmask its tricks. Henceforth it becomes necessary to join a critique of false consciousness to any rediscovery of the subject of the *cogito* in the documents of its life; a philosophy of reflection must be just the opposite of a philosophy of consciousness.[1]

Continental philosophy, especially hermeneutics, phenomenology, and post-structuralism, beyond their methodological and ontological disagreements, has nonetheless manifested a common effort to "deconstruct" the *cogito* and renounce its solipsist attempt to discover objective truth in the solitary act of its reflections.

The rejection of the Cartesian cogito and its ambition to grasp the infinite in the contemplation of its own possibilities is motivated by the existential acknowledgment of our finitude and the opaqueness of our desires and motivations. From a historical point of view, the philosophical and epistemological separation of the soul from the *psyche* in the post-Nietzschean world of subjective values and meanings expressed this repatriation of the spiritual dimension within the thickness of its embodied expressions. In this sense, the philosophical question of interiority seems to have been marginalized, if not relegated to the philosophy of religion, becoming itself, as tantamount to speculating on the soul, a matter of faith. Moreover, the self has also been denounced as a fallacy, as if it were meant to designate the "I" that dwells in one's interiority.

However, such a philosophical shortcut, which would read the question of the self's constitution in continental philosophy along the lines of a dichotomy between interiority and exteriority, misses precisely the complexity to which the hermeneutics of Ricoeur and others point, as well as the intertwining between the anthropological, the metaphysical, and the ethical levels of our experience that forbids us to reduce the subject either to its ability to reflect and constitute meaning or to its failure to master completely the forces and the life that make it exist. In other words, the contemporary primacy given to space and exteriority[2] and the consequent rejection of interiority reveal a misunderstanding about what these dimensions refer to once they are mapped out as territories rather than lived-through experiences. The constructive and positive part of the task proposed by Ricoeur, namely the "rediscovery of the subject of *cogito*," is yet to be undertaken.

Certainly, the spatial metaphor distinguishing exteriority from interiority has been used consistently throughout the history of philosophy, as it is closely linked to the affective life that inhabits the human psyche. As Jean-Louis Chrétien observes,

> Not only thought, but affectivity itself can only be understood spatially: anguish constricts, contracts, and petrifies, joy and hope expand, dilate, mobilize, this being so little metaphorical that

> the narrow or the broad, absolutely speaking, are not physically observable (on what scale and by what measure?), but originally existential and affective terms. There is no need in this to want to escape our condition, any more than to see it as a degradation. But of course, interior space should not be hypostatized as if it always existed by itself but led back to acts of speech and consciousness which open it up to various horizons.³

In other words, the inner world points to our ability to live our experiences through our individuated bodies and, at the same time, distantiate ourselves from that very experience by reflecting on it.

The emphasis on spatiality is related to the necessity to delineate and communicate the content of the experience that is described, and it fits with the movement of "return" implied by reflection and introspection. This framework indicates the paradoxical dynamics of a "space" that is yet never fixed or "hypostatized" and that expands and retracts itself as it breathes in and out its experiences of the surrounding world. Consequently, one of the major contributions of Chrétien's work, and of the phenomenological work on interiority for which Ricoeur's diagnosis calls, is precisely to cancel the dichotomy or strict separation between two allegedly heterogenous domains, namely interiority and exteriority. As Heidegger already explained in his characterization of Dasein: "For the Dasein there is no outside, for which reason it is also absurd to talk about an inside."⁴ In fact, Heidegger refers here to the very structure of intentionality brought to light by phenomenology and according to which subjects as monads are not closed off entities—with or without windows—but rather always already engaged and attuned to the world through their relations to objects and other subjects. The task, then, as Ricoeur mentions, lies more in a critique of the philosophy of consciousness proposed by transcendental idealism than in a rejection of the individuating and individuated imprint on the lifeworld left by the self through its words, feelings, values, and actions.

Consequently, reopening the question of "interiority" means rethinking these dynamics of alteration and appropriation that constitute the subject and its interpretations, while analyzing these dynamics in relation to what precisely resists and transcends them: the lifeworld, the other, or God. Recovering one's inner dimension implies a recognition that it is "already always there" as the inner world of experiences and meanings that infuse, and are manifest in, the expressions of the lived body, the intentionality of the sentiment, or the constitution of values. A quick reading of Maurice Merleau-Ponty's foreword to the *Phenomenology of the Perception* might lead us to believe his critique of Augustine is a condemnation of interiority:

> The world is there prior to every analysis that I could give of it, and it would be artificial to derive it from a series of syntheses that would first link sensations and the perspectival appearances of the object together, whereas both of these are in fact products of the analysis and must not have existed prior to it. Reflective analysis believes it moves in the reverse direction along the path of a previous constitution and meets up with—in the "inner man," as Saint Augustine says—a constituting power that it itself has always been. Thus, reflection carries itself along and places itself back within an invulnerable subjectivity, prior to being and time. Yet this is a naïveté, or if one prefers, an incomplete reflection that loses an awareness of its own beginning.[5]

Merleau-Ponty's claim consists less in denying the very experience of interiority than in reconnecting it with the expressivity of the flesh—in all its dimensions—thereby overcoming both idealism and materialism. According to Merleau-Ponty, materialism and idealism suffer from the same reductive gesture that leads to objectification and misses the dynamic and vivid dimensions of human experience: "While the living body became an interior without an exterior, subjectivity became an interior without an exterior, that is, an impartial spectator. The naturalism of science and the spiritualism of the universal constituting subject, to which reflection upon science leads, share in a certain leveling out of experience: standing before the constituting I, the empirical Myselves are merely objects."[6] A similar diagnosis can be found in the working notes of the *Visible and the Invisible*, written fifteen years after the publication of *Phenomenology of Perception*, in which Merleau-Ponty insists on the need to describe "the spiritual part" of the human being and characterize phenomenologically the interiority of Being itself: to "redescribe the all interhuman and even spiritual life."[7]

As a result, Augustine's words, according to which God is "more inner to me than I am," sound less outdated than they seem and point to a profound metaphysical and anthropological experience of an account of interiority that resists the self-transparency of the Cartesian cogito while it opens a dimension in which encountering resistance and opacity, or conversely a vivid presence, seems like a new form of *epoché*. To Augustine, the revelation of interiority precisely overcomes the subject's attempt to consider itself the source of all acts and realities. As Chrétien explains, "The way to interiority, to the center of the self, far from leading to recognizing oneself as a source, invites me to go beyond what I have higher or deeper, to discover myself, in the strong sense, inhabited or inhabitable by a presence other than mine."[8] And further, "the path to interiority is therefore not the loss of the immense, but the plunge into an even more disconcerting immensity, because its excess is in me, it is me. The Augustinian privilege of interiority does not lie in excluding exteriority, but in including and exceeding it."[9]

In other words, a closer consideration of our lived-through experience of time and intersubjectivity leads us to go beyond the spatial and sequential figuration operated by diachronic consciousness and turn to the critical transformation and individuation a renewed account of interiority may generate both at the personal and collective levels. This non-objectifying account of interiority may fit well with what Ricoeur calls the dimension of the "sentiment," which describes a qualitative relation to the world, to oneself and others, at the intersection of the cognitive and the affective domain, beyond the dichotomy between mind and body—a relation that intertwines the "intentional" and the "intimate" (*l'intentionnel et l'intime*) and features the being-in-the-world of a vulnerable subjectivity, marked by its openness to life and others:

> Feeling is the felt manifestation of a relationship to the world that is deeper than that of the representation which institutes the polarity of subject and object. This relationship to the world goes through all these secret threads, "stretched" between us and beings, which we precisely call "tendencies." We can only grasp these pre-predicative, pre-reflexive, pre-objective links in two broken languages, that of behavior, that of feelings; but they are the common root of these two languages; a tendency is both the objective direction of conduct as feeling; the felt manifestation of that "to what" is approaching, "far from what" is moving away, "against what" our desire fights.[10]

One may already find this intertwining of intentionality and intimacy and this porosity over against which desire constitutes itself in the phenomenological descriptions of empathy (*Einfühlung*) elaborated by Edmund Husserl, Edith Stein, or Erwin Straus. Indeed, the phenomenon of empathy reveals a phenomenon of interaffectivity and intercorporeity that does not abolish the frontier between the inner world and the outer/other world. Rather, it points to a relational ontology—a kind of alterology—that makes the other really present to the self as other, as the one that paradoxically opposes itself as other yet communicates its feelings and inner world to the subject.

Erwin Straus also described a process of *Einfühlung* with the world itself—a process that overcomes, as well, the dichotomy between interiority and exteriority without merging plurality and difference into one single identical and homogenous world. Inner states relate us to the world. They are like dynamic shades that shape the subject's individuation process as well as the world: "The states of mind hidden in the interior are not for us isolated states of mind, separated from the world, locked in their interiority: they all have a communicable meaning. . . . The states of mind hidden in the interior are not in themselves interior states, they are in communication with the world, and are not thoughts about it."[11]

This universal form of sympathy is not another form of hidden idealism or panpsychism but rather the utmost reality felt through human interactions. In other words, instead of locking down the subject, interiority reveals the interdependency and connection between it and other beings in such a way that the latter are presented to the self without abolishing its sense of radical freedom and individuation. One hypothesis to be investigated could be phrased as follows: overcoming the philosophy of objectifying consciousness clears the way for new accounts of the self that are dissociated neither from the lifeworld nor from the ethical need for personal conscience actualized through human agency.

As this volume will show, these various layers (metaphysical, anthropological, and ethical) can offer a promising renewal of the question of interiority. We have briefly sketched a reorientation of the philosophical reflection that enables it to question further: What can interiority bring to current debates in critical phenomenology, as well as in social and political philosophy? The lived-through experience of shared alienating feelings confronts the subject with the inner creative resources they can use and appropriate for themselves and with others to transform their environment and lifeworld. Also, and more fundamentally, a reflection on interiority opens a range of considerations on the nature of our relation to the lifeworld and other living beings.

Specifically, this volume examines the constitutive aspects of interiority, including the lived body, subjectivity, affectivity (e.g., joy), gender, power, intersubjectivity, world, meaning, God, and transcendence. The essays not only contribute to an understanding of the rich, constitutive aspects of interiority but also mine and expose new and/or understudied phenomenological sources, from recent interventions in French phenomenology to insights from early women phenomenologists including Edith Stein, Gerda Walther, and Hedwig Conrad-Martius. The limits of interiority will be explored by engaging with Japanese philosophy while also teasing out social and ethical implications that stem from a phenomenological account of interiority. To this end, the volume is divided into three parts: interiority and subjectivity, alterity and transcendence, and interiority and world.

Part 1 explores the relationship between interiority and what it means to experience oneself as a subject, an I and/or a self. Starting from a renewed investigation of the main authors of the phenomenological tradition, namely Husserl and Heidegger, this section further explores phenomenological approaches to interiority and the self by referring to the works of Conrad-Martius and Henry, who both investigated our inner life in contrast with corporeality, affectivity, and the general phenomenon of incarnation.

Carla Canullo's "The Spatiality of Acosmic Interiority: A Phenomenological Attempt to Rethink 'Lived Space'" presents a new account of what it means to live spatiality. Interiority has often been associated with the intimacy of the subject and understood as the opposite of exteriority. Consequently, it is thought to have emerged, for the most part, from the inside/outside opposition and the Kantian distinction between time/inner sense and space/outer sense, and its fate has been linked so closely to the subject's fate that it has been undone by its own crisis. To rethink interiority, Canullo suggests we leave behind this conception in order to grasp interiority and the subject together within a spatiality that characterizes the subject's interiority conceived as a "lived space." She argues that the Husserlian conception of interiority is largely premised on positing a distinction between the inner and outer, the inside and outside. The interior is justified insofar as it is distinguishable from its opposite, namely exteriority. Also, the different senses of time that accompany the interior and the exterior reinforce the distinction between the two realms. This Husserlian model, Canullo argues, is overcome by Michel Henry, who identifies the interiority of the subject as manifest not in time but in life and in the flesh. This immanent interiority is "acosmic" because it is not grasped in the outside of the world. "Acosmic interiority" does not mean, however, interiority without space. To rethink the subject's interiority, Canullo posits a new kind of spatiality, a "lived space" that does not contrast with, and ultimately rely on, exteriority.

Hans Rainer Sepp's chapter, "Interiority, Exteriority, Being-In: A Concise Analysis" draws upon Eastern philosophy and phenomenology to further discuss the unique relationship between inner and outer, interior and exterior. Engaging Buddhist thought, as well as thinkers including Hedwig Conrad-Martius, Sepp highlights the role of the corporeality in shaping the aforementioned relationship. Two modes of being-in are distinguished: in the first, an anonymous self relates to itself and its experiences, whereas in the second, a world is constituted by relations to and with others and objects—a world of meanings. But these two primary senses of being-in, which are lived from within our interiority, are distinguishable from historically conditioned forms of subjectivity and interiority. One realm is not reducible to the other, nor is one realm given priority over the other. They are unique but related realms, but the significance of the historical realm and its external force can only be grasped from within the realm of our interior being-in, from the very experience and resistance the interior is living through its externalization. Sepp observes,

> Both, the real (*reell*) subjective of the self and the real, which I am not, are not relative to the historical world of being-in-the-world. Therefore, it would be inadmissible to designate this difference with the relation of inside and outside. Such a relation limited to sense would miss the fact that both the self-performance of the absolutely subjective and the original experience of the absolutely real—that is, the pure experiencing of the primal interior and the original experience of a primal exterior—transcend any context that would govern the meaning of historical situation.

Consequently, far from being relegated to idealist accounts of the self, this phenomenological exploration of interiority requires a realist perspective that paradoxically includes the overcoming of any attempt to reify the inner experience and the acknowledgment of its vivid reality.

In "Self-Owning, Self-Transparency, and Inner Nudity: Hedwig Conrad-Martius on Interiority," Christina Gschwandtner analyzes, along these lines, the rich phenomenological legacy of the philosopher Hedwig Conrad-Martius, one of the founding yet understudied figures of the phenomenological movement. After completing her studies with Alexander Pfänder, Conrad-Martius left the University of Munich to study with Husserl. Part of the Göttingen School of Husserl's thought, she defines phenomenology, against more idealistic accounts, as a realist project that seeks to uncover the real being of reality. Gschwandtner examines Conrad-Martius's thought to uncover an account of inner subjective life, described as an inner nudity, in which the self comes to appear as it is, making possible real and meaningful self-disclosures and ownness. It is these possibilities of the self, manifested inwardly, that distinguish humans from other forms of animal life. Our human souls, as opposed to other animal souls and spirits, have a unique capacity of self-understanding that can guide and shape the way we stand in relation to ourselves and in our comportment toward ourselves. Gschwandtner argues that the possibility of self-awareness, as well as one's relationship to oneself, can help foster relations between the individual and other beings, including other animals and God. She sees in Conrad-Martius, especially on account of the philosopher's deep interests in biology and cosmology, an inner awareness that can transcend traditional substantializing and objectifying views of human and animal nature.

Part 2 investigates the very possibility of transcendence contained within interiority, albeit in limited and shifting ways, and the way it is also a space of encounter, relationality, and alterity. Angela Ales Bello ponders the important role of interiority in discovering who and what we are. She argues in her chapter "'*In interiore homine*': The Presence and Absence of the Divine in the Human" that searching within ourselves allows us to analyze the structure of the human being. Drawing upon phenomenological insights, in particular those of Edmund Husserl and Edith Stein, she investigates the lived experience of interiority to understand the following question: What is the human being? The answer is drawn from within through analyses of lived experience, rather than from the "outside." This mode of inquiry reveals the existence of an all-powerful *something* that transcends us, that lives within us as presence/absence; it is the means by which we understand our limits and finitude. We call it the divine. For Ales Bello, interiority is also a place of radical encounter where human beings can come to transcend the human and find the divine, a space where we meet that which is radically other to ourselves, ultimately giving rise to religious experience.

Brian W. Becker's "'It Is No Longer I Who Do It': Interiority and the Foreign-Body" explores the relationship between the lived body and interiority. He analyzes the unique phenomenon of the phantom limb, which many phenomenologists have written about, most famously Merleau-Ponty in his *Phenomenology of Perception*.[12] The phantom limb creates a unique relationship between the subject and one's own lived body. Becker chronicles how psychology, phenomenology, and theology analyze the experience. In some individuals the phantom limb is lived as a separate, foreign being, one over whom control is not possible. If the experience of the phantom limb is inwardly lived as an experience of the foreign other, the relationship has implications for the ways in which one lives the experience of the other person: the other's presence is to be viewed not only as an object that stands outside and against me but as most traditional views of the object also maintain. The other, however, establishes a new relation between me and the other, as lived inwardly, as internalized. To understand how the other may be uniquely positioned within me, Becker suggests three important phenomenological aspects that characterize the inward relation to the other: time, space, and identity. Ultimately, the foreign other is understood as thanatonic; that is, like the phantom limb, it is not something I can control according to my own will. As Becker concludes, "The foreign-body belongs to another logic, which shall be called the *thanatonic phenomenon*. It reveals, like the erotic phenomenon, an alterity that meets me in my bodily existence, but this time in its lived *and* material dimensions where I confront an originary fissure and alienable origin. . . . In the thanatonic phenomenon, the foreign-body that comes from elsewhere collapses all distance in excorporating my body and flesh, consuming my space, my time, and my identity."

Emmanuel Housset's chapter "Inner Distance and Surreptitious Patience According to Jean-Louis Chrétien" mines the work of the recently deceased French philosopher Jean-Louis Chrétien for its phenomenological implications for interiority. One of Chrétien's last books, *L'espace intérieur*[13] (*Interior Space*), explores the writing of ancient and medieval thinkers to show how the concept of an interior space is developed and defended in their works, ultimately creating an inner space for God to dwell in human beings. Housset phenomenologically develops Chrétien's idea to show how the creation and cultivation of an inner space and an inner life require a specific kind of questioning, namely patience, understood as a kind of deep listening and waiting for a response. Here, in this new configuration of patient listening, the centrality of an active I, who is the central figure and actor, is displaced. The other is given priority, and it is the other who transforms us. In patient listening, meaning emerges. "What exceeds all expectations," Housset observes, "is the foundation of surreptitious patience, and this excess of the immemorial and the unexpected is both what divides our present and what gives it its true thickness, one that is much more decisive than the thickness resulting from retention and recollection. Therefore, interiority is not primarily the place where a passive and active subject master meaning and where their presence is loaded by a past and holds no future. On the contrary, it is the place where meaning emerges while confronting alterity, which is not overcome but encountered." The idea of an I who is in control of its own inner sphere of ownness is displaced by the other, to whom we patiently and surreptitiously listen through questioning and response.

Drawing on the relational dynamics that shape our inner experience, the part 3 of the volume focuses on the relation between interiority and world in metaphysics and ethics.

In "The Self-Awakening (*jikaku* [自覚]) from the Citadel of the Self: Everything is Interconnected with Everything," Steve G. Lofts, like Sepp, draws from Eastern philosophy to rethink the relationship between interior and exterior. Lofts considers the radical possibility that the Western concept of interiority is largely influenced by the identification of substance with identity, thereby reducing the interior realm to the domain of the substantial I of identity. Interiority, then, is simply the experience of the I living its own reality. The other is also subsumed and defined through the life of the I. Lofts discusses the categories of interior and exterior, self and other, and subject and object and their dependence on Western constructs of substantial identity. These constructions have had deep and often dire social and political consequences. To overcome the simultaneous identification and bifurcation of the aforementioned concepts, Lofts proposes that we engage with Zen philosophy to understand that, in fact, exterior and interior must be thought in relational rather than oppositional terms. The Western claim of the existence of two distinct zones of immanence and exteriority is false; everything is interconnected. As Lofts notes,

> To the degree that we can speak about interiority and exteriority, we must always speak about them as reciprocal and relational notions that exist only in reference to the other. They must not be conceived as autonomous regions that need to be bridged, but rather as two relational limits of a single reality. Thus, it is not a question of finding a way out from interiority to the exteriority of the world, to the realm of objects, or to the other self, nor is it a question of explaining how the exteriority of the world enters the interiority of the self.

Christian Lotz, in "*Ultima Ratio* Decisions and Absolute Interiority: From Hegel to Bonhoeffer" investigates one of the classically defining aspects of interiority, namely conscience. His chapter seeks to give a phenomenological account of conscience, not simply as a form of knowledge, as more traditional forms of conscience conceive of it, but as a mode of action, what Dietrich Bonhoeffer calls the "a-rationality of moral agency" or what Hegel terms "the very practical form of self-consciousness." Lotz's phenomenological discussion of conscience reveals it to be a unique form of human activity that can engender action capable of resisting evil. Analyzing the writings of Hegel and Bonhoeffer, Lotz discovers that the agency of consciousness produces not simply the awareness of acting subject or self but the very possibility of an absolute responsibility that makes an appeal to be heard, to be enacted, with the knowledge that one is never capable of fully answering the absolute nature of the call of responsibility. The rise of the call of responsibility for action is a sign of concrete hope that seeks to resist an evil or compromising situation. The inner reality of conscience makes possible both resistant hope and action.

Ann Murphy's "Critical Phenomenology and the Rehabilitation of Interiority" introduces the perspective of critical phenomenology while it reconfigures the contemporary meanings of inside and outside, considering social and political shifts. Critical phenomenology is phenomenology that takes power seriously. Even as it maintains fidelity to phenomenology's methodological commitment to the first-person description of the basic structures of experience, it draws attention to the broader power structures that frame these accounts. For this reason, phenomenology's critical turn has emphasized the ways in which power structures experience, exteriority shapes interiority: the external world determines psychic life. She argues here that a properly critical phenomenology must also consider the importance of interiority for our ethical and political analyses, against the Foucauldian claim that phenomenology cannot do so. Drawing on the works of Maurice Merleau-Ponty, Frantz Fanon, and Lisa Guenther, Murphy argues for an understanding of critical phenomenology that foregrounds a relational yet conscious limit of the phenomenological ego, capable of grasping constitutive inner states like pain, vulnerability, and affectivity while dwelling within the complex forms of conditioning intersubjectivity that are part of a meaningful world.

The aim of this volume, in part, is to shed light on important phenomenologists whose works and ideas have not been fully investigated. We conceive of our work here as helping scholars and philosophers become familiar with understudied but valuable sources of thinking on the question of interiority, in particular Edith Stein and Gerda Walther, two important figures in the early phenomenological movement. To this end, Elodie Boublil's chapter, "Joy, Interiority, and Individuation: A Steinian Account," notably relies on the works of Edith Stein to argue that joy unveils the dynamic process of subjectivity's individuation through the expansion of the subject's vital force and the awareness of an inner sense of being. Joy, a particular feeling that emerges from the depth of our beings, namely from our hearts, reveals the meaningfulness of our relation to the lifeworld through the movements of our hearts (*Gemütsbewegungen*) and our attunement to Being and the living. More specifically, a phenomenological analysis of joy uncovers the link between intentionality and creativity. Joy reveals the structure of the inner sense of subjectivity. In a reciprocal movement that intertwines passivity and activity, the subject expresses, through joy, openness to the world and others, as well as irreducible transcendence. Joy becomes the ontological marker of our individual capacity for freedom and hope.

Antonio Calcagno's "Gerda Walther's Phenomenology of Interiority and the Idea of a Fundamental Essence" looks at the work of Gerda Walther, a member of the phenomenological movement as it took up residence in Freiburg, where Husserl occupied a tenured, full professorship in philosophy. Like Conrad-Martius, Walther arrived from Munich, sent by her teacher Pfänder, to study with Husserl, and like her contemporaries Conrad-Martius and Edith Stein, Walther's phenomenological approach is distinct. But though these thinkers developed their own respective views, they shared a deep concern for the question of what it is to be human and a commitment to justify the possibility of interiority or an inner life. Calcagno argues that one can find in Walther's writings on mysticism, and in other texts as well, a robust account of interiority. But what distinguishes her account from others is that the self and the I can be radically displaced, for example in intense experiences of community, telepathy, and mystical experience, such that the I becomes fused with others, a we, or God. The interior is often conceived as a deep, almost impervious realm of identity, an inalienable I. Walther shows how interiority is more porous than traditional accounts maintain, thereby allowing us to grasp how we can truly bond with others in the world or suffer great distress caused by external forces or even mental illness. Interiority, then, is not simply a realm of I or personal life but also a communal and social realm.

The chapters contained in this volume expose and help develop a phenomenology of interiority, expanding received phenomenological and philosophical accounts by uncovering important constitutive layers of the phenomenon. It is our hope that readers will find novelty and inspiration in the chapters, ultimately making possible both critical dialogue and further research.

Notes

1. Paul Ricoeur, *The Conflict of Interpretations: Essays in Hermeneutics* (Evanston, IL: Northwestern University Press, 1974), 18.

2. For example, see the recent work of Roberto Esposito, *A Philosophy for Europe: From the Outside*, trans. Zakiya Hanafi (Cambridge, MA: Polity Press, 2018).

3. Jean-Louis Chrétien, *L'Espace Intérieur* (Paris: Éditions de Minuit, 2014), Kindle ed., 354.

4. Martin Heidegger, *The Basic Problems of Phenomenology*, trans. Albert Hofstadter (Bloomington: Indiana University Press, 1982), 66.

5. Maurice Merleau-Ponty, *Phenomenology of Perception*, trans. Donald A. Landes (New York: Routledge, 2013), xxiii.

6. Merleau-Ponty, 56.

7. Maurice Merleau-Ponty, *The Visible and the Invisible*, trans. Alphonso Lingis (Evanston, IL: Northwestern University Press, 1968), 232. This philosophical attempt to think together interiority and the world has also been undertaken by Jan Patočka. See Jan Patočka, "Das Innere und die Welt," *Studia Phaenomenologica* 7 (2007): 15–70.

8. Chrétien, *L'Espace Intérieur*, 2057.

9. Jean-Louis Chrétien, *La Joie Spacieuse* (Paris: Éditions de Minuit, 2007), 37.

10. Paul Ricoeur, *A l'école de la phénoménologie* (Paris: Vrin, 1986), 252.

11. Erwin Straus, *Du sens des sens* (Grenoble: Millon, 1993), 242.

12. Merleau-Ponty, *Phenomenology of Perception*, 78–80.

13. Jean-Louis Chrétien, *L'espace intérieur* (Paris: Éditions de Minuit, 2013).

PART ONE
Interiority and Subjectivity

1

The Spatiality of Acosmic Interiority
A Phenomenological Attempt to Rethink "Lived Space"

CARLA CANULLO

Inside/Outside: An Irreducible Binary?

Some models of thought undoubtedly frame the way we think about spatiality. The "inside/outside" binary is one of them. Depending on grammatical use, the two terms are deployed either as an adverb or a preposition, ultimately expressing the *localization* of something "inside" or "outside." Aristotle already referred to this localization when he used the terms "containing" and "contained" within the context of his definition of "place," understood as a contiguous boundary. He expands on this definition in his *Physics*, in which the issue of place is discussed along with the issue of "movement," which denotes not only "shift" but also "increase" and "diminution."[1] According to the Stagirite, place refers to the boundary of the containing body, which is in contact with the contained body. The contained body refers to what can be moved by way of locomotion. Since only contiguous and continuous parts can move, the place is the motionless boundary that is contiguous with the movable body.

After the so-called spatial turn in contemporary philosophy, does it still make sense to start from Aristotle, especially when "lived space"[2] is set forth as a specific kind of spatiality to characterize interiority? In this chapter, I will indeed argue for such a starting point in our attempt to "rethink the lived space." I will put into question the binary "inside/outside" to rethink *interiority* as *original spatiality*, without reference to exteriority. The notion of *contiguity* described by Aristotle serves as a key concept to demonstrate the foregoing thesis.

The concept of the "continuous" does not admit interruptions and, therefore, maintains the inside/outside as uninterrupted. On the contrary, the "contiguous" implies the difference made by the interruption. Contiguous here means "bordering, adjacent," or "closely connected," but never "without stopping" or being "uninterrupted" like the continuous. In my view, the concept of interruption is fundamental to rethink interiority. This notion can help us consider the genuine phenomenon of interiority without necessarily referring it to its contrary, namely exteriority. Hence, it can be considered as contiguous but not continuous with exteriority. Moreover, I will not consider "what/*was*" interiority is. Rather, I will investigate "how/*wie*" an internal spatiality manifests itself, and I will consequently refer to phenomenology, which (as Husserl or Heidegger taught us) does not deal with what appears but with how it happens.

We can now answer the question that opens this introduction: Is the spatial localization "inside/outside" an irreducible reference? Yes, perhaps, but it can be rethought through the tools of philosophical tradition such that these adverbs and the spatiality they outline as exteriority and interiority are grasped not in continuity but in contiguity. Furthermore, if they are contiguous but not continuous, first, one will not be the contrary of the other, and second, each of the two determinations will be grasped starting from its *originality* and not in the background of a unique conception of space establishing the criteria of both what is exterior and what is interior. To rethink this original *way* of considering spatiality, I will start with Husserl, who also questioned two different ways of conceiving exteriority and interiority, ultimately linking these dimensions of spatiality to the givenness of the phenomena, in the context of his discussion of space and time.

Edmund Husserl: The Phenomenology of Space and Time

The "inside/outside" distinction certainly conditioned the way Immanuel Kant conceived of exteriority and interiority. In his *Transcendental Aesthetic*, space is defined as the formal and pure intuition of "outer" sense, whereas time is understood as the formal intuition of the "inner sense."[3] It is a "fundamentally incorrect expression," Husserl says about this distinction, which "implies . . . a fatally erroneous position." Kant inevitably split what must not be split, namely, sensation and perception.[4] Instead "space is a necessary form of things and is not a form of lived experience, specifically not of 'sensuous' lived experience."[5]

Husserl's difference with Kant is, therefore, clearly stated. It is even more explicitly stated in the pages dedicated to the relation between space and time in the former's *On Phenomenology of Internal Time Consciousness* and *Thing and Space: Lectures of 1907*. In the former text, while highlighting the meaning of the "suspension of objective time," Husserl writes that this can be illustrated by a "parallel with space," "since space and time exhibit such significant and many noted analogies."[6] To explain those analogies, Husserl writes: "The consciousness of space . . . belongs to the sphere of what is phenomenologically given. . . . If we refrain from every interpretation that goes beyond what is given, and reduce the perceptual appearance to the given primary contents, the latter yield the continuum of the visual field, which is quasi-spatial, but not space or a surface in space. Roughly speaking, the continuum of the visual field is a twofold continuous multiplicity."[7] In the latter text, the parallelism is even clearer, and time is connected to extension, as in the case of the perception of a house.

If perception lasts a minute, every minute can also be split into several other time intervals (e.g., half a minute). However "if we carry out the phenomenological reduction, the Objective time, the determination as minute and half-minute falls away. Thereby, however, the extension and the divisibility indeed pertain immanently to what is given, to the perception as a phenomenological datum. We will speak of pre-phenomenal or transcendental temporality, *versus* phenomenal temporality, the one attributed to objects, the one that, in virtue of the apprehension of things, is constituted as the time of things."[8] We can see this time continuity as an *extension*, "which falls to the lot of perception or, more precisely, perceptual appearance."[9]

In section 20 of *Thing and Space*, Husserl confirms the foregoing claim: "Temporal extension is a sibling of the spatial . . . (and) like temporality, spatiality pertains to the essence of the appearing thing. The appearing thing, whether changing or unchanging, endures and fills a time; furthermore, it fills a space, its space."[10] Husserl continues: "We have a spatial form and a spatial filling. What fills the space is the matter, a term we must take here in a quite *naïve* sense, namely, in the sense perception prescribes for us: that which stands in perception as filling space."[11] In order to explain this observation, Husserl deploys an example.

This example, which could be read in parallel with the one proposed in the 1905 lessons,[12] shows that sound points not only to its related physical source (e.g., the sound that comes from a violin) but also to the fact that it fills the room with the content it produces. Indeed, the sound

> fills the space insofar as it is heard everywhere in the space, e.g., that of the hall. The point, however, is that in hearing, in perceiving, in general, we do not and cannot perceive any space filled by a sonic quality. The space of the hall visually appears as determined in such and such a way through is corporeal limits and its surface limits. The floor, the walls, and the ceiling are covered with visual qualities. That is how they appear. Nevertheless, nowhere does a quality appear in the case of a sonic covering or another sonic filling.[13]

How, then, do the spatial determinations constitute themselves? To answer this question, Husserl distinguishes between temporal and spatial extension. The latter differs from the former as its continuity is of a different kind: it is a continuous and unitary extension. If the different, sensitive data do not appear in a dispersive way, it is because "they have a rigorous unity and rigorous form, the form of pre-phenomenal spatiality,"[14] which develops together with the pre-phenomenal temporality described earlier. Moreover, Husserl distinguishes between two kinds of continuity: the continuity "that belongs to spatial extension as such, and that comes to consciousness as an immanent moment,"[15] as, for example, when we move from one point to another experiencing continuity in discontinuity and the continuity that refers to "the continuity of the filling determinations, for example, the flowing over from one quality to another quality, perhaps from the transition from the red through purple to violet."[16] Therefore, "whereas the continuity of spatial, objective extension is a thorough one, allowing no leap and no hiatus, the continuity of the filling is such that it can be broken up by a discontinuity."[17]

After having established this continuity, Husserl sorts out the following "problem" in section 25, namely the possibility for an apparition to constitute itself as an apprehension of something in the unity of space holding in itself the bodies without being itself a body.[18] The philosopher notices that even in the case of temporal continuity, the same problem occurs. He speaks about a "spatial environment" and "temporal environment" to characterize this special continuity. Both are "co-perceived" together with the thing, and both space and time perceived simultaneously with the thing are the space and time of "that thing" but also different from it. This temporality and spatiality—and herein lies the Husserlian problem—must be joined with another temporality and spatiality understood as "order," which develops among things while appearing through kinds of reference (e.g., "central idea," reconnections, the memory that brings us back) that are the intuitive "armor" of mundane spatiotemporality. Husserl writes, "The environing objects, with their properties, changes, and relations, are what they are for themselves, but they have a position relative to us, initially a spatio-temporal position and then also a 'spiritual' one."[19] Therefore, "actual perceptions thereby are connected to possibilities of perception, to presentifying intuitions; the nexuses of immediate perception contain conductors which lead us from perception to perception, from a first environment to ever new ones, and thereby the perceptual gaze attains things in the order of spatiality."[20]

But one phenomenological question remains: *How* can such spatiality grant us access to givenness? According to Husserl, spatiality constitutes itself "in the movement of the object itself and the movement of the Ego."[21] Furthermore, he specifies that space appears immediately to our perception. Nevertheless, in order to talk about "evidence according to identity" and about the "unity of the object," many perceptions need to be unified in a synthesis that is at the base of the logical one, and "the perceptions must be integrated as phases into the synthesis, and we see that precisely only if we carry out the synthesis."[22] This claim is of the uttermost importance, as Husserl writes, for it means that an "identical and unchanged spatial body demonstrates itself as such only in kinetic series of perceptions, which continually brings to appearance the various sides of that thing. The body [*Körper*] must rotate or be displaced, or I must move, move my eyes, my body, in order to see it from all around, and at the same time, I must keep approaching it and receding. . . . That is how the state of affairs is expressed from the standpoint of the appearing thing."[23]

The foregoing passage opens the chapter dedicated to the "phenomenological concept of kinaesthesis."[24] Husserl mentions in the very first lines that spatiality is made and that it appears in movement. The kinesthetic system, however, has a decisive role not only for the perception of the objects but also for the body itself that perceives them, as we have already seen.[25] In these pages, the linking-role of the body starts to be investigated before being addressed extensively in *Ideas II*.[26] Indeed, the issue of kinesthesia and movement will be central not only for highlighting the special manifestation of corporeality as *Leib*[27] but also for establishing that "in all experience of space-thingly Objects, *the Body* 'is involved' as the perceptual organ of the experiencing subject."[28] Such a role explains why Husserl starts to investigate how corporeity is constituted. Grasping this corporeity becomes possible if the body (*Leib*) is different from the "corporeal body itself" (*Körper*). Most of all, the body is characterized by the special positioning that renders it an "object/subject" of sensations, as evidenced by the phenomenon of touch: "Touch-sensations belong to every appearing objective spatial position on the touched hand when it is touched precisely at those places."[29]

Now that the main arguments made by Husserl about spatiality have been introduced, I would like to return to the main question I raise about the possibility of conceiving a specific mode of givenness associated with the spatiality of interiority.

By calling us to return *zu den Sachen selbst!* ("to the things themselves!"), Husserl leads us to the fundamental givenness of spatiality at stake in the adverb/preposition "inside/outside." His investigation of space is decisive to this binary. Husserl seems to conceive interiority and exteriority only in terms of inside and outside. Indeed, if on the one hand he shows that time is an *affaire* of interiority (as suggested in 1905 by the expression "internal time") and that space is, on the other hand, related to the outside, Husserl places time and space parallel to one another. Hence, the boundaries between the interiority of the body that gives us spatiality and the exteriority of things that are perceived spatially are entwined when the (phenomenological) way of their givenness is at stake. Therefore, through Husserl, we grasp the specific kind of givenness that shows interiority and exteriority as they are, namely as irreducible to a spatial property. However, they are grasped as they manifest themselves together with the phenomena. This is undoubtedly the strength of the position, in which the distinction between *Körper* and *Leib* occurs.

Nevertheless, does the way in which interiority and exteriority show themselves enable us to grasp the features that distinguish them and make them original? Are we now able to grasp them according to their originality and not as one being the negation of the other? Probably not, even though Husserl distinguished the ways of being of corporeality in his distinction between *Körper* and *Leib*: *Körper* manifests itself as visible from the outside and *Leib* manifests itself from the inside. Yet, this distinction draws on a homogeneous conception of space that pertains both to exteriority and interiority. The same idea of the continuous and continuity characterizes both temporality (and therefore every *Inner Zeitbewusstsein*) and spatiality. Even though interiority/exteriority are grasped in their ways of manifestation, they give themselves according to continuity. This makes their manifestation homogeneous. Consequently, one manifests itself only as the contrary of the other. Husserl does not certainly deny that there is discontinuity or fragmentation. Even if fragmentation can refer to time and space, it is still the fragmentation of a continuity that is the same and only horizon of the manifestation. Now, without leaving the phenomenological field, we have to look for the possibility of a manifestation that gives itself while acknowledging the contiguity of exteriority and interiority and therefore refers their manifestation back to the same horizon.

The Discontinuity of Appearing: Michel Henry

Perhaps it is not by chance that Michel Henry referred, albeit heretically, to phenomenology in order to think about an *original* manifestation of interiority. He distinguished two different kinds of manifestation: one proper to the world and one proper to life. While participating in a conference dedicated to the publication of *Incarnation*,[30] Henry presented his work as an investigation of the foundation of "his" phenomenology (known as a "phenomenology of life"), "characterized by what one can call a 'phenomenological dualism' or the 'twofold nature of appearance.'"[31] According to Henry's thesis, the body manifests itself in two ways: as a corporeal body appearing among things and as living flesh revealing itself only "through the immanent and pathetic self-impression of life."[32] Therefore, he says, "This is just the beginning of an analysis written for the first time in the years 1946–1950. . . . Subsequently, phenomenological dualism has been applied to various philosophical issues: Marx and the economy, the unconscious, culture, the work of art, the phenomenological method, and the phenomenology of the twentieth century in general."[33]

This "twofold nature of appearance" is reaffirmed through his entire work. In *I Am the Truth*,[34] Henry sets the world and life in radical opposition. The world belongs to the outside, and life manifests itself only in the inside, that is to say, in the sphere of pure immanence. Indeed, the word "phenomenon," whose etymology refers to the word φως (*phos*), which means light, motivates such a difference. A phenomenon is what appears, what shows itself. However, how does this showing happen? It appears in the outside of the world and "for the eyes of those who can see it." "World," according to Michel Henry, is spatiality, understood as "outside," a space where everything happens in an impersonal way.[35] Therefore "a thing exists for us only in that primordial 'outsideness' that is the world"; again "the 'world's truth' is nothing other than this: a self-production of 'outsideness' as the horizon of visibility in and through which everything can become visible and thus become a 'phenomenon' for us."[36] If the horizon of manifestation were the world's exteriority, even the difference between space and world would disappear, as if the truth of the world would consist in manifesting "this self-externalization of externality where the horizon of visibility of the world is formed, its 'outside' as another name that we know still better: it is called time. Time and the world are identical: they designate the single process in which the 'outside' is constantly self-externalized."[37]

This is a strong and certainly questionable claim. Nevertheless, it should be read in light of Henry's general argument. Actually, Henry wants to show that, first, time and space are the conditions through which the phenomenon shows itself, therefore they are "conditions" and they do not belong to the phenomenon itself. Second, the "outsideness" of the world not only points to its location but also shows *how* something manifests itself. In other words, it guarantees the condition of possibility of its manifestation. Life, however, cannot be perceived in the outside. If the "world" is the condition through which exteriority manifests itself, it is necessary to reflect on the specific mode of manifestation of interiority. According to Henry, as we said before, life manifests itself in the living flesh.

Life "designates a pure manifestation, always irreducible to that of the world, an original revelation that is not the revelation of another thing and does not depend on anything else. Rather, it is a revelation of self, that absolute self-revelation that is Life itself."[38] Therefore, interiority, according to the French philosopher, refers to the life that does not manifest itself "outside"—in the world—but that manifests itself within. How is this possible? How does the manifestation of an interiority that does not appear in the world, and that is an acosmic interiority, happen? According to Henry, life is total immanence to itself and does not suppose anything else apart from its movement and rhythm. It is self-affection; it is itself the original feeling. This self-affection, according to Henry, is interiority, which manifests itself through its *pathos*. In other words, interiority does not manifest itself as "something" but as it is passively experienced. Hence, Henry writes,

> *Pathos* designates the mode of phenomenalization according to which life phenomenalizes itself in its original self-revelation; it designates the phenomenological material out of which this self-donation is made, its flesh: transcendental and pure affectivity in which everything that experiences itself finds its

concrete, phenomenological actualization. . . . If life originally reveals nothing but its reality, this is just because its mode of revelation is *pathos*, which is this essence entirely concerned with itself, this plenitude of a flesh immersed in the self-affection of its suffering and joy.[39]

Therefore, interiority is the possibility of the manifestation of the same consciousness, and consciousness manifests itself starting from itself, and hence it becomes aware of itself in the very moment it receives impressions. So, such self-manifestation is possible because consciousness is impressive (*impressionnelle*) and "consciousness would impress itself, so that it would be this original self-impression that would reveal it to itself, making thus possible its own revelation."[40]

An impression (*Empfindniss*) is a self-modification. It is the *original* feeling, the primordial way of thinking. Henry arrives at this original feeling while examining the hyletic moments of consciousness assumed as moments that individualize consciousness itself. But what makes possible every original impression of consciousness and consciousness itself? The answer is life. This term designates the invisible feature that gives itself in the manifestation; life is the flesh of the phenomenon. It is *phenomenality*, that is, the only condition of interiority's manifestation. It is also the reason why *phenomena* are what they are and give themselves to us; it is the phenomenological material, and, finally, any initiative of the manifestation is exclusive to phenomenality. Furthermore, two features characterize this "phenomenological material." First, it is different from the "outsideness" that is always transcendent. It is immanent to interiority. Second, such *pathic* immanence is what Henry calls the flesh, that is, the only "substance" that can feel itself because it gives itself its own impressions. It can do this because it "is life" (that manifests itself *in* such self-impressions without resorting to anything external). Every manifestation, therefore, is an act "which appears as independent of its forward movement, independently of the movement whereby it projects itself outside itself, reveals itself in itself, in such a way that this 'in itself' means: without surpassing itself, without leaving itself."[41]

There exists a radical difference between the ways exteriority and interiority manifest themselves. Hence, the manifestation of interiority avoids the topical localization of the inside/outside binary. Besides, such a manifestation is "acosmic," without world, as appearing in the outside means appearing thanks to the conditions of space and time. Instead, Henry's interiority is the life that manifests itself in the pathos that the flesh lives in the total immanence to itself.

Having "theorized" the "twofold nature of appearance," Henry reflects on the original difference of the manifestation of exteriority and interiority. However, if on one hand this originality (looked for from the beginning) is finally gained, then on the other hand spatiality is completely lost (the one that Husserl instead enabled us to think and that Heidegger, as shown by Didier Franck, did not ignore).[42] Even if the French philosopher offers an original way to conceive of the givenness of interiority starting from itself (i.e., an interiority that gives itself as living flesh and life), he confronts us with new difficulties, as he urges us to think the manifestation of life and interiority *without space*. Nevertheless, one may wonder whether the "acosmism" of interiority necessarily needs to be *aspatial*. Are space and world necessarily identical? The answer is no. Spatiality should not be put aside; rather, it must be reconsidered in light of the spatiality designated by the concept of the "contiguous" instead of being systematically referred to the spatiality of the continuous that puts forth a unique and same horizon for every *locus*. The idea of the contiguous allows us to consider the distance required by the manifestation of different spatial dimensions.

Consequently, Michel Henry's phenomenological dualism fails to reframe the spatiality of such acosmic interiority. Even if Michel Henry enables us to grasp a kind of interiority that is no more contrasted with exteriority, namely a kind of interiority that refers to the living flesh and the immanence of life, his phenomenological dualism fails to reframe the kind of spatiality required by what we call acosmic interiority. Indeed, his acosmism too quickly renounces lived space, which is the proper space of interiority.

A Spacious Interiority

To renounce taking the world as the horizon of manifestation does not imply that one rejects the concept of space and, therefore, the idea of interiority's acosmism. Furthermore, rethinking lived space is required on account of the fact that the living being and the flesh in which life feels itself are interior to themselves without being non-spatial. If interiority amounted to non-spatial acosmism, living concreteness would be taken away from interiority. No finite life can grow outside spatiality. Otherwise, all phenomena related to living beings would be perceived simply as "events of exteriority," turning the word interiority into nonsense. Such a transformation would ultimately be false.

We need to consider whether it is possible to think of a space that is not the horizon of manifestation of life but that would give itself in the *manifesting and happening* of a living and incarnated interiority. To put it differently, we need to examine whether a spatiality that is intrinsically instituted through interiority's manifestation is possible *while manifesting itself*. Finally, we have to consider whether spatiality specific to acosmic interiority is possible. Jean-Louis Chrétien offers some solutions to these issues.

In *Spacious Joy*, Chrétien refers to an interiority that is not described in localizing terms (inside/outside)[43] but in terms of how it reveals itself while we experience it. Chrétien describes a phenomenon that shows the constitution of space, namely "dilation," which can characterize either exteriority or interiority, though it manifests itself in a different way. Indeed, the former dilates itself in an extensive way, whereas the latter exhibits itself in an intensive manner. The former dilation reflects the increase of space, whereas the latter one shows an intensification that allows the appearing of the phenomenon to be felt and experienced.

Chrétien starts his reflection by recalling the meaning of the verb "to dilate" in different European languages found in the analyses of Pierre Kaufmann, Gaston Bachelard, and other philosophers.[44] Chrétien then elaborates the concept of the spatial dilation of interiority by connecting dilation to joy. Joy is certainly an "affective tonality" that dilates interiority when it manifests itself. Joy is felt while it manifests itself dilating. We feel joy, like a breath that expands the chest, when we experience a feeling of dilation. The space of joy is realized *while* it is dilating, that is, *through this act of dilation*. According to Chrétien, joy happens, and is therefore to be understood, as a "spatial joy." Such dilation coincides with a true movement through which interiority also occurs, a movement that gives itself according to the rhythm of the increase and decrease.[45] So, intensifying joy amplifies itself.[46] Moreover, it generates a unity that, being continuously in movement, continuously unifies the life of the spirit. In accordance with Bergson, Chrétien writes that "one's own experience as a living self cannot be divorced from experiencing life as such, in its unity."[47] Furthermore, the inner space that joy dilates is continuous and unitary, much like the exterior space described by Husserl. The binary of "inner space/exterior space" reappears in another text, *L'espace intérieur*,[48] in which interiority is investigated in light of this twofold spatiality.

Like Henry, Chrétien shows that interiority owns its original way of being and is different from exteriority, but *contra* Henry, he shows that it can be acosmic without being aspatial. Rather, interiority owns its original spatiality as it is space that dilates together with what happens in it, for example, the experience of joy. This affective tonality broadens the space of our interiority, making it feel wider, and this happens because this dilating movement is *intensive* and not *extensive* (as in the case of exteriority). Moreover, while the dilating is manifesting itself, interiority appears because it is felt, thereby becoming capable of experiencing itself. This dilating effect of joy reflects itself in inner space. Chrétien resorts to metaphors of external space to describe this phenomenon. The metaphor of the "chamber" describes the interiority of the heart; the metaphor of the inner temple, the interiority of the sacred; the dwellings "of the house, the castle, and the flat," depict the interiority of the soul. This, once again, brings us back to the binary "inside/outside," which, however, in this case, is grasped through the original phenomena of interiority and exteriority. Nevertheless, the impossibility of describing interiority without resorting to exteriority raises once again the question: If it is impossible to renounce to the language of exteriority, can we say that space has been radically rethought? Certainly, Chrétien (and Henry before him) create an original way of thinking the givenness of interiority, and Chrétien's spacious interiority "responds" to Henry's conception of acosmism. However, could we ever rethink the space of interiority without resorting to the inside/outside model?

The Spiral of Space

If the foregoing possibility has not been achieved thus, it is because neither Henry nor Chrétien (nor Husserl before them) seek a phenomenon that would enable us to think of space in a different way from homogeneity and continuity, to think of the trait that was grasped by Aristotle, namely *contiguity*. Perhaps such a phenomenon manifests itself in a figure that geometry, which rationalizes space, receives from mechanics, that is, the spiral. This figure manifests itself as welding together both inside and outside (without resorting to their juxtaposition) and brings forth a new model in which everything is at the same time inside (like the line that develops in the different spirals) and outside (the circles of the spiral are infinite and develop in any direction of space—from bottom to top or the opposite, from the right or left). Like the interiority investigated by Chrétien, the spatiality of interiority that the spiral outlines is instituted through movements of *intensification*. As the spiral stretches and contracts, what we call "interiority"—which is differentiated from continuous, external space—is characterized by the varying of the intensity through which we experience it. However, since it is a metaphor that does not grasp the originality of interiority, we have to show how it is possible that the spiral institutes a space.

It does so because geometry can find the formulae that describe a phenomenon after it occurs in the reality studied by mechanics. The spiral belongs to mechanics and not to geometry. René Descartes and Marin Mersenne[49] understood that the specificity of the spiral lies in the fact that it is not a line (e.g., the circle or the ellipse) but that even if it portrays a flat figure, it "describes" how the different points of the "living" world are linked together and interrelated. Descartes, for example, discovered the logarithmic spiral while studying the inclined plane as a tool to lift weights; the line he drew among the points of the plane and the ground was, indeed, a spiral that varied when the inclination of the plane itself varied, generating with each variation different speeds and energies. The spiral, therefore, is "discovered" as it manifests itself as a way of outlining space, not according to an inside/outside topic but according to the development that manifests itself while happening in nature.

One will object that the logarithmic spiral is a continuous series of spires and that consequently it is impossible to escape the continuity we have tried to avoid since the beginning of our reflection. In reality, such continuity is only apparent; even if the line that represents the spiral is uninterrupted, the energy that manifests it and with which one speaks about a spiral, including in mechanics, is characterized by different and discontinuous levels of intensity, due to either the contraction or extension of the spiral itself—a reduction or an extension that, in the case of Descartes, depends on the inclination of the plane related to the ground determining the different relationships of acceleration and deceleration. Moreover, the spiral appears in natural phenomena such as flying birds, the arms of the galaxies, and many other phenomena. If therefore the spiral defines the way in which varying masses accelerate on an inclined plane or the way birds follow trajectories, it is also possible that it is the "shape of the space" where the *acosmic spatiality of interiority* is outlined.

From the beginning, we have tried to grasp the spatiality of interiority beyond the inside/outside binary—a kind of spatiality whose manifestation happens in an original way and not as the opposite of exteriority. The stages of our reflection have focused on the spatial exteriority developed by Husserl, the acosmic interiority of Henry, and the internal spatiality of Chrétien. The latter philosopher demonstrates this internal spatiality by showing that an affective determination, for example, joy, can be "spatial." To do so, he argues that dilation is how joy spatializes itself. Nevertheless, in order to describe interiority, Chrétien also resorts to metaphors of exteriority. Our hypothesis, by contrast, is that instead of interiority, there exists a space that occurs *through* the manifestation of interiority itself. It is confirmed by the fact that one speaks about interiority with reference to affective phenomena that, though they are felt, bring into existence what we generically call an "internal world." The intensity through which "affection" shows itself to us is how it "takes or occupies some space" and, therefore, manifests itself.

Henry would say that "affection" can do so for the living flesh that characterizes the interiority versus the exteriority of the world; Chrétien would say that it does so because affection is able to dilate and, therefore, to "make itself felt." Neither of these two cases consider the "lived space," which the spiral brings to manifestation. Instead, it is shown by an application of such a geometric figure that a "spiral spring" exists. This is a "body" able to stretch when it is provided with a given force only to return to its natural state. By doing so, it shows the way of being of "something" that by its very nature *releases being*. The *Sache selbst* of the "spiral spring," in the end, manifests itself when such a spring gathers energy that is released at the moment the spires release themselves. Now, nothing forbids us to think about the spatiality of interiority in this way.

This latter is not an empty space in which things happen; rather, we grasp it only when we experience phenomena not visible in exteriority and that therefore manifest themselves when they modify us and our perceptions of the external world. For example, when we say, "Space is narrow," we do not mean that it is small; rather, we express its quality by depicting it as suffocating. This perception is given not in exteriority (where we see the boundary of a room) but only in our interiority. It is an intensive perception and not an extensive one, as we could perceive as "open" a narrow space in which one lives out of choice, as witnessed by those who experience monastic life or other forms of meditation. We have a "living perception" of space, which is linked to the way it is "lived." "Living" and "lived" do not express something that is happening (living), nor something that has happened (lived): they happen synchronically, they intensify one another as the spiral does that "is" both while it gathers energies (and therefore it is living) and while it releases what it has gathered (and therefore it is lived). The space of interiority is conceived in the same way as that of the energy of the spiral.

We know neither what is "inside" ourselves nor what is "inside" things, and for this reason, we think every interiority against exteriority that we see. However, thanks to the path opened by phenomenology and its guiding principle, "*Zu den Sachen selbst!*," the interiority of the thing as the thing itself or eidos has avoided the question about what it is to question instead how interiority gives itself (and therefore its *Gegebenheit*). Following the path of phenomenology, "grasping interiority" in its givenness is possible because its *Sache selbst* does not give itself as something, but it gives itself *as* a phenomenon of spatiality experienced differently from an externally perceived experience. In fact, as mentioned earlier, inner space is different than an exteriority that quantitatively expands itself; inner space manifests itself in the "intensive" phenomena of modification, phenomena that speak about interiority. However, we can still ask: *How* does the spatiality we subtracted from the localization of "inside/outside," and that we do not want to conceive as "inner world," happen?

Perhaps it manifests itself just like the spatiality of a spiral that traces the space that emerges around it, without outlining boundaries (as any other geometric figure would do), making us feel its intensifying movement. It manifests itself by composing a "space of energy," which is analogous to the magnetic field; it is not "something," but it is generated by the movement of energies. In this sense, the spatiality of interiority will not be the opposite of exteriority; rather, it will be contiguous to it, as is shown by the fact that its intensification also modifies how exteriority is perceived. Finally, it may be understood as a spatiality that neither preexists nor is felt regardless of the phenomenon that manifests it, by intensifying and reducing it, according to the movement of the spiral. Therefore, while interiority is felt through this intensification, it first manifests itself as a space that is *lived* while it is being lived, and therefore while it intensifies itself, and second, it gives rise to the thought of an inner space grasped *originally* and not as *counter-posed* to exteriority.

The spiral can achieve the foregoing intensification because it is a figure that generates spatiality. It does not outline any boundaries, but it singles out trajectories and therefore movements that create themselves for the energy that the spiral generates, as shown by the study of mechanics that discovers it and that then gives it to geometry, in the same way that it outlines interiority not in opposition to exteriority but *as* a space that is instituted. At the same time, the spatiality of interiority can intensify, and its boundaries need not cease dilating or contracting, thereby starting their expansion again. From beginning to beginning, according to beginnings, this will never end.

Notes

1. Aristotle, *Physics*, ed. Jonathon Barnes (Princeton, NJ: Princeton University Press, 1991), IV, 4, 211 a–b, and 5, 212b–13a.

2. See Robert T. Tally Jr., *Spatiality* (London: Routledge, New Critical Idiom, 2012). About the "lived space" see also Henry Lefebvre, *The Production of Space*, trans. D. Nicholson-Smith (Oxford: Basil Blackwell, 1991); and Edward W. Soja, *Postmodern Geographies: The Reassertion of Space in Critical Social Theory* (London: Verso, 1989).

3. See Immanuel Kant, "Transcendental Aesthetic," in *Critique of Pure Reason*, trans. Marcus Weigelt (London: Penguin Books, 2007).

4. Edmund Husserl, *Thing and Space (1907)*, trans. R. Rojcewicz (Dordrecht: Kluwer, 1997), § 14 (HUA 16:43).

5. Husserl, § 14 (HUA 16:43).

6. Edmund Husserl, *On the Phenomenology of the Consciousness of Internal Time (1905)*, trans. J. Barnett Brough (Dordrecht: Kluwer, 1991) 1, 5 (HUA 10).

7. Husserl, 1, 5 (HUA 10).

8. Husserl, *Thing and Space (1907)*, § 19, 52 (HUA 16:62).

9. Husserl, § 19, 52 (HUA 16:62).

10. Husserl, § 20, 55 (HUA 16:66).

11. Husserl, § 20, 55 (HUA 16:66).

12. See, for example, "The Identity of the Tone, of the Temporal Object, and of Each Phase of the Temporal Object in the Flow of the Time-Consciousness," in Husserl *On the Phenomenology of the Consciousness of Internal Time (1905)*, 220 ss.

13. Husserl, *Thing and Space*, § 20 (HUA 16:67–68).

14. Husserl, § 21 (HUA 16:69).

15. Husserl, § 21 (HUA 16:70).

16. Husserl, §21 (HUA 16:70).

17. Husserl, 59 (HUA 16:71).

18. See Husserl, § 25 (HUA 16:83–84).

19. Husserl, § 1 (HUA 16:5).

20. Husserl, § 1 (HUA 16:5).

21. Husserl, § 44 (HUA 16:154).

22. Husserl, § 44 (HUA 16:155).

23. Husserl, § 44 (HUA 16:155–156).

24. Husserl, § 44 (HUA 16:154).

25. The unpublished works by Husserl translated in French by D. Frank, D. Pradelle, and J.-F. Lavigne in the volume "La Terre ne se meut pas" also face the kinesthetics-spatiality matter. See Edmund Husserl, *La terre ne se meut pas*, eds. D. Frank, D. Pradelle, and J.-F. Lavigne (Paris: Les éditions de Minuit, 1989).

26. Husserl (= Idee II).

27. Husserl, § 38: The Body *(Leib)* as the organ of the will and as the seat of free movement, 159–60.

28. Husserl, § 36, 152.

29. Husserl, § 36, 152.

30. Michel Henry, *Incarnation: Une philosophie de la chair* (Paris: Seuil, 2000). Henry's quotations are from Philippe Capelle-Dumont, *Phénoménologie et incarnation*, in *Transversalités* (Paris: Janvier-mars, 2002), 1–124.

31. Henry, 88–89.

32. Henry, 88–89.

33. Henry, 88–89.

34. Michel Henry, *I Am the Truth: Toward A Philosophy of Christianity*, trans. S. Emanuel (Stanford: Stanford University Press, 2003).

35. Henry, 12.

36. Henry, 15, 17.

37. Henry, 17.

38. Henry, 34.

39. Michel Henry, *Phénoménologie et langage (Ou: pathos et langage)*, in *Michel Henry: L'épreuve de la vie*, eds. A. David and J. Greisch (Paris: Les éditions du Cerf, 2001), 25.

40. Henry, *Incarnation*, 70–71.

41. Michel Henry, *The Essence of Manifestation*, trans. G. Etzkorn (The Hague: Martinus Nijhoff, 1973), 226–27.

42. See Didier Franck, *Heidegger et le probleme de l'espace* (Paris: Minuit, 1986).

43. See Jean-Louis Chrétien, *Spacious Joy: An Essay in Phenomenology and Literature* (Lanham, MD: Rowman and Littlefield, 2019).

44. Chrétien, 6.

45. Chrétien, 3.

46. Chrétien, 3.

47. Chrétien, 18.

48. See Jean-Louis Chrétien, *L'espace intérieur* (Paris: Minuit, 2014).

49. See René Descartes, *Correspondance* (Paris: Vrin, 1996), letter on October 5, 1637, and September 12, 1638.

2

Interiority, Exteriority, Being-In
A Concise Analysis

Hans Rainer Sepp

The Primal Interior

In everyday life, but also in scientific observation, we usually set inside and outside against each other as a matter of course. But we should bear in mind that this opposition is relativized or reinterpreted in other cultures, such as in East Asia. Is the relationship between inner and outer, then, a European positing? And if so, what motivates this positing, and what is the genealogy of its meaning? "European" points to a mode of reflection that thematizes explicitly the relation between outside and inside. This becomes clearer when we take into account that this form of reflection correlates to the relation of subject and object. But if the inside denotes the "here" of the center of experience, and the outside, the "there" of the thing to which the experience refers, this concerns not only Europe in a general, nontheoretical-thematic sense—although this structure of reference was radicalized in Europe in the formation of objectification theory—but also, arguably, every human practice that is directed toward any thing that is relative or "other" to me.

Thus, it is necessary to distinguish, first, that every day, worldly practice already deals with the difference between inside and outside in its reference to things. Practice entails interest, which is always determining, and grasps the external object from its own specific perspective. Second, the dominance of this interest-led grasp of the real forms the central motif for both European and Eastern philosophy, especially Buddhism.

European philosophy recognizes in the thing-interest of practice a myopic worldview—and correlatively—an arbitrary, subjective attitude. In order to counter this subjectivist attitude, European philosophy first develops a radically objectivist attitude that strives to overcome the limited purview of individual perspective. In modernity, the latter is surpassed in the recourse to the background subjectivity of the Kantian transcendental subject, in which both the perspectival subject's attitudes are to be integrated and the practical and theoretical termination in the object is to be avoided. Thus, European *theoría* is confronted with the basic problem that not only the object-related attitude but also the transcendental approach as theorizing reflection have to deal with the reproach of objectification. The reproach that subjective experience is still localized in the canon of object-oriented European science by a radicalized, transcendental theory characterizes, for example, the entire engagement of Heidegger's early philosophizing with Husserl's transcendental phenomenology. To mainstream objectifying, thematic reflection, however, there have been a few counter-positions that first appeared in ancient skepticism and later expressed especially in Eckhart or, in the present time, in Michel Henry, whose *phénoménologie de la vie* seeks to uncover an original interior that lies before any inside-outside difference. This interiority can be understood, as in Henry, simply as life—as the self-movement of the subjective; to Eckhart, it is the innermost of the timeless and spaceless, as well as the unnamable, the "ground of the soul."

A parallel can be observed in Buddhism; although here it is precisely about the change of practice, about the practical elimination of the functioning object-related subjectivity, the handling of subjective perspectivity is not oriented to the opposition of practice and theory. Thus, Zen Buddhism in particular—contrary to the usual style of human practice—seeks to reach that basic mode of existence that lies below any "discriminating," distinguishing consciousness and thus also a thematic inside-outside relation, for instance—as already referred to by Dōgen—in the concentration on the present in the experience of the "here" through the sitting posture of zazen. Zazen is the attempt, through a corporeal posture,[1] to suspend the reference point of the object-oriented world guided by self-interest and experience the originary "experiencing" itself that carries this reference. The essential point is that through this practice, no state is attained that did not exist previously; rather, the experiencing experience itself, which had earlier disguised itself with the escape into the object, emerges.[2] In his early work, Nishida Kitarō treats this original inner being as the pre- and extra-discursive "Pure Experience" lying before all activity of consciousness.[3]

In recourse to schools of Buddhism as well as to authors of European mysticism and finally to phenomenology, such an original kind of inner being can be conceived as a basic interior, as the self-movement of life, which is always in function but which rarely becomes thematic in the contexts of the practice in which we are related to "this" or "that." This interiority is prior to any meaning of inside and outside and thus also to their relation of reference. And when this interiority becomes thematic, it cannot be thought through a simple, objectifying view but only in such a way as to try to grasp what *cannot* be grasped objectively in itself. The peculiarity of this interior consists, consequently, in the fact that it is reflexively not capturable: it stands in no correlation to any experience that gives it originally. Even if we are aware that every one of us is experiencing something at this moment, we are not able—if we want to name it—to meet it one-on-one with words. In this sense, it is *a primal interior*: there is obviously no inside that we experience more originally than our experiencing itself; as a primordial experience, it represents the ground of all being able to experience. Since this original interior is that of experiencing itself, which everyone carries out for themselves, it is absolutely individuating: it cannot be experienced communally. Levinas's concept of *séparation* refers to this state of the in-dividual, ab-solute, and absolutely separated.[4]

The interior thus appears in at least two ways: on the one hand, as the not object-related—and in itself speechless—self-movement of our experience, which, as a primordial inside, does not already stand in parallel to an outside and, on the other hand, as the meaning of an inside, which we use to contrast with the meaning of an outside. If one asks in what relation that primal interior stands to the pair of inside and outside, the following thesis can be formulated: the primal interior on the one hand and the relation of inside and outside on the other hand are *not on the same level*; they are not comparable and thus do not represent an alternative. But they are not without connection because the former is in the latter as its basic element. This means *experiencing* as an accomplishment—which already functions in any experience of *something* but usually does not become thematic—is the former with respect to any reference to the object. This will be clarified in what follows.

In order to substantiate the expressed thesis, we must first take a detour and ask whether *the outside* is not also experienced in an original way. If the thematic inside-outside relation already begins too late, that is, if it always has the primal interiority of pure experiencing as its precondition, there is perhaps an outside that is also not experienced originally in the realm of (practical or theoretical) meaning, such that one can perhaps say that the "outside" of sense formation constitutes precisely the original concept of the exterior. Is there, then, an outside reference that is *not cognitive* in a broad sense? In other words, is there also a primal outside, just as we speak of a primal inside? And if there is, how do the two primordial forms relate to each other?

The Primal Exterior

The question of the original experience of the outside must begin at a deeper point than where "outside" is already understood in some way, regardless of whether it concerns a worldly/practical or epistemological understanding. For the original experience of the outside—of a primal exterior—consists precisely in the fact that the corporeal interior reaches its absolute limit: "there," where my bodily experience encounters *resistance*. "Outside" is experienced first and foremost as the sense-*less* influence on my basic corporeal ability, in such a way that the movement of my inner being is prevented by something that either does not originate from my corporeal state or is experienced in such a way that it exceeds its normal functioning, such as a pain that assaults me.

Max Scheler was probably the first to clearly point out that *the real* in the strict sense is not originally experienced by meaning but on the path of resistance. Following from this, we can say: the experience of the real—and with it the primal experience of an outside—is based on the experience of a limitation when acting out my interiority, whether the surface of my corporeality is touched or pressed by something that is absolutely alien to it or whether a resistance arises in me, for instance, when my wish to remember is inhibited. As a result, within the inner being a resistance directed against it builds up or, in other words, the inner being experiences in itself its outside becoming—its being oriented to the outside. Thus, the original experience of the outside can first be understood, in general, as a suspending of the interiority in itself by a confrontation with something other than itself, something that transcends my momentary experience. Any meaning of "outside" and "inside" is founded in this experience.

The problematic of the outside, which encounters my corporeality from within and transcends it at the same time, is closely linked to the European discussion of the reality of the "outside world." This is the context in which Scheler speaks of the original, sense-*less* experience of the real. In his unfinished treatise "Idealism and Realism," he emphasizes that both points of view—that of idealism and that of realism—are subject to an incorrect basic assumption. Both cases tacitly assume that the reality of an object is a *datum of knowledge*, which idealism transfers to subjectivity and realism to the real.[5] The *próton pseúdos* of both idealism and realism consists in the fact that both the meaningful and reality "are considered *inseparable* with respect to their possible immanence of knowing and consciousness"[6]; in other words, in the tacit presumption that the real can be spoken about in the same way as the non-real, that is, all sense-based objects and ideas. While any sense can—in principle—be immanent to knowing and consciousness as itself, albeit in different degrees of adequation, this is not the case of the nonetheless *experiential* real, which remains "*alien* to consciousness and *independent—essentially* transcendent."[7] The experienced real cannot find entrance into knowledge and consciousness as such, since it is only given by resistance but has its genuine mode of being experienced.

This means experiencing and sense-related experiencing do not coincide. As far as it can be experienced originally only by resistance, one cannot speak about the real itself. But if one speaks of the "real," it is about *the meaning* of the real. Terminologically, *the real*, which is originally experienced as only sense-*less* by pure corporeal pressure, can be distinguished from *reality*. "Reality," in this regard, concerns the way of making the subject *the realness* of the real; that is, not to subjugate the real to the meaning, since the experienced real itself cannot be represented by sense directly, but to determine the realness of the real by linguistic expression, and in such a way that this realness is not relative to consciousness.

Hedwig Conrad-Martius,[8] in particular, undertook the latter in phenomenological-ontological terms by locating the meaning of the realness of reality neither in the context of the belief in an *Ansich* in the lifeworld, philosophy, and science nor in the transcendental consciousness that constitutes all forms of meaning. Her ontological analysis of what reality is differs from the traditional, epistemologically motivated question of the reality of the external world in that she advocates leaving the question of whether there is reality in abeyance and instead tries first to grasp what *reality* actually means. She finds the starting point for this in everyday experience, but without following its attitude of belief: "We ask what makes or would make a reality, *if* it is factually found or even only thought to be found, into such a reality in itself."[9]

So if we ask what the original experience of the outside is, the answer can be that it is the corporeal experience of resistance, the "real" that encounters us "inside" or "outside" ourselves, consequently motivating the topos of "inside and outside" and therein preceding the distinction between an inner and outer world. This being approached by the real is not mediated by meaning, but it provokes the genesis of sense, indeed of the world as an imaginative, temporal-spatial context. This imaginative terrain, opening up with and for the sense, makes it possible to escape the encroachment by the real into a relatively protected realm and to encounter the real with an entirely different capacity: *understanding*. Security against the danger of being delivered to the real promises structures that form the net of a time-space as independent from the *hic et nunc*, that is, the world as a transcendental-imaginative one.

Such spanning of worldliness, however, has a marginal zone in which the limit of the formation of sense is still experienced in itself, for the natural world-attitude already contains a transcendence of the subject's own circle of sense. At this point *world* becomes ambiguous: it is the transcendental-imaginative totality of positively available sense, a reflection of our existential place, giving us a practical/worldly certainty and, at the same time, something that transcends us and escapes our dispositive grasp. This worldly experience of transcendence can become the starting point for philosophically questioning the state of the "world as such," that is, to try to determine, for example, the autarchic meaning of its being-real, which is not relative to our constitution of sense. To ask for the reality of the "world" in its cosmic state does not contradict that the real is originally to be experienced always in resistance and that the ability to form a coherent net of sense is motivated by this very experience of resistance.

Thus, the worldly belief in a real "outside" proves to be a conglomerate that is located in the horizon of sense but at the same time is rooted in the experiencing of the primal interior and the experience of a primal exterior. On the one hand, this belief is based in the interior movement of life that not only takes place in absolute self-affection but also, at the same time, drives beyond itself and generates meaning in life. The action of this driving beyond oneself can be grasped with the concept of *desire*. On the other hand, belief bears witness to the fact that what is desired is not readily attainable, as its attainment meets with resistance. Belief thus becomes a witness and an implicit expression of the experience in which reality cannot be subjugated in the orientation toward the desired object and thus remains unavailable. The fact that reality is discovered in its surplus potential points to the connection between *belief* in reality and religious *faith*.

The epistemological question concerning the extent to which our experience meets external reality is thus subject to a twofold inadequacy. On the one hand, it addresses its concern to an inapplicable medium by seeking to answer the question in the context of sense. On the other hand, it is subject to the same limitation that it wants to overcome: the subjective-lifeworld orientation to reality. For the question still remains bound to this subjective outlook in which it realizes itself in the form of a desire by *striving for* the demonstration of an access to reality. However, it is not about searching for criteria in how far human existence meets reality but about *showing* how it is always already affected by reality and how this reality thus witnessed in its independence.

Thus, the topic of reality will no longer be an epistemological one but one that questions the core content of our worldly experience and ultimately forms a concept of reality or of the outside that leaves it in its absolute alterity: namely, how the outside—which initially encounters me sense-*lessly* as the real that resists me—correlates to that which transcends me (or as reality, or cosmos, or the world "itself") with worldly experience or with theoretical comprehension, without being reducible to either. In this sense, the outside, the world, reality, are grasped in a *meontic* way. "Meontic" here refers not to the alternatives of either cognitively appropriating that which encompasses me or to postulate it as unknowable; rather, it refers to the possibility of recognizing the absolute withdrawal of the real, and of *not* approaching its structure ontically as positively given but meontically as an Other entirely in relation to my understanding of the world and, under this presupposition, of designing the possibility of a *speculative* access[10] to its independence.

One essential point remains open: if every formation of sense takes place in the context of sociality, then in contrast, the experience of resistance is bound to a singular corporeal existence, which is respectively mine. If one admits the fact of an a-social, separated, in-dividual existence, it is no longer possible to start with the formation of sense and the world as *intersubjective* facts. It is rather necessary to show how sociality generates itself in view of this radical single existence. Here it can only be hinted that the rescue by the protective umbrella of sense takes place at the same time as an emergence of the social. The communal creation of meaning rescues the single existence not only from the resistive unpleasantness of nature but also, through norms and laws, from the intrusiveness of others and from the resistive abysses in one's own self. The creation of meaning and language not only saves the single beings but saves them *together*.

Preliminarily summarized, the experience of a primal exterior has a threefold foundation: first, it presupposes a *functioning inside* (primal interior), which, second, *desires* at the same time—it does not only remain within itself in the realization of its experiencing and permanently rests in itself—and third, it creates the *borderline experience of resistance* through the attempt to realize its own desire. The corporeal experience of a primal exterior marks the beginning of a path on which—through the establishment of sense—the interpretations of "inside" and "outside," or of an inner and outer world, finally emerge.

The most important result of the considerations so far, however, consists in the closer explication of the thesis expressed above: that it is not enough to juxtapose "inside" and "outside" and to attribute every interior or exterior to a part of this pair of opposites. Rather, the primal interior is the real—or, to use Husserl's term, the *reell*—precondition for the experience of a primal exterior, just as it is the condition for the founding of sense, which splits the real into inside and outside. A common level, on which an outside confronts an inside, is created only by meaning. As related to sense, this common level is socially constituted from the beginning, just as it presupposes, at the same time, an original interiority and the experience of an original exteriority acquired on the basis of resistance, both of which are founded in the sense-*less* realization of an a-social, *in-dividual* existence. Radical in-dividuality, in the sense of *separation* on the one hand and sociality on the other, therefore do not contradict each other; here, too, both act on each other on different levels that can never be congruent. Only recently, and at first probably only in the regional cultural development of Europe, did the *individual* come to be segregated in the context of the social, even to the point of becoming individualistic, and thus opposed to the social in the latter itself.

Being-in

Here, further questions suggest themselves: What is the difference between the original, primal interior as the subject's self-completion and the Being-in (*Insein*) that Heidegger speaks of in *Being and Time* in relation to Being-in-the-world (*In-der-Welt-sein*)?[11] What is the relation of the inner, which is opposed to an outer in the context of social formation of meaning, to both forms of being-in: the being-in as the primal interior and being-in as being-in-the-world? And what follows from such a splitting of the being-in into these two forms or our behavior toward them?

As is well known, the Being-in in *Being and Time* does not designate for Heidegger a being-in of the kind that one thing is in another, but it is the "formal existential expression for the Being of Dasein, which has being-in-the-world as its essential state."¹² As "being-alongside-with" (*Sein-bei*), Dasein is "always 'outside' " with the objects of its interest to be taken care of, whereby this being-in-the-outside itself still represents a mode of that "inside" that is formed by the structure of Being-in to which the ecstatic turning outside still belongs.¹³ The inside (of Being-in), which encompasses its outside-being, underlies any formation of sense, and thus also that which distinguishes an inside from an outside, in such a way that any concrete meaning is tied back to the structure of Being-in, which Heidegger explicates as the mutual interpenetration of state of mind (*Befindlichkeit*), understanding (*Verstehen*), and discourse (*Rede*).¹⁴ However, the conditional of concrete meaning is still subordinated to that which is sense-related, and the question becomes whether Being-in is sufficiently grasped when it is located in the *logos*: in discourse, which originally determines both state of mind and understanding.¹⁵

When Heidegger puts the determination of the Being-in at the center of his *Daseinsanalytik*, he brings to the concept what had already become apparent a hundred years before. From the eighteenth to the nineteenth century, we see the beginning of a process that can be described as a profound change of the subject. In the course of this process, the absolute, autonomous subject of idealistic philosophies loses its prominent position. It no longer faces the world but finds itself *in* the world. With the establishment of transcendental philosophy, the subject had gained an exclusive position. Fichte still locates everything in the ego: "The I should . . . set itself *for itself*; it should set itself *as* set by itself. It should therefore, as certainly as it is an I, have the principle of life and consciousness merely in itself."¹⁶ With the "in itself," the figure of a founding center is implied, even if no center of experience is yet conceived into which the "I" itself would still be embedded.

Friedrich Schlegel drafted his concept of a "universal poetry" (*Universalpoesie*) a few years later under the direct impression of Fichte's definition of the ego. In the *Athenaeum*, he writes about "romantic poetry" as "progressive universal poetry" (*progressive Universalpoesie*): "Only it can, like the epic, become a mirror of the whole surrounding world, an image of the age. And yet it too can *hover* most *between* the represented and the representing, free from all real and ideal interest, on the wings of poetic reflection *in the middle*, always potentiating this reflection and multiplying it as in an endless series of mirrors."¹⁷ Even if universal poetry as "transcendental poetry" (*Transzendentalpoesie*)¹⁸ is still ascribed the central position of the absolute subject, the idea of a middle realm between subjectivity and objectivity is, at the same time, already formulated, and poetic reflection is shifted there.

This middle, however, leaves its inhabitants placeless in the sense that they are not rooted in it but left afloat. The centrality of subjectivity is weakened, but at a price: the new place of the Romantic worldview, up to its radical form of Romantic irony, promises no real foothold. The subject threatens to be torn apart in the process. Existing only as a hollow form, the subject's habit of perceiving itself as the reason for everything still chains it to itself, while the non-subjective real has already become independent. Thus, suspended in a quasi-airless space, the subject is stretched out in an in-between whose edges mark, on the one hand, its lost home and, on the other, the reality that has become largely unavailable in its real contents and their ideal foundations.

In Wilhelm von Humboldt's work, the subject is newly located by language, but in such a way that the subject finds its place in the middle between its capacity to dispose of language and being disposed of by it. Thus, in his study "On the Diversity of the Human Language Structure and Its Influence on the Intellectual Development of Humankind" (*Über die Verschiedenheit des menschlichen Sprachbaues und ihren Einfluß auf die geistige Entwicklung des Menschengeschlechts*), published posthumously in 1836, he writes: "In the way language modifies itself in each individual, a power of man over it is revealed in contrast to its . . . power."[19] The subject has found a new anchorage at the price of giving up its absolute position; the center of its existence is the narrow gap between a dependence on language, which the subject can no longer control, and a freedom that is still possible under these circumstances.

With the "Great Noon" (*der Große Mittag*) in his *Zarathustra*, Nietzsche unfolds the experience of a middle that has gained breadth so that one can literally settle down in it. Here, the reconciliation of subject and reality is thought, but in such a way that this reconciliation has to be formed again and again as something that can only be realized instantaneously and fleetingly: Zarathustra's settling down unintentionally under an old vine at the noon hour leads to an experience of presence that is as simple as it is intense. The pretending, purpose- and *télos*-driven life process is interrupted. In this pause a unique moment opens up as an in-between that no longer indicates a directional dimension rooted in the subject and reaching out to the world but in which, in a con-creative balance, subjectivity is already permeated by reality, which is also shaped by the experiencing subject.[20] The interruption of temporal course ("still") makes a temporally-spatially unique experiencing and its worldly content emerge completely ("perfect"). However, it is not only the tendency toward a fixating, monotonous synchronism that is disturbed: this moment also has absolute boundaries, a beginning and an ending. Thus, a middle is conceived in which the subject is completely absorbed in its con-creative exchange with reality, but only for this moment. The opening of a middle—which grants a settling down and fulfillment therein—and the subsequent turning away from it do not form an indissoluble contradiction for Nietzsche; they are, rather, the undistorted mode of the self-realization of life.

Heidegger's transformation of the subject, first to Dasein and later to the human being, who as a mortal (*Sterblicher*) is embedded in the world, puts the emphasis on the insertion (being-in) of human existence into an event encompassing it, for which Heidegger later, after his *Kehre*, uses the word "enowning" (*Ereignis*) or more commonly in English: "event." Thereby it becomes clear that only the center itself, and only a certain type of being-in, is favored: one that establishes the being-in in a context formed by language and understanding. Being-in then means to stand in an "understanding of being."[21]

Here, therefore, a question inevitably arises about the radicality of the "in" and the middle formed by it. Is it a middle that has the tendency to homogenize itself by keeping itself *on this side* of Being and, moreover, is only aligned to the area of (opening/closing) sense, whereby the total figure of being-in-the-world or of the time-play-space is not itself still under or transgressed toward that which cannot be grasped with the means of this middle area, that is, the corporeality and the real itself? The only crossing over that can take place here is obviously that from a being-alongside objects to the conditions of this being-alongside revealed in its preliminarily functioning by the fundamental-ontological analysis or by means of thinking and poetry in Heidegger's later work. Heidegger's thinking of being, however, is then still subject to Nietzsche's criticism of European Apollonianism—in *Birth of Tragedy*—as a radicalizing independence of the center, insofar as he has shown not only world constitution as the formation of a centered area of sense but also that every such process of becoming-the-world as becoming-sense—not only that of an objectifying attitude—carries the tendency to absolutize itself: every center, which no longer knows a *radical outside*, tends toward totalization. But in what do the radical abysses of sense consist? Is there an alternative being-in, and what role does the subject play in its emergence?

Since the juxtaposition of a subject that is autonomous from the world and a subject or Dasein that is in the world is not sufficient, the alternative is not a traditional subject versus event (*Ereignis*). For already in the nineteenth century, as indicated, a different conception of the subjective had emerged.

This new subject fits neither into the template of the idealistic tradition nor into that of a social being in the world grounded in understanding. To account for this new subject, it is necessary to point out more precisely the character of the inner being and to ask to what extent the primal interior provides, in fact, an alternative being-in to the being-in-the-world.

The crucial point is this: from the perspective of the primal being-in, the corporeal interiority, the sense genesis of the being-in-the-world can be understood—a vice versa movement or reversal does not lead from the latter to the former. The necessary modules for the outline of the being-in-the-world lie, on the one hand, in that original being-in of the self-movement of the living, bodily subject and, on the other hand, in the experience of its absolute limit in the resistive contact with the real, through which the formation of the outside first takes place. The constitution of an imaginative world—a world of sense—emerges as a counter-resistive response to the encroachment of the real, which is perceived only as pressure. As already indicated, the connection, based on language and meaning, that leads from the experience of the in-dividual corporeal subject to the formation of a world grounded in sense can only be comprehended as a social one. As mentioned above, it is sense itself that effects the mediation: each individual subject makes the experience of the resistant violence of the real, but in the mastering of this experience sociality is founded, namely, by means of the sense, which thereby produces and stages itself in the ground plans of a world by which it is formed. This process takes place directly such that it roots the radical in-dividuality within a network of social references, out of which the "individual" first understands herself or himself as a social one.

The positionality of the corporeal in-dividual, the real experience of a resistant outside acting on this positionality, and the social-imaginative foundation of the world taking place within the purview of the positionality, are three components that interact and form a sequence. However, each stage is not created by the previous one. The positionality of the in-dividual does not produce the real experience; for this, a real is required that is not dependent on the original self-movement of a corporeal subject. On the contrary, the fact of the primal interior can be described in its reality as a real (*reell*) immanent fact, which explains why the subject can experience itself as resistant. This then entails the paradoxical experience of the outside in itself, and this paradox is mostly reflexively grasped when I actually locate the experienced resistance in myself.

In the same way, the experience of the real does not bring forth an imaginative world. Rather, it must be seen as the prompting moment that gives birth to a sense-related, mental potency. From this side, too, it can be said that the experience of an original interior and an original exterior is not compatible with the meaning of "inside" and "outside": that is, that imagination and real experience are not on the same level, neither forming opposites nor polarities but operating on completely different fields. All of humanity's cultural achievements exhibit this asynchronous relationship between the imaginative and the real, which is particularly evident in cultural creations that are localized in real space, such as the house, the city, and the territory: they are as much imaginative products as they are real facts. They exist, however, because they are based not only on a drive to form meaning but also on a corporeal experience of the real, which, moreover, accompanies every formation of sense.

Consequently, it is not sufficient to speak only of being-in-the-world; rather, *two* forms of being-in are to be distinguished, which are not reducible to each other in their factual content but of which the one, being-in-the-world, is grounded in the other in the sense that it is released from the latter in its effectiveness. Here one can see how philosophical approaches have given preference to either the one or the other mode of being-in. While Heidegger allows human existence to be unilaterally grounded in being-in-the-world, by contrast Henry grounds it unilaterally in the being-in of transcendental self-affection. Nishida's early reference to "Pure Experience" is close to the latter, whereas the later Nishida with his "logic of place" tries to think of both together under the traditional titles of the "single" and the "general" in such a way that the interaction of both each forms a "place."²² However, this interaction is understood in such a way that both the single and the general produce a middle. Such a middle, however, that as "contradictory self-identity," it forms in itself a field of tension, in which one side constantly experiences itself confronted with a completely other and vice versa. A pretended self, be it a single existence or a community, is thus only itself to the extent that it simultaneously touches all that it is not, but *ex negativo*, in a meontic way, without being able to appropriate the other. This form of thinking can be found against the background of Zen Buddhism not only in the entire Kyōto School but also in Adorno's *Negative Dialectics* and Fink's *Meontics*.

From the interior of the experiencing life there are thus three forms of the outside: first, that which leads one's own capacity to its real limit, which in the experience of the resistant "indicates" a sense-*less* real; second, the manifold meanings of the outside in the contexts of sense, which are created by normative socialization; and third, the meontic boundary experienced in these contexts to that which encompasses me. Since that which encompasses cannot be represented positively by any given convention, its outside can only be named in negativity—in the extreme form of the negation of meaning in itself. Or, in other words, the socialized, sense-related, being-in of being-in-the-world harbors two abysses in itself, both of which cannot be accounted for by Heidegger's ontological difference: on the one hand, there is the abyss of the absolute withdrawal of sense, which means that a *totum* that encompasses or supports human existence can never be phenomenally given in a positive way with the means of sense, but only negatively, meontically, as an absolute outage; on the other hand, there is the abyss of sense in general, which consists in the fact that every reference to sense finds its absolute limit in the resistive experience of the sense-*less* real.

The twofold meontic and real abyss of the being-in-the-world concerns both the reference to one's own corporeal self and to the "world" as such in its real status that is not relative to the worldliness of inner-worldly being. Consequently, the conception of the *identity* of the personal self becomes problematic for the determination of the self. Two proofs can be given for the thesis that there is no identity that is self-identical in the social. First, the ostensible identity of a group (family, clan, people, nation, etc.) is either the "style" or "type" of a way of life that emerges through a process of meaning or the forced will to the identical. To call a style or type of a factual being an "identity" would be wrong, since every style or type has its indeterminate and indeterminable marginal zones and is therefore fragile and open to the constant reconstruction of its meaning, and precisely because there is nothing self-identical in the first place, the will arises to make identical that which is non-identical.

Second, even a single, personal self does not have identity, insofar as it too is subject to the ongoing creation of meaning; as Levinas recognized, in the self's lowest level of Pure Experience (using Nishida's term), and only here, one encounters an absolute identity in such a way that *only I* make and can make this experience *here and now*. However, this self-realization of life cannot be lifted up to the higher level of a temporally enduring sense of positivity and marks, rather, the boundary of the imagination of such positive stock of meaning in a meontic, as well as in a real, respect.

From this follows a twofold way to relate to oneself: the first is in the acceptance of the absolute, real (*reell*) identity preceding sense and constantly manifesting itself in the mere carrying on of my everyday life—an identity which, as real facticity, cannot be positively inserted into worlds of sense but can only be described meontically; the second is in the acceptance of the possibility to come to know myself in its social dimension. In this way, I come to know myself personally, as an established sense of my person, and as a continuously establishing self. This constant establishing of the self and one's person means that there is no absolute identity; rather, here, there we find open-ended process of self- and personal-becoming. The first is the confrontation with my being-in in the context of the primal interior; the second is my confrontation with myself in the context of its socialized being-in-the-world.

A parallel applies to the abyss of the "world" as such. If the worldliness of my being-in-the-world is the totality only of its respective horizon of understanding, the absolute borderline of the abyss is not only in the outside that results from the experience of a real resistance provoking its outline. Here also arises the possibility of extending the concept of the world beyond this abyss of sense and, as has already been sketched, of asking for the *totum* of the world or reality in general, which in the framework of phenomenal givenness can only be again meontically applied. And, if necessary, one can make use of the tool of speculation in the controlling consciousness of this border or limit transgression.

Inside-Outside

Finally, to return to the initial question: To what extent do East Asian perceptions relativize the relationship of inside-outside and thus also the talk of an interior? A threefold answer could be given. The first answer would be to undertake a genealogy of sense that would try to show what exactly this conception refers to and what motivates it. (Zen) Buddhism understands the relation of inside-outside as a dichotomous distinction to be abolished like all "discriminations." As we have shown, this distinction correlates with certain social setups and concerns a specification within the framework of being-in-the-world, but not with the underlying pre-forms of a primal inside and primal outside. One could say that the concentration on the center (being-in) of human existence from Nietzsche to Heidegger was already an attempt to prevent the independence of the inside-outside relation and the tendency toward objectification in relation to things and the world.

The second answer refers to a concept that has been tried out both in East Asia and (albeit only selectively) in Europe: namely, to think of the middle as a tense *in-between*, in the way that in the worldly being, the very Other to it, the encompassing of the "world," or the depth of the self, appears negatively or meontically. Since here the abyssal is not positively determined, it escapes both externalizing objectification and subjective appropriation. In Europe this may have been intended by Heraclitus when he refers to the all-embracing as logos and consequently refuses to de-*fine* this everyday word in its meaning, that is, to fix it. Also, Zen Buddhism's reflection of the *satori* experience is not about a turning away from an area marked as "outside" to an "inside," as Augustine's phrase *in te redi ipsum* suggests for Europe.

Satori is experienced and cannot be expressed linguistically in a positivistic way. It can be expressed only negatively: the self becomes accessible only as something inaccessible to predicative, determinative speech. The place where this extreme position can be realized—apart from the dichotomy of inside-outside—is basically an incessant movement that realizes the in-between first in the resistance to being attached to things (to determinative speech), which is then followed by the awareness of the "absolute nothingness" as becoming free from this being-attached-to, and finally results in the renewed, transformed "turning back" to the concrete world. Against this background, it is indeed no longer appropriate to distinguish an outer from an inner world.

The third answer to the initial question consists in pointing out that in East Asian views there is nevertheless an original outside, the outside that defines itself in the resistance of the real but does not become thematic as such. An example of this is the story of Bodhidharma, who is said to have spent nine years in a cave in order to attain enlightenment by staring at the face of a rock. He famously achieved this when, after a long period of sitting on the ground, his limbs fell off. The satori, which made the linguistically and sensually structured world sink, was brought about by something nonlinguistic, nonsensual: corporeal pain and its radical overcoming. The satori is therefore based on a corporeal confrontation with the original, pure resistance occurring outside, which has no name, because its experience is extra-linguistic or sense-*less*.

As far as the relation of inside and outside is concerned, these four determinations would have to be made and are briefly summarized below.

One: The relation of inside and outside in its common use is relative when the relational elements occur on the same level, that is, that of language and the conventional formation of sense, which does not catch up with the borderline or liminal character of sense and language. Here the demarcation of inside/outside can be questioned, as well as the difference of the self-contained and the foreign, of the self and the other, and, in general, of the subject and the object. The alternative to these commonsense, binary oppositions, however, does not consist in a holism of whatever kind since every conception of wholeness bears the traces of its genesis from the partial. Also, the wholesale abolition of this opposition does not represent an alternative. As the East Asian example proves, it is rather a matter of dissolving the presuppositions of thought and language that underlie this opposition so that it is possible to make recourse to the opposition of inside and outside without substantively solidifying it.

Two: the relation of inside and outside is not relative where corporeality comes into play. The original inside is, as a real (*reell*) interior experience, the precondition for experiencing a resisting primal exterior, in the encounter with a real that I am not, which is "outside" insofar as "I" am not the originator and cause of this experience of resistance. This experienced "outside" is not yet a predicatively grasped or even named outside. Both forms—the original inside as my absolute (experienced here and now [*reell*], possibly resisting) primal interiority, as well as the original outside as my absolute (not to be derived from something else) outside experienced in the resistance of the real acting on me—are not only transcendent, as far as language and sense are concerned; as already explained, they are also not on the same level, in the sense that the primal exterior would be the outside to that primal interior, even if this experience of the outside presupposes a living organism equipped with the interiority of an original inside. It is now clearer that the primal interior and primal exterior are not correlative: they do not correlate insofar as the former is *I myself* and the latter is experienced with the means of the I-self. What is experienced is *not* the same as the I-self. Only in the context of sense formation—which is not yet at stake at this stage—could one speak of a correlation of the mode of *cogitare* and *cogitatum*. My real corporeal experience, however, has no correlate at all. Thus, only this latter experience yields that which is identical in itself.

The Buddhist modification of existential experience is directed against the first determination but implicitly accords with the second, without this becoming explicitly thematic.

Three: on the basis of the second determination, my real (*reell*) transcendental self (to which I am absolutely bound) and the real non-self (which absolutely transcends myself) separate. On the one hand, the self is transcendental not only because it can transcend itself in the context of sense (and has always transcended itself); since it cannot actually leave itself, it is transcendental in an even more original way—it *is* prior to any sense: it is always ahead of me and I can never catch up to it by means of sense. Yet, it remains *my self* in this absolute withdrawal. In its transcendental ability to let me transcend by means of sense in the direction of what I am not, I cannot dispose of the real (*reell*) inside; but I can reconstructively reveil the sense-sedimentations triggered by it piecemeal up to a certain degree—and this all the more radically, the more I am able to take a free stand on the conventions of that being-in-the-world to which I belong. The not-self, on the other hand, is transcendent not only because it transcends the sense *meontically* in itself but also because it is encountered in such a way that it *really* meets me before, and outside of, any sense as the real that I am not.

Both the real (*reell*) subjectivity of the self and the real, which I am not, are not relative to the historical world of being-in-the-world. Therefore, it would be inadmissible to designate this difference with the relation of inside and outside. Such a relation limited to sense would miss the fact that both the self-performance of the absolutely subjective and the original experience of the absolutely real—that is, the pure experiencing of the primal interior and the original experience of a primal exterior—transcend any context that would govern the meaning of my historical situation. Both this radical subject and the real are divorced from the subject-object dichotomy underlying the context of the historically or socially determined being-in, as well as from any "event" (*Ereignis*), which moves these dichotomous links into a middle realm as the center of the respective historical world; coextensive with such a dynamic would be the idealistic retracing of all meaning to an absolute, sense-constituting subjectivity that becomes just as absurd as the traditional question about the existence of the outside world so that a realism of whatever variety does not represent an alternative.

Four: if one asks how one can relate to these abysses of the historical world, both practically and theoretically, the answer would be in the realization of an *in-between* that meontically advances from the equally concrete and narrow center of a respective world into two border areas: both into the depths of the respective personal self, but always already over-formed by the social, and into the depths of one's own historical world, always already over-formed by the alien. At the periphery of these border areas, the uncapturable reality of the self and the completely other of the real—the real Other and the real Reality itself—appear, which nevertheless implies the constant demand for an unceasing process of illuminating the self and reality, starting from one's own historical being-in-the-world and in constant reconnection to it.[23]

Notes

1. The terms "corporeal" and "corporeality" used here are meant to express the idea that experience is always this two in one: on the one hand, our inner bodily experience, which is, on the other hand, an experience by means of our own physicality. This does not refer to an objectified body but designates the physical firmness and mass of the corporeity with which we encounter the resistant real with resistance on our part.

2. Thus Lin-Chi I-hsüan (Linji Yixuan, ninth century) emphasizes that where the object-related attitude ("You look outside yourself, going off on side roads hunting for something, trying to get your hands on something. That's a mistake.") is interrupted, the simple life process itself emerges: "Just act ordinary, without trying to do anything particular. Move your bowels, piss, get dressed, eat your rice, and if you get tired, then lie down." *The Zen Teachings of Master Lin-Chi: A Translation of the Lin-chi lu*, trans. Burton Watson (New York: Columbia University Press, 1993) 29, 31.

3. Cf. Kitarō Nishida, *An Inquiry into the Good, Zen no kenkyū, Tokyo 1911*, trans. Masao Abe and Christopher Ives (New Haven, CT: Yale University Press, 1990).

4. Cf. Emmanuel Levinas, *Totalité et Infini: Essai sur l'Extériorité (Phaenomenologica)*, vol. 8 (Den Haag: Martinus Nijhoff, 1961) chap. B.1, 23ff., *et passim*.

5. Cf. Max Scheler, "Idealismus–Realismus," in his *Späte Schriften (Gesammelte Werke)*, vol. 9, ed. Manfred S. Frings (München: Francke, [1976?]) See also, Max Scheler, "Idealism and Realism," in *Selected Philosophical Essays*, trans. David R. Lachterman (Evanston, IL: Northwestern University Press, 1973), 288–356.

6. Scheler, "Idealismus–Realismus," 185 (my translation).

7. Scheler, 186 (my translation).

8. Conrad-Martius undertakes a first systematic analysis of what "reality" actually means in an extensive study that she titled "Realontologie" and which appeared in 1923 in Husserl's *Jahrbuch*, the *Yearbook for Philosophy and Phenomenological Research* "Realontologie," in *Jahrbuch für Philosophie und phänomenologische Forschung*, vol. 6 ([Max Niemeyer?], 1923), 159–334. Later, she took up the theme of reality primarily in her book *Das Sein* published in 1957 (München: Kösel) and based it on studies she had already done in the 1930s.

9. Conrad-Martius, "Realontologie," 159 (my translation).

10. Concerning the possibility of a speculative philosophy on a phenomenological basis, see Hedwig Conrad-Martius, "Phänomenologie und Spekulation" (1956/1957) in *Schriften zur Philosophie,* ed. Eberhard Avé-Lallemant, vol. 3 (München: Kösel, 1965), 370–84. Cf. also the similar project of Eugen Fink, for example, presented in his article "Die intentionale Analyse und das Problem des spekulativen Denkens" (1951) in *Nähe und Distanz: Phänomenologische Vorträge und Aufsätze*, ed. F.-A. Schwarz (Freiburg: Karl Alber, 1976) 139–57.

11. Cf. Martin Heidegger, *Being and Time*, trans. John Macquarrie and Edward Robinson (Oxford: Blackwell, 2001; first ed. 1962), §12.

12. Heidegger, 80.

13. Heidegger, 89.

14. Heidegger, §§ 28–38.

15. Heidegger, 172.

16. "Das Ich soll sich . . . *für sich selbst* setzen; es soll sich setzen, *als* durch sich selbst gesezt. Es soll demnach, so gewiß es ein Ich ist, das Princip des Lebens und des Bewußtseyns lediglich in sich selbst haben." Johann Gottlieb Fichte, *Grundlage der gesammten Wissenschaftslehre*, in *Sämmtliche Werke*, ed. Immanuel Hermann Fichte, vol. 1 (Berlin: Veit, 1845/1846), 273 (my translation).

17. "Nur sie kann gleich dem Epos ein Spiegel der ganzen umgebenden Welt, ein Bild des Zeitalters werden. Und doch kann auch sie am meisten *zwischen* dem Dargestellten und dem Darstellenden, frei von allem realen und idealen Interesse auf den Flügeln der poetischen Reflexion *in der Mitte schweben*, diese Reflexion immer wieder potenzieren und wie in einer endlosen Reihe von Spiegeln vervielfachen." Friedrich Schlegel, Fragment 116 in *Athenaeum: Eine Zeitschrift von August Wilhelm Schlegel und Friedrich Schlegel*, ed. Curt Grützmacher, vol. 1 (Reinbek: Rowohlt, 1969), 118f (my translation, my emphasis).

18. Schlegel, Fragment 238, *Athenaeum*, 1:144.

19. "In der Art, wie sich die Sprache in jedem Individuum modifiziert, offenbart sich, ihrer . . . Macht gegenüber, eine Gewalt des Menschen über sie." Wilhelm von Humboldt, *Werke*, ed. Wolfgang Stahl, vol. 5 (Rheda-Wiedenbrück: Mundus RM Buch and Medien Vertrieb GmbH, 1999) 57 (my translation).

20. "Still! Still! Didn't the world become perfect just now? What's happening to me? . . . Still! The world is perfect." *Thus Spoke Zarathustra: A Book for All and None*, eds. Adrian del Caro and Robert B. Pippin, trans. Adrian del Caro (Cambridge: Cambridge University Press, 2006), 223f.

21. In Heidegger's *Contributions to Philosophy*, the being of Dasein is grasped as "inabiding" (*Inständigkeit*): the Da-sein is the "inabiding *carriability*" (*inständige Ertragsamkeit*) of the clearing of the "be-ing itself" (*Lichtung des Seyns selbst*). Martin Heidegger, *Contributions to Philosophy (From Enowning)*, trans. Parvis Emad and Kenneth Maly (Bloomington: Indiana University Press, 1999), 210. In the "inabinding removal-unto the t/here" (*inständliche Entrückung in das Da*), it is the "*understanding of being*" that as "*staying within the openness* . . . shifts man into the openness of being." Heidegger, 213f.

22. See, for example, Nishida's essay "Sekai no jikodōitsu to renzoku" "Self Identity and Continuity of the World" (1935), in *Nishida Kitarō zenshū*, complete work ed., vol. 8 (Tokyo: Iwanami Shoten, 1988), 7–106.

23. This article was written at the *Central European Institute of Philosophy* in Prague (Faculty of Human Sciences of Charles University).

3

Self-Owning, Self-Transparency, and Inner Nudity

Hedwig Conrad-Martius on Interiority

CHRISTINA M. GSCHWANDTNER

"Aber daß es eine innere Nacktheit gibt, ist mir freilich noch nie eingefallen."

(But it never occurred to me that there could be such a thing as inner nakedness.)

—Hedwig Conrad-Martius[1]

In much of her work, Hedwig Conrad-Martius, a student of Husserl and early phenomenological thinker, develops careful distinctions between various kinds and levels of beings that would be sustainable in light of contemporary biological, physiological, botanical, zoological, medical, and psychological insights. Although she uses the traditional language of body, soul, and spirit—and in fact strongly criticizes thinkers, including Heidegger, who dispense with the notion of the soul—she does not simply adopt an Aristotelian, scholastic, or modern approach.[2] Rather, she engages in thorough phenomenological descriptions and creative thought experiments that enable her to show the similarities between various types of beings and transitional points from one kind of being to another in order to be able to define their respective essences or natures (*Wesen*). A particular construction of interiority plays an important role in her analysis of the human being and its nature.

This contribution will seek to unfold how interiority functions for Conrad-Martius, both in terms of her distinction of the human from other kinds of beings and in her analysis of absolute interiority as a form of "inner nudity." It will suggest that this notion of interiority is able to articulate a notion of human distinctiveness that is in productive continuity with that of other living beings, thus overcoming some of the sharp separations drawn not only in medieval thinkers (only humans have the *imago dei*), early modern thinkers (animals as machines but without soul or *mens*), and late modern thinkers (only humans have dignity and are to be treated as "ends in themselves" because they alone are rational beings) but also in more recent postmodern positions that, despite attacks on the Cartesian subject, continue to maintain firm distinctions between human and animal.[3] In fact, Conrad-Martius responds explicitly to some of these positions and is especially critical of contemporary attempts to eliminate the soul or to make it a mere "flip-side" of the body.[4] Furthermore, she advocates consciously for greater continuity between human and animal without giving up on distinctions altogether. She recognizes—and explicates—that both humans and "higher" animals have a soul or interiority that distinguishes them significantly from plants and "lower" animals (such as insects), while she also draws distinctions between animal (as *sichhaft*) and human (as *ichhaft*) that are about continuity more than absolute distinction. Her work on interiority consequently opens new possibilities for phenomenology more broadly and for eco-phenomenology more specifically, which helps us understand human consciousness more fully and articulate its nature with more nuance than is currently the case.

Interiorization (*Innerung*) and Self-Owning Interiority (*selbsthafte Innerlichkeit*)

Parsing the differences between types of beings (nonliving, plant, animal, human, etc.) is central to Conrad-Martius's project and a theme to which she returns often. The early *Metaphysische Gespräche* already engages the issue, with two conversation partners trying to ascertain the essence or nature of the human vis-à-vis plants, various animals, and even disembodied spirits.[5] She refines the distinctions the two dialogue partners work out in this early 1921 text in many later lectures (such as *Bios and Psyche* and the various lectures brought together in her collected works)[6] and other books (such as *Das Sein* or *Die Geistseele des Menschen*).[7] The distinctions between *Körper*,

Leib, Seele, Gemüt, and *Geist* become ways of distinguishing various beings from each other: plants in contrast to nonliving entities have *Leib,* not only *Körper*; animals in contrast to plants have *Seele,* not only *Leib*; spirits are *Geist* but have no *Leib* or *Seele*; humans have all of them, including *Gemüt.* Yet these are not simply terms for ontological categories; she carefully depicts how they are expressed phenomenologically in behavior, action, affect, and so forth. Ultimately, whether a being can interiorize and how it does so plays an important role in delineating these differences between kinds of beings.

The ability to interiorize is most frequently associated with the soul, thus it is an ability shared by humans and animals, though—interestingly—not by spirits or angels, who Conrad-Martius contends have no souls.[8] The soul's relation to the body is precisely one of interiorization (*Innerung*). She stresses this relationship between soul and body, which is often pictured as a "spatial" interiority. Indeed, she frequently uses language of "depth," "room," "realm," or "ground," and speaks of the soul as "spreading throughout" or "sinking into" the body—all of which connote an interiority that is placed *within* another space or place and involves a movement to the inside. The soul is spread into or illuminates the body; it reaches every part of the body and is on some level mirrored within it.[9] This is possible through an inner owning of the self via the soul that descends to its depth and from there operates on the entire body and all of its parts.[10] The body is the ground of the soul; it is rooted within it (rather than shaping it in Aristotelian fashion). The soul sinks into the body, into its innermost depth. Even animals search for this kind of interior depth.[11] The language she employs serves to cement her conviction that both soul and body are intimately connected, and, in some sense, even spatially coextensive. She often points to the psychosomatic dimensions of emotions and illnesses to show how an experience is expressed in both body and soul at the same time.[12]

Conrad-Martius consistently attributes this type of interiority to both humans and animals. Both animals and humans can live out of their interiority and, consequently, have a soul.[13] Plants may have a "soul-like principle," but no soul in the sense of feelings (*Empfindungen*) or a "selbsthafte Beherrschung von Leib."[14] This "possession" or "mastery" of the soul over the body is effected precisely through a process of interiorization. Plants consequently lack interiority: the plant "has no inner standpoint from which it could stand over against its own corporeality as shaped by itself."[15] An animal being is "interiorized" (*geinnert*) in a way that "attaches" to, expresses, or owns a self (*selbsthaft*).[16] The animal not only "has" interiority but shapes it actively, extends into it, fills its space. She speaks of this repeatedly as a "soul space" or "soul realm" (*Seelenbereich*), which functions as the interior space or room (*Innenraum*) of the self.[17] This realm or space can be filled by two kinds of feelings: on the one hand, "corporeal" feelings (*Leibgefühle* or *sinnliche Triebe*, i.e., sensory drives) such as hunger or fatigue (she calls them *leibseelisch*), and, on the other hand, affective feelings or emotions (*Gemütsbewegungen*) such as anger or joy (she calls these *seelisch-seelische* or *seelisch* in the proper—*eigentlich*—sense). The latter dwell in the inmost depth of the soul (*eigenster Innenraum der Seele*), while always also being expressed in bodily fashion through gestures, facial expressions, bodily postures, and so forth.[18]

She goes on to develop this even more fully by distinguishing between a kind of soul that enables self-owning or self-attachment (*selbsthaft*) in a form of interiority that all animals share and a form of the soul that opens up a unique interior space that is shaped by this soul in feeling or affect and which is found only in higher animals: "The plant becomes an animal being when the entelechial soul gains a 'seat' within itself and through this is able to separate from its own lived body in interiorily, self-owning fashion. If this self-owning principle of the soul that has become autonomous, beyond this also contains an inner 'space,' if it is so to say spread throughout its own interior and formed into it, then a soul of feeling or affect develops. This region of feeling is the owned inner realm of formation of a soul that has become self-owning."[19] Only animals own themselves in this way; such owning is possible only through a process of interiorization. If there is no "inner space," there can be no owning of the self.

Conrad-Martius elaborates this space more fully in a later text, in which she stresses the special process of interiorization more thoroughly. It is an absolute inner space that stands in marked contrast to the outside.[20] This true life of the soul, the depth of inner affect, including genuine affective impulses and movements, is found possibly in fish, reptiles, and birds but especially in mammals. She speaks of this unique interior life of the soul as a kind of "self-realization" of the soul.[21] This self-realization of the soul is an absolute interiority that responds and corresponds to the corporeal expressions of the soul and enables it to react to experiences and events.[22] It also constitutes a "self" that is able to respond to stimuli, move, make spontaneous decisions, and so forth, in a way that is self-motivated or self-directed. Although she often stresses the importance of such a space of interiority in higher animals, she acknowledges that an inner self is present even in "lower" animals (her example is an amoeba).[23] Thus, this ability to interiorize in self-owning fashion and the ability to control one's own body from an inner standpoint are already present in the simplest animals but not lost in more complex species.[24] Higher animals are able to find a balance between a mastery of the lived body and deepest possible dwelling within interiority.[25]

She calls this process "in-carnation" in contrast to the mere "excarnation" of lower species. That is to say, while plants only move outward, animals and humans also move inward. In her earlier work she puts this in terms of externality (*Äußerlichkeit*) and internality (*Innerlichkeit*). She stresses that these two are not just the reverse of each other—as several of her contemporaries claim—they cannot be transformed into each other, designate two different movements, and yet they are closely connected.[26] The soul is the very interiority as such of the body (*seine Innerlichkeit schlechthin*). Later she will define *Exkarnation* and *Inkarnation* as follows: "Excarnation is the bodily, selfless, outwardly oriented formation of the primordial self in the form of a species-specific substance, incarnation is the bodily, self-owning, inwardly oriented formation of the primordial self into itself. These two directions of being have absolute significance. They cannot be relativized, cannot be exchanged with each other."[27] She frequently insists on the distinctiveness of these movements, which—while complementary in some form—are neither simply two sides of the same coin nor interchangeable.[28]

Conrad-Martius argues that these distinctions show that body and soul are ontologically different. Feelings, affects, moods, and impulses are interior in a unique sense. They fill the depths of the soul's self.[29] This process of interiorization refers to deepening or lowering the self into its own innermost core. She reiterates the idea that any animal is able to do this on some level[30] but that only the highest animal and the human have a corresponding interior space in which the self can shape itself in various ways. Animal and human are entirely alike in this respect: "But we haven't stressed the most important thing yet: the selfless inhabitation (*selbstlose Durchwohnung*) that all vegetative and thus also animal and human have in common, as much as the self-owing inhabitation (*selbsthafte Durchwohnung*) that characterizes only animal and human, have the very same ground and source of being (*den gleichen Seinsgrund und Quellpunkt*)."[31] She stresses the interiority of this psychic space: "This is a space that is wholly interior (*ein ganz und gar und absolut innerer*), wholly and entirely owned by the self (*ein ganz und gar und absolut selbsthafter*)."[32] Through this inner center the self comes to itself and enters into existence.[33] It stands "upright" (*seinsselbstständig*) with an "inner posture" (*innere Haltung*).[34]

Doubled Interiority and Inner *Retroszendenz*

Human and animal, then, are closely connected and share similar kinds of interiority. What distinguishes human from animal is that the human has not only soul but also spirit (*Geist*). The human not only sinks into the self but also rises up from it. Conrad-Martius consistently identifies the soul with a deepening and lowering, while the spirit (*Geist*) designates a lifting and moving upward.[35] The spirit can govern the soul and guide the body.[36] Hence, there are three stages (or three ontic constitutions): first, the principle of entelechy operates outward on the material body (*Exkarnation*); second, an inner attachment to and owning of the self works *into* the lived body and permeates it from inside in terms of feeling and animation (*Inkarnation*); and third—and only in the human—the self rises up via spirit in personal freedom.[37] It is important to reiterate that both ex-carnation and in-carnation are, in some sense, forms of interiority: one is a movement outward from the interior self (albeit without a distinct "space" of interiority), and the other is a movement inward to the interior self, although they are operative in this full or absolute sense only in higher animals and humans.[38] Even the spirit will turn out to be a kind of interiority. Spirit rises up and transcends its own self, but in a manner that returns to itself and is self-reflective. Only humans can be located within, or return to their center in this specific way.[39] Humans have a unique capacity (both positive and negative) for interior self-concentration and self-absorption. The human capacity for spontaneity is unique in its capacity for deeper levels of interiority.[40]

In contrast to the animal, then, the human has a dual interiority, not only in regard to the lived body (as is true of the animal as well) but also in regard to the self. Humans confront themselves in doubled fashion and thus self-transcend into the interior in a twofold manner.[41] Later, Conrad-Martius will call this the "spirit-soul" (*Geistseele*) of the human, as distinct from the animal soul. In the human spirit this leads to an absolutely immanent "*Retroszendenz*" (i.e., a transcendence that works backward), in which the "I" can be related to itself by being separate from itself and referring back to itself. This distinction between the personal I and the self—and their possible relationship—shows an essential interior depth of human personhood.[42] While animals are in possession of their bodies via their souls, the human is in possession of this possession, which turns the "self" into an "I."[43] That is to say, the human is distinct from the animal by being aware of its own mastery and self-consciousness.[44] Humans are able to be self-transparent in a way that the animal, entirely absorbed in its own interiority, is not.⁴⁵ Humans, therefore, own themselves as an "I" and not just as a "self"; they are *ichhaft* rather than only *sichhaft*. This self-referred self-transcendence is absolute interiority in its deepest sense.⁴⁶ The acts and experiences of spirit are grounded in this inner *Retroszendenz*.⁴⁷ In fact, a being that owns itself as an "I" (rather than just as a "self"), that is, a being that is personal, is impossible without such a self-transcending and self-returning self-foundation.⁴⁸

The main capacities associated with spirit are freedom and personhood. Although "higher animals" can have certain levels of understanding and even a kind of distance from the self, they are not related to their own thinking or understanding:

> The animal cannot make the secondary move of thinking about its own thinking, understanding its own understanding. It cannot make a second step of spirit behind itself (*geistig hinter sich selber treten*), because it does not stand behind itself in this secondary way in being-constitutive fashion. This is precisely what makes the person, what makes for the psychic-personal (*das seelisch Personale*). In this personal manner of being lies the abyss of freedom (*Abgrund von Freiheit*). . . . The human as person owns an abyss of freedom, despite all of its corporeal-psychic ties (*bei aller leiblich-seelischen Gebundenheit*). This is why the human has free choice and decision-making power (*freie Wahl- und Entscheidungsmöglichkeit*).⁴⁹

That is to say, humans are able to perform a second step of interiority that relates them to their own interiority, to their thinking, understanding, and feeling, and enables them to take a position in regard to it: to choose it or refrain from it. This does not make their freedom or choice separate from the body—the human always remains embodied and the soul intimately wrapped up with the body—but they are able to shape their relations with soul and body from an interior perspective, a *process* of interiorization, not just an interior dwelling.⁵⁰

What is particularly fascinating is that Conrad-Martius distinguishes this human ability to interiorize from that of spirits who—in contrast to humans—*are* spirits, rather than *having* spirits.⁵¹ (She is very clear that this is a phenomenological thought experiment within the *epochē* and that no claims are being made about the "existence" of specific spirits.) Such spirits, whether those of fables and traditional folk tales or biblical angels (fallen or not), have no inner life; they are "hollow" inside, cannot enter within themselves, and are therefore incapable of interiority.[52] She is insistent throughout that the human, rather than *being* a spirit—which would turn us, literally, into mere "spirits"—*has* a spirit.[53] The human has weight and can transcend itself in various ways, while spirits are naturally light and thus cannot have the same depth or capacity for self-transcendence. The human must bear the soul and make it a task.[54] If spirits are hollow, in some sense, a pure shell, animals always live within their shell. While animals remain attached to the souls they own and in which they are entirely absorbed, humans can transcend this "shell" (*Hülle*) and have an inner nakedness—naked, but not hollow.[55] While the animal is, so to say, "clothed" in its nature[56] and spirits are so identified with theirs as to be unable to separate from them in any form (they *are* their very natures as spirits), humans are able to relate to their natures and even divest themselves of them in some form; they are able to transcend them via self-relation as a form of self-transparency and inner nakedness. In some sense, while the animal is pure interiority, and the spirit has no interiority, the human is related to its interiority, able to move and develop within it.[57]

Conclusion:
Possible Phenomenological Implications and Applications

Conrad-Martius is thus able to maintain much greater continuity between human and nonhuman animals than most philosophers (past and contemporary) have been able to do and to give a full account of our animal being that, at the same time, does not collapse all distinctions or deny any sort of interiority to other animals.[58] Consequently, her account may be able to point a way forward for one of the crucial dilemmas in environmental—and indeed in broader philosophical—thinking today: on the one hand by stressing the ways in which humans are part of the natural world, not only dependent on it but intimately connected to it on various levels (biological, genetic, ecological, etc.), and on the other hand by maintaining a role for human responsibility for the destruction wreaked on the planet and for addressing its dire consequences—consequences that affect not only humans but all species. Deep ecology (and some of the recent proposals in various forms of transhumanism, new materialisms, and speculative feminisms)[59] with its enfolding of the human entirely into the natural that erases all meaningful distinctions between them has been unable to develop a sustainable ethics for responding to the ecological crisis. Merely feeling part of the ecosystem and organically connected to it is not necessarily sufficient for articulating any sort of responsibility for it and often results in a kind of ecological quietism.

At the same time, traditional notions of human agency tend to rely on versions of human subjectivity that draw absolute lines between the human and the natural world (including animals) and thus are not all that useful for proposing environmental responsibility. They are also usually unable to formulate why animals, for example, might have moral standing, while not necessarily qualifying as independent, individual moral agents. Conrad-Martius develops notions of interiority that show the human in full continuity with the animal in terms of relation to the body and expression of affect and even spontaneity, while she develops a realm of action and agency that allows for self-reflection and self-transparency, such that faults can be confronted and new ways of acting and living become possible. The shared types of interiority she shows to be present in all animals may well provide better arguments against factory farming, cosmetic testing, and gratuitous medical experimentations, or, more positively, for protections of lands necessary for the flourishing of plants and animals. Simultaneously, the distinct type of interiority she elucidates in human experience provides grounds for speaking of agency and ethical responsibility in ways that do not draw absolute distinctions between humans and other animals and yet show humans' unique capacities both for causing destruction and for exercising compassion or restraint.

Beyond its ecological implications, there is also rich potential here for more nuanced discussions of human interiority in terms of affect, emotion, self-reflectivity, and other aspects of consciousness. Her articulation of the psychosomatic enmeshment[60] of affectivity provides possibilities for more accurate accounts of mental and emotional illness that overcome some of the artificial distinctions often drawn between bodily and psychological impairment, as well as helping us work out the particular sorts of interiority at work in experiences of depression, schizophrenia, and other illnesses in which differing types of interiority play an important role. If pushed further, her account may also have potential for making a contribution to current phenomenological discussions on the moral emotions—such as pride, humility, or shame—that rely significantly not only on a notion of interiority but also on the possibility of articulating self-transparency and interior self-critique.[61] Her notions of the self-realization of the soul and of the "inner nudity" of the human may open new paths here.

Notes

1. Hedwig Conrad-Martius, *Metaphysische Gespräche* (Halle: Verlag Max Niemeyer, 1921), 94.

2. For example, she disagrees with Aristotle over whether plants have souls—in her view they do not—and how exactly soul and body are related (i.e., she thinks the human is "rooted" in the soul rather than "formed" by it). She also applies the term "logos" to all beings, not reserving it only for humans. She is strongly critical of Descartes in various places (especially in *Bios and Psyche*). Indeed, her retrieval of soul-language is due largely to what she perceives as a false dualism in Descartes and some contemporary thinkers (including Jaspers).

3. Such as the contentions that only humans are fully self-conscious (Husserl), only humans "exist" (Heidegger), only humans have auto-affection and thus they alone participate in "Life" (Michel Henry), only humans have the "face" or discourse of absolute alterity (Emmanuel Lévinas), only humans are "adonné," undefinable and fully devoted to the wholly other in mutual erotic abandon (Jean-Luc Marion), or seeing the "animality" of humans as utterly distinct from that of "animals" (Emmanuel Falque).

4. See her critiques of Heidegger, especially in "Heideggers 'Sein und Zeit,'" "Dasein, Substanzialität, Seele," and "Existenzielle Tiefe und Untiefe von Dasein und Ich," in *Schriften zur Philosophie*, vol. 1 (München: Kösel Verlag, 1963), 185–244; of Karl Jaspers, especially in "Seele und Leib" and "Die menschliche Seele," in *Schriften zur Philosophie*, vol. 3 (München: Kösel Verlag, 1965), 107–43; of Herbert Fritsche, especially in "Bios und Logos," in *Schriften zur Philosophie* 3:157–62; and of Edgar Dacqué in "Edgar Dacqués verlorenes Paradies," in *Schriften zur Philosophie* 3:163–83.

5. Hedwig Conrad-Martius, *Metaphysische Gespräche* (Halle: Verlag Max Niemeyer, 1921). One of the conversation partners at first finds the introduction of such spirits ludicrous and it is made clear throughout that this is a phenomenological thought experiment to enable a more careful delineation of the nature of the human and not a claim about the actual "existence" of spirits, angels, or other such beings.

6. Hedwig Conrad-Martius, *Bios und Psyche: Zwei Vortragsreihen* (Hamburg: Claassen und Coverts, 1949). See also various lectures and unpublished texts in her three-volume *Schriften zur Philosophie* (München: Kösel Verlag, 1963, 1964, 1965).

7. Hedwig Conrad-Martius, *Die Geistseele des Menschen* (München: Kösel Verlag, 1960); *Das Sein* (München: Kösel Verlag, 1957).

8. Conrad-Martius, *Metaphysische Gespräche*, 41–51.

9. Conrad-Martius, 36.

10. "Das tierische 'von innen her sich selber Haben und bewegungsmäßig Beherrschen' geschieht von jener in sich selbst hineinvertieften Stelle des seelischen Grundes her, die dadurch zu einem seelischen Selbst oder einem Seelenselbst geprägt ist. Nur wo ein solches, von der lebendigen Körperlichkeit, die eben dadurch zum Leibe wird, abgelöstes seelisches Selbst oder Seelenselbst verbunden ist, kann die

Körperlichkeit mit dem, was sie betrifft oder an ihr geschieht, innerlich 'gehabt,' d. h. empfunden und selbsthaft bewegt werden." Conrad-Martius, *Bios und Psyche*, 87. "Tier und Mensch greifen von der selbsthaften Innerlichkeit oder dem inneren Selbst her in den Leib hinein, bzw. zu den Gliedern hindurch." Conrad-Martius, *Bios und Psyche*, 88.

11. Conrad-Martius, *Metaphysische Gespräche*, 204.

12. For the most detailed account, see "Die menschliche Seele," *Schriften zur Philosophie* 3:126–28, although she frequently returns to this claim in later texts and gives many examples, both phenomenological descriptions and instances drawn from contemporary physiological, psychological, and medical research.

13. Conrad-Martius, *Metaphysische Gespräche*, 149.

14. Conrad-Martius, *Bios und Psyche*, 83.

15. Conrad-Martius, "Seele und Leib," *Schriften zur Philosophie* 3:108.

16. The term "selbsthaft" is crucial to her thought but difficult to translate. It implies both a "having" of the self (she contrasts it to *selbstlos*/selfless or without self) and an adhering to it (*haften* means to attach or adhere to). I translate it as "owning" here because that seems to hold these aspects together and possibly captures best her use of the term.

17. Conrad-Martius, "Die menschliche Seele," *Schriften zur Philosophie* 3:129.

18. Conrad-Martius, *Schriften zur Philosophie* 3:132–33.

19. "Die Pflanze verwandelt sich, wie wir sahen, in ein animalisches Wesen, wenn die entelechiale Seele einen Sitz in sich selbst gewinnt und dadurch vom eigenen Leib innerlich-selbsthaft abgelöst wird. Enthält nun dieses selbsthafte, dieses autonom gewordene Seelenprinzip überdies noch einen eigenen inneren 'Raum,' wird es sozusagen in sein eigenes Inneres hinein ausgeweitet und hineingestaltet, so entsteht die Gefühls- oder affektive Seele. Die Gefühlsregion ist der eigene innere Ausgestaltungsbezirk der selbsthaft gewordenen Seele." Conrad-Martius, *Bios und Psyche*, 91.

20. "Erst wo sich ein 'Selbst' in sich selber 'hineinvertieft' zeigt, kommt es zu einer Psyche. Ich habe diese ontische Sachlage als 'Innerung' bezeichnet. Sie führt bei niederen Tierarten zunächst zu einem selbsthaften Empfindungs- und Selbstbewegungszentrum und bei höheren Tierarten zu einem förmlichen Innenraum. Es ist dies ein ganz und gar selbsthafter, ganz und gar 'innerlicher' Raum, ein *absolut* innerlicher Raum, der zu dem absolut äußeren in polarem Gegensatz steht. Aber es ist eben doch ein wahrer 'Raum'!" Conrad-Martius, *Geistseele des Menschen*, 19.

21. She suggests that this is a novel idea that has not been examined so far: "Jenes selbsthafte Durchwohnen des Leibes ist eine Art und Weise seelischer Selbstverwirklichung, die, soviel ich sehe, noch nirgens herausgestellt worden ist." Conrad-Martius, *Bios und Psyche*, 93.

22. "Die leibliche Verwirklichung der Seele, die eine absolut äußere ist, steht im polaren Gegensatz zur affektiv seelischen Verwirklichung der Seele, die eine absolut innerliche ist; und eben deshalb können sie in genau analoger, parallelistischer

Weise auf irgendein das tierische oder menschliche Selbst betreffendes Ereignis oder Erlebnis reagieren." Conrad-Martius, *Bios und Psyche*, 109.

23. She goes back to this example frequently and argues that in some ways this is clearer in the amoeba than in a horse (a reference to Uexküll). The more complex an animal becomes the more difficult it is to see the connection between soul and body and the particular process of interiorization at work. Conrad-Martius, "Die menschliche Seele," *Schriften zur Philosophie* 3:130.

24. Conrad-Martius, *Bios und Psyche*, 95–96.

25. This goes "bis zu den wunderbaren Gestaltungen höchster Tiere, in denen ein vollkommenes Gleichgewicht zwischen höchstmöglicher Beherrschbarkeit des Leibes und tiefstmöglicher Ein- und Inwohnung in sich selbst erreicht zu sein scheint. Hier führt der leitende Logos, aus dem die leibende Potenz unerschöpflich strömt, nicht zur Höhe, sondern zur Tiefe." Conrad-Martius, *Metaphysische Gespräche*, 205.

26. "Die Innerlichkeit des Psychischen verhält sich zur Äußerlichkeit des Physischen wie *das* Innere zu *dem* Äußerlichen. Nicht geht es hier um eine relative Innerlichkeit und Äußerlichkeit, so wie innerhalb der physischen Welt ein Inneres immer und immer wieder das Äußere einer weiteren Innerlichkeit ist. Mit der ureigenen Tiefe des Seelenraums kommen wir vielmehr zu der absolut inneren Gegenseite der äußeren physischen Welt, und diese Äußerlichkeit und Innerlichkeit können niemals ineinander verwandelt werden. Um so mehr sind sie ineinander ausdrückbar! Wenn schon der Fels die Form des ihn durchbrechenden und auswaschenden Stromes annehmen muß, der Ton die Züge der ihm eingeprägten Plastik, wieviel mehr muß der Leib das sich ihm statisch und dynamisch einprägende seelische Geschehen ausdrücken, das seine Innerlichkeit schlechthin darstellt. Nur weil man diese Innerlichkeit gänzlich entvitalisiert, sie zu einem spiritualistisch verblaßten Konglomerat von 'Bewußtseinsinhalten' und 'Empfindungen' gemacht hatte, weil man ihre ureigene reale Dynamik nicht mehr begreifen konnte und wollte, erschien eine wahrhaft kausale Ausdrücksmöglichkeit unverständlich." Conrad-Martius, "Seele und Leib," *Schriften zur Philosophie* 3:117–18 (emphasis hers).

27. Later she will define *Exkarnation* and *Inkarnation* as follows: "Die Exkarnation ist die leibhaft selbstlose Hinausgestaltung des Ursprungsselbstes in der Form einer arttypischen Stoffsubstanz: die Inkarnation ist die leibhaft selbsthafte Hineingestaltung des Ursprungsselbstes in sich selbst. Diese beiden Seinsrichtungen haben absolute Bedeutung. Sie sind nicht relativierbar, können nicht relativ zueinander vertauscht werden." Conrad-Martius, *Geistseele des Menschen*, 51.

28. See the graphic examples in "Die menschliche Seele," where she also vigorously argues against Jaspers whom she accuses of turning soul and body into merely two sides of the same coin; soul and body become mere aspects of each other ("der Unterschied zwischen Leib und Seele als ein bloß aspekthafter gefaßt wird"). Conrad-Martius, *Schriften zur Philosophie* 3:127.

29. Conrad-Martius, *Bios und Psyche*, 108.

30. "Halten wir dieses Wesentlichste fest: das Tier reicht auf doppelte Weise durch seinen Leib hindurch: einmal, indem es ihn herausgestaltet wie die Pflanze, zum anderen Mal, *indem es ihn von innen her als Selbst beherrscht*: es kann ihn bewegen und durch ihn Eindrücke empfangen." Conrad-Martius, "Seele und Leib," *Schriften zur Philosophie* 3:108–9 (emphasis added). Again she gives *Mimose* and *Amöbe* as examples.

31. Conrad-Martius, "Seele und Leib," *Schriften zur Philosophie* 3:109.

32. Conrad-Martius, *Geistseele des Menschen*, 52.

33. "Mit dem selbsthaften Innerungszentrum ist das Ursprungsselbst selber erstmals zu sich selbst gekommen, das heißt ins aktuelle *Da*sein getreten. Was hier demnach im speziellen aktualisiert werden muß, ist die eigene innere Selbsthaftigkeit des Usprungsselbstes." Conrad-Martius, *Geistseele des Menschen*, 52.

34. Conrad-Martius, "Die menschliche Seele," *Schriften zur Philosophie* 3:134.

35. "Die Standortsverlegung in den Geist scheint eo ipso eine Erhebung, die in das seelische Zentrum eo ipso ein Versenken zu sein." Conrad-Martius, *Metaphysische Gespräche*, 218.

36. Conrad-Martius, "Bios und Logos," *Schriften zur Philosophie* 3:162. She insists that this is not arbitrary control or dictatorial domination but the sort of guidance that inspires trust and puts body and spirit into harmony with each other. She argues strongly against notions of soul or spirit that separate them from corporeality or denigrate the body.

37. Conrad-Martius, *Bios und Psyche*, 90. She suggests that ultimately, the entelechial soul has a fourfold formation: bodily (*leiblich*), ensouled-bodily (*leibseelisch*), affective (*affektiv*), and spirited (*geistig*). Together with the "ground of the soul" there are five expressions or realms: three psychic (the ground itself and its two realms of expression) and two in reference to the body (excarnate and incarnate). For an early formulation of this, see Conrad-Martius, "Die menschliche Seele," *Schriften zur Philosophie* 3:136–37.

38. "Die Ausrücke 'nach außen' und 'nach innen' gewinnen so einen klaren ontischen Ansatzpunkt: aus dem Selbst heraus und in das Selbst hinein. Hier stehen sich *absolute Äußerlichkeit* und *absolute Innerlichkeit* gegenüber." Conrad-Martius, *Bios und Psyche*, 108. See also Conrad-Martius, "Seele und Leib," *Schriften zur Philosophie* 3:118.

39. Conrad-Martius, *Metaphysische Gespräche*, 69.

40. Conrad-Martius, 119. She argues that animals also act spontaneously. Human spontaneity is characterized by levels of self-reflection and self-transcendence that are not present in animals in the same way.

41. She says: "Durch die selbsthafte Eigenposition gewann das Tier eine Art innere Selbständigkeit von seinem Leibe oder seinem Leibe gegenüber. Der Mensch aber besitzt darüber hinaus und überdies eine existenzielle Selbständigkeit seinem eigenen entelechialen Ursprungsselbst gegenüber. Der Mensch hat, so könnte man

sagen, eine doppelte Innerung: in bezug auf den Leib und in bezug auf das eigene Selbst. Oder auch: er ist in doppelter Weise sich selber vorgesetzt, seinem Leibe und sich selber. Man kann auch sagen: er transzendiert sich selber nach innen hinein in zweifacher Weise." Conrad-Martius, *Bios und Psyche*, 124.

42. Conrad-Martius, *Geistseele des Menschen*, 11. She is quite emphatic in several places that human, person, I, and self ought not to be equated with each other and that none of these terms reduces to body, soul, or spirit. Each designates different elements or aspects. Conrad-Martius, "Bios und Logos," *Schriften zur Philosophie* 3:160.

43. Conrad-Martius, *Das Sein*, 120.

44. "Wir würden—in einer entsprechenden Anthropologie—weiter sehen, daß sich der Mensch von dem Tier gestaltlich dadurch unüberbrückbar abgrenzt, daß er diesen 'Bezirk der Innerlichkeit' selber wiederum 'innerlich' in die Hand bekommt, daß er auch diesem noch einmal 'vorgesetzt' wird und dadurch des Selbstbewußtseins und freier Willensentscheidung fähig wird. Hiermit ist die *Person* konstituiert." Conrad-Martius, "Die 'Seele' der Pflanze," *Schriften zur Philosophie* 1:359.

45. Conrad-Martius, "Die menschliche Seele," *Schriften zur Philosophie* 3:136–38. Even here she will admit degrees of consciousness of interiority in various species of animals.

46. "Mit der Ichverfassung ist eine Stelle absoluter innerer Rücktranszendenz gegeben. An eine noch tiefere Seinsstelle hinter ihr kann wesensmäßig nicht mehr zurückgegangen werden, weil es eine solche nicht mehr gibt." Conrad-Martius, *Das Sein*, 123.

47. Conrad-Martius, 122.

48. "Ein ichhaft Seiendes existiert überhaupt nicht ohne eine sich selbst übersteigende transzendentale Selbstbegründung." Conrad-Martius, *Das Sein*, 137.

49. Conrad-Martius, "Die menschliche Seele," *Schriften zur Philosophie* 3:138. She is quite critical of existentialism, which she thinks takes such freedom out of context, separates it from human corporeality and absolutizes freedom.

50. See also the distinctions she draws between soul and spirit in her "Wirkender und empfangender Geist [Geistlicht und Geiststoff]." Conrad-Martius, *Schriften zur Philosophie* 3:295–314.

51. She similarly argues frequently that it is wrong to say that humans *are* bodies—as Heidegger, Merleau-Ponty, and other phenomenologists did—but that instead we *have* bodies. This point is already made in the earliest texts (e.g., *Metaphysische Gespräche*, 40) and she still insists on it most forcefully in her late work. This form of self-owning is crucial for her, as we have seen above. Maurice Merleau-Ponty, for example, maintains that "the body is our general means of having a world" and therefore "I am not before my body, I am in my body, or rather I am my body." Merleau-Ponty, *Phenomenology of Perception*, trans. Donald A. Landes (London: Routledge, 2012), 147, 151, respectively.

52. Conrad-Martius, *Metaphysische Gespräche*, 125.

53. Conrad-Martius, *Geistseele des Menschen*, 11.
54. Conrad-Martius, *Metaphysische Gespräche*, 77.
55. Conrad-Martius, *Metaphysische Gespräche*, 94.
56. Conrad-Martius, *Metaphysische Gespräche*, 95.
57. "Develop" in the sense of maturation and growth, not in the sense of social Darwinism, of which Conrad-Martius is extremely critical. See her texts "Zum gegenwärtigen Stand naturwissenschaftlicher Welterfassung," "Abstammungslehre, Geschichte und Metaphysik," and "Geistige Vorgeschichte und Ideologie des Darwinismus," in *Schriften zur Philosophie* 2:219–52; "Individualität und Fortpflanzung" and "Menschenzüchtung," in *Schriften zur Philosophie* 3:144–56.
58. She also does not simply collapse all animal species together but makes distinctions between kinds, drawing on various kinds of biological insights to which she often refers in her treatment. Philosophers tend to speak of "the animal" as if all animals were alike and as if there were no distinctions between insects, fish, birds, and mammals. Genetically, behaviorally, and in many other ways, surely the great apes and various other mammals are considerably more like humans than they are like spiders or fish. To speak simply of "the animal" disregards all such distinctions.
59. Such as the work of Bruno Latour, Donna Haraway, and others.
60. "Seele und Leib," *Schriften zur Philosophie* 3:111. At one point she speaks of "vielfacher Verschlingung" (manifold entanglement).
61. See especially Anthony Steinbock, *Moral Emotions: Reclaiming the Evidence of the Heart* (Evanston, IL: Northwestern University Press, 2014).

PART TWO

Interiority Alterity, and Transcendence

4

"In interiore homine"

The Presence and Absence of the Divine in the Human

ANGELA ALES BELLO
TRANSLATED BY ANTONIO CALCAGNO

The citation from Augustine of Hippo contained in the title of this chapter directly leads us to the question I wish to explore: How does the concept of the divine come to enter or be "in" the human mind? We often use the expression "come to mind" to signify something that we do not perceive as coming from outside the human mind; rather, it conveys something that is already in us, but about which we are not aware or to which we pay no attention. Nevertheless, something appears to us; it shows itself. Often, the concept of the divine is hidden or latent in us. One could say, perhaps, that the divine lives in us passively, and yet it unconsciously pushes us to desire to know and understand the finitude of our own being. Why are we aware of our own impotence or powerlessness? Why do we desire to know "everything" and whence comes this desire? Through such questions we enter into the profound realm of our constitution as human beings, and we begin to explore "religious experience."

What is Religious Experience?

Let us begin by examining the sense or meaning of religious experience rather than the various theoretical aspects of the traditional proofs for the existence and nature of God, which the Western philosophical-theological tradition treats within a largely rationalist framework. I do not deny the validity of such a mode of investigation, for such questions can certainly be explored through the use of human reason. But even before we can proceed in this manner, we have to establish the origin of the foregoing mode of questioning. In order to tackle the question of the sense of religious experience, we certainly have to deploy our intellectual and rational capacities, but they are incapable of capturing and describing something deeper than what they can grasp, namely, the "feeling" of a trace of the presence of something that supersedes, makes true, and justifies the human being—a presence that can or must be brought to reflexive awareness.

My claim here may appear to fit within a traditional rationalist framework, especially within the Western cultural context that is moving toward ever greater secularization, ultimately distancing itself from the divine while rendering it superfluous, noxious, and nonexistent. Nevertheless, let us commence with an analysis of a phenomenon that can be considered to lie in opposition to religion, namely, atheism. In particular, let us explore the thought of Ludwig Feuerbach. Even if his thought may not be well known, his ideas were deeply influential for thinkers like Nietzsche and Marx. His arguments are often used to justify the negation of God's existence, as well as the illusion of religion and religious experience.

One often hears religion described as a "projection" of fantasy and therefore as lacking in any validity. Feuerbach, in his *The Essence of Christianity*, argues that we must free ourselves from submitting to such self-subjugating behavior, for it lacks consistency. He understands religious experience as the fruit of alienation and the projection of what one desires to be but is not. He maintains that if we accept that the attributes of God are a human projection, as in arguments from analogy, which I will address later in this chapter, we also have to admit that the attributes assigned to God are invented by human beings who do not wish to accept certain limits about themselves: we do not wish to see ourselves as limited and impotent, for we see God as without limit and omnipotent.

According to Feuerbach, "Such as are a man's thoughts and dispositions, such is his God; so much worth as a man has, so much and no more has his God. Consciousness of God is self-consciousness, knowledge of God is self-knowledge. By his God thou knowest the man, and by the man his God; the two are identical."[1] It is clear that the human being cannot know God as He is. When one speaks about God, one uses one's own words with all their limits. As Saint Paul remarks, we hold our truths in clay pots, for if we were to know God perfectly, we would be God. But human beings are capable of knowing things without identifying themselves with the content of their knowledge. This happens daily, but the object God, as Feuerbach identifies it with the human, is not human. This is demonstrated by the fact that the philosopher strives to make God human. He wrote two books, *The Essence of Religion* and *The Essence of Christianity*, to show that God does not exist, which indicates he certainly does possess a notion of God. Again, the question arises: How did this notion come to be in Feuerbach's mind? He would say that God is the object of our desire.

The philosopher's argument, at first sight, seems convincing, but when it is examined more closely, it proves to be fallacious for various reasons. Feuerbach's thesis has as its focus the human psyche: he discusses desire, that is, the desire to surpass a limit, the desire to be loved, and he argues that Christianity's success is connected to this desire. We must ask, however, why do we desire to be omnipotent, and why do we believe there is someone who is? How does the notion of God arise?

Desire is understood as an attitude, a mover of psyche, and therefore something we live, an *Erlebnis*, understood in the phenomenological sense, that derives from the experience of a "lack," a lack of something we know, though vaguely and perhaps obscurely so. Perhaps we desire it because we do not possess it. Nevertheless, we have before us something desirable. We could ask why the human being refers to "God" in such cases, ultimately ascribing to Him attributes the human being does not possess: omniscience and limitlessness. Hence, it is not true that the knowledge we have of God is the knowledge we have of ourselves, for we would then have to say that God is "finite" or "limited." God would be limited in His powers to do things. We experience ourselves in these limited ways. Furthermore, Feuerbach affirms that it is this very experience of limit that allows us to project an unlimited being that exists outside of ourselves. But the experience of the limit is possible only if one "knows" that a limit exists. It delineates itself when we intuit something that exists beyond this limit. But what is a limit? It is a boundary or border, and in this case, it borders with the unlimited. If we admit that there is a limit, we also intuit that there is the unlimited.

Desire is born out of a lack of a perceived fullness, and limit simultaneously arises with our awareness of the unlimited. And if we are finite beings, how can we think of the unlimited? The only valid response here is that we already know, albeit imperfectly, something that exceeds us, that configures itself as Powerful and Absolute. Such an awareness cannot arise from our limited selves; rather, it is given by the Unlimited Itself. This kind of reasoning we find in Plato, Augustine, Anselm of Bec, Descartes, Edmund Husserl, and Edith Stein.

Though Feuerbach's arguments are fallacious, they are nonetheless important, for they permit the delineation of a territory or realm in which we can move not only to demonstrate that an omnipotent God exists but also to understand the sense of religious experience by means of desire. The capacity to desire is human and concretizes itself in particular desires, but all desired things, once obtained, never completely fulfill our desires, for we want more of them, or want them "totally" or "completely." It is not enough to keep desiring more things, for even this constant desiring will leave us wanting. But what pushes us? Whence comes this impulse? Augustine and Anselm understood the ontological sense of this deep desire that pushes us to search not only for the satisfaction of needs but also for the sense or meaning of existence.

It is clear that the structure of desire can operate as an exchange of sorts insofar as something obtained, such as success, a frenetic or tranquil life, money, an absolutized knowledge of a field, can fulfill something we can define as an opening to a Power. But we also know that this kind of exchange between desire and fulfilment is transient, and this is why we fear losing what we have obtained. By contrast, the encounter with the Other completes desire because it totally fulfills human expectations, especially as it pertains to all particular situations or circumstances. This encounter illuminates the aforementioned situations, giving to them a transcendent meaning while making them feel real and true.

The Divine in Human Interiority

Let us delve into our interiority to try and grasp the presence/absence of the divine. This form of self-inquiry permits us to analyze the structure of the human being. The thought of Edmund Husserl and Edith Stein provides a useful guide for unpacking this structure. The investigation of interiority does not simply confine us to the study of the sense of religious experience, as it also allows us to tackle the question: What is the human being? Such a question can be answered from an outside or external perspective by other sciences and fields of inquiry, whereas phenomenology deploys lived experience. Husserl maintains that lived experiences, in their structural purity, make manifest essential modes and aspects of the human subject. In fact, he observes that the human being lives both as a subject and object of phenomenological investigation. The human being is capable of perceiving, remembering, imagining, loving, suffering, desiring, thinking, valuing, reflecting, and so on and acts within these various capacities both as a subject and an object. Human capacities or potentialities are discovered to be transcendental, experiential structures that come to the fore in consciousness, which is a mirror that displays the complex, articulated stratification constitutive of the human being.[2]

One of the principal ways that philosophy and religion have described the structure of the human being is by introducing the categories of body and soul. If a universal structure of the human is posited, how can we justify the claim that the encounter between human beings is defined by an encounter between singular individuals? Certainly, philosophical reflection can lead one to grasp the defining universal elements of humans, and this capacity for universalization guides our search for evidence of common traits shared among humans that allow one to recognize one as similar to the other: the other is similar to me. Empathy or intropathy allows us to see this shared similarity. Community is possible, but its foundation lies in a non-transcendent singularity or individual. Stein justifies this irreducible singularity by defining it as a personal core or personality (*Persönlichkeitskern*), which she also calls the "soul of the soul." If we pause to consider how this sense of singularity may be understood in terms of the "I," which refers to but is also distinguished from a self, we can better grasp human interiority, for we move beyond the restricted conceptual confines of the body-soul binary. Body and soul become more complex realms than the standard philosophical models present.

The complexity and stratification of the human being may be used to describe the sense of religious experience. Drawing upon Augustine of Hippo, Anselm of Bec, Husserl, and Stein, I wish to begin to delineate an opening onto understanding the divine. Saint Teresa of Avila's image of the interior castle provides a useful model of the unity and complexity of the human being. All the rooms that Saint Teresa deploys may be understood as steps along the interior path that mark the diverse strata of the human being. Stein, from the time she was a young philosopher, understood the value of this image. When, after reading Saint Teresa's autobiography, Stein exclaims, "This is the truth!," she not only refers to her rediscovery of the religious experience she originally had in her adolescent years, but she also confirms the essential description of the human being that she develops on the basis of Husserl's method.

The personal core, which may be understood in Teresian language as the "seventh room," is a concept that Stein develops in different works.[3]

It also represents a line of thought that runs from her early work in phenomenology to her later metaphysical work on the human being. In fact, one could read Stein's understanding of the personal core as one of the key bridges that unites her early and late work. She initially develops the concept within a descriptive, essential framework and later attributes to it a metaphysical, ontological sense, understood in Duns Scotus's terms as an ultimate substantial form. Here, Stein deals with and presents a solution to the controversial medieval question about that nature of the principle of individuation.[4]

Stein's discussion of the personal core provides the ontological ground of Augustine's and Anselm's arguments. Where does one find the truth that dwells in one's interiority? Where do we find the source of that idea of "that which no greater can be conceived"? In other words, where do we find a trace of the divine? I maintain that the personal core is the place where we can begin to search for God. And though we can speak of the development of a personality or personal core, the core itself does not develop or change, as Aristotle pointed out. The core itself remains simple and eternal. It gives impetus to development and manifests itself through the growth or diminution of personality or personal traits/character, through the body, psyche, and spirit. The personality core must be "preserved" as it is given at the moment of birth. It is the trace of the eternal in human beings. Stein observes: "The end of earthly life and the entry into eternal life would mean that 'darkness' fades away and the entire personal core becomes actual and transparent. However, it is clear at the same time that the core has already been in eternity throughout the entire duration of its earthly life."[5] The foregoing citation shows her understanding of the Gospel's words that all must enter the celestial realm as children, that is, they must preserve and guard the core they received at birth, a core that marks their singularity and its unique characteristics. The fact that humans live contemporaneously in time and eternity must not be viewed as contradictory, for Augustine indicated the human soul was supratemporal, and this aspect of the soul, Stein argues, is justified through the concept of the personal or personality core.

In *Potency and Act*, the question of the core is related to the complexity of the human being. Stein distinguishes between what is peripheral and what is deep. Plumbing the depths of the human soul permits us to see and come into contact with the core, which also tells us what the person is. "What is the person, if we disregard all the things that play out one after another in the course of his life? He is something put into the world as a center to engage the world—in the form of the intellect—in such ways that he is either beset by the world or penetrates into it by overcoming it. This either-or is not exclusive."[6] The personal core is distinguished by its simplicity, as it is not constituted by a series of parts. It lies in a state of potency, as opposed to one of actuality, with regard to the spiritual life. In order to actualize the spiritual life, the person must act, that is, move from a state of potency to the actualization of acts. Certainly, the core may remain hidden to an individual; nonetheless, it has its actuality insofar as it exists and it is active and real, even though it may never be completely actualized. The experience of one's own individuality occurs in one's lived experience. But if all lived experiences are individual, "they do not all have a personal particularity. Only those that arise from the depths of the soul are imprinted with singularity. As these lived experiences unfold, I live this 'note of individuality.' I feel the source of such individuation to be deep and I feel its depth to be of a certain degree."[7] Furthermore, in her *Einführung in die Philosophie*, Stein notes that "the personality core unfolds in the psycho-physical development of the empirical person, making the individual a whole person with individual qualities."[8]

All persons manifest inclinations, dispositions, and different reactions. They express themselves in particular ways. If one could map the interior complexity of the human being while distinguishing the operations and acts that characterize the essential natures of the spirit or psyche, one would be able to foresee which lived experiences could be activated by singular subjects because subjectivity is truly unique and non-repeatable. We can certainly ask ourselves whence this impossibility of repetition comes. The answer lies in the personal core, but only in the horizontal sense and when we situate human beings within the framework of the relations between human beings. If we examine what we know transcends human beings, and if we ask about the origin of such transcendence, we discover that the personal core has a second function: it serves as the meeting point of the divine and the human.

Given that the core is the distinctive element of the human being that actualizes itself fully in the spiritual life, one could hypothesize that in the earthly life actualization may always face certain menaces. In the *status termini*, the core of the human person could be actualized:

> And I dare say we should also understand the *status termini* [state "of the end," i.e., in the afterlife] of human persons in an analogous way. I mean, as the enduring, highest attainable actuality of what they are in themselves, in such ways that nothing

dark and unknown any longer lies behind their actual spiritual living, and in the person's core the alternation of potentiality and actuality is superseded, the core in eternity throughout the entire duration of its earthly life. Time is in eternity and never ceases therein. And what is in time is for this very reason in eternity, but it is in eternity in a way other than it is in time. The person's earthly life is temporal; it has a beginning and an end in time and fulfills the duration between them.[9]

The Ground of the *analogia entis*

Stein notes that "the person's core is the be-ing which she is in herself and through which she is a *similitudo* [likeness] of divine being. It is what positively lies behind the *analogia entis* [analogy of being] as its basis."[10] Her observation affirms my claim about the personal core: if it is the ground of the analogy of being, the core must be the locus where one finds the trace of the divine, understood in the Augustinian sense, that is, it is the locus of presence/absence because we find there a *similitudo*, or likeness, that prevents the core from being understood as a pure act (*actus purus*), even though we recognize a potentiality or capacity for the growth or increase of being of the conscious, spiritual life.

Thomas Aquinas certainly takes up the theme of the analogy of being, but so too do the phenomenologists insofar as they have discovered, Stein claims, the experiential source of it. The first "analogue" that the human encounters is the other, who is similar. In Stein's *Introduction to Philosophy*, we find an extraordinary discovery about intropathy. After she explains the claim that empathy, in part, consists of the presentification of an originary vital movement of another person who has no relation of continuity with my own living or life, she attempts to "draw out" what is typical in the other, as well as what is common with what I live. This "drawing out" that characterizes the empathic act is an autonomous act that permits one "to infer from the givenness of a typically communal part the presence of an analogous completion." She continues, "Here, we find the legitimate core of the theory of analogical inference."[11] Stein argues that the aforementioned theory is based on lived experience. In other words, analogy, understood as a conceptual instrument, presupposes the experiential dimension of the knowledge of the other, who is similar and, therefore, analogous to me. It is this similarity that makes the conceptual theorization possible

Let us turn to the question of the modality of "feeling" the other, which is related to the experience of "feeling oneself." Phenomenological analysis shows that knowledge of the other is achieved at different levels through a particular empathic feeling in which one's own individuality is related to the individuation of the other. One not only feels in oneself the other, who one tries to know, but also feels the Other, who supersedes and transcends all particular configurations. The Other cannot fit into the same empathic act we use to know the other. And though we "see" the other to be similar to us, we cannot "see" a transcendent God, who is nevertheless present in us. Here, the meaning of the Incarnation becomes clear: God, through an extraordinary act of goodness, wants to show Himself to us and others. Stein claims that God continues to show Himself through the Eucharist and that Jesus is recognized as God because he is inscribed on the personal core.

The core is the locus of the divine's manifestation. And faith, from which natural knowledge about God stems, is born from this contact with the divine who is "felt" in that act, which unites in itself knowledge, understood as understanding as well as love and action, as Edith Stein taught. One can accept or reject this act. One who accepts can simply follow God and, in Thomas's language, when this happens, what is accepted is done so on the grounds that it is "credible." Alternatively, one could deploy a demonstrative, rational proof—the argument from analogy.

The foregoing claim helps distinguish the faithful believer from the arguing philosopher. If argumentation utilizes analogy, it moves from the plane of experience of the similitude with the other to the intellectual plane of reasoning. Here, we find ourselves in the domain of "proofs" and "demonstrations" for the existence of God. Between beings and the One who imparts and is the source of existence, namely God, a relation must exist. This relation, however, does not only remain at the level of existence. In addition to the foregoing aspect, Stein maintains that an analogy, understood as "quality," is also given. The human being, who receives existence, is characterized by its core, which is spiritual. Analogy, then, works in the spiritual realm. God, the existing Spirit, gives an origin to all spiritual beings in more or less perfect forms. This affirmation may seem shocking, but we must recall that Stein claims that the presence of God, of the Spirit, understood as "objective" (i.e., as quality), can also be attributed to material things. For example, the Platonic-Aristotelian concept of form is also linked to material things, but it is in no way reducible to it.

The human being is the closest creature to God, created in the image and likeness of God, and this image resides as God's imprint upon the personal core. This permits Stein to conclude that though the core is eternal, it also dwells in time while simultaneously containing the trace of the Eternal. And as the core is not capable of development, though it can increase in being in the form of an augmentation of the being of spiritual life, the recognition of the foregoing presence falls to the spirit. If the spirit is primarily grasped as a locus of decision-making, of acts of will and intellection, the spiritual lived experiences that constitute it manifest these acts as free. So, one is free to accept or reject the presence of the divine. Given that stratifications of the human being exist and that it has its own unity, the divine presence must "move" through the acceptance or rejection of the psyche, which offers to the human spirit material to sort and evaluate, ultimately receiving or correcting the psychic impulse. Even the body comes to be involved, for the acceptance of the divine presence allows the body to adopt certain habits and dispositions that manifest a relation to this presence in the life of the human being. One can see this relation when observing various liturgical rights that seek to express, through the body, the intimacy and uniqueness of the relation of the human to the divine presence.

The Acceptance or Rejection of the Divine According to the "Phenomenology of Religion"

At this point, two hypotheses emerge. First, there must be someone who, feeling the presence of the divine, accepts God at the psychic level while consciously accepting Him at the spiritual level. Both psychic and spiritual acceptance also manifest at the corporeal level. Second, there are those who refuse to accept the divine presence, for God is not desired at the psychic level. This individual will often, through the use of intellection, offer justifications to prove that the divine presence is illusory. As mentioned earlier, this is the atheistic way to approach the question of the divine presence.

Stein indicates that atheism can be understood as a negation or as a "flight into theoretical negation that leads, however, only to another form of angst in the face of the nothing."[12] Her position runs parallel to that of Gerardus van der Leeuw. The two thinkers can help us understand what religious experience is and what it means to refuse it. Both positions allow for the integration of two perspectives. The first is based on an essential description, philosophically understood, which is the fruit of investigating the depths of human interiority. The second is the result of a historical analysis related to so-called religious manifestations that "indicate" or "show," through ritual acts, invocations, and various elaborations of doctrine, the reference to something that transcends human beings. They also show that religious phenomena are not only individual phenomena; rather, they are intersubjective and communal.

Reading van der Leeuw's writings, one notes that the history of religions is more than a legitimate and distinct field of study; it also presupposes and connects to other disciplines. Even if these other disciplines are unaware of religion's involvement in their own field, they remain no less vital and important for religion. Van der Leeuw's work seeks to establish what religion is in order to be able to indicate which fields are properly religious and, say, not political, artistic, or linguistic, for example. The merit of his work lies in its conscious engagement of the foregoing problem, especially as outlined in his phenomenology of religion, which treats the specific phenomenon of religion.[13] His claim that religion can be studied as a historical phenomenon pushes van der Leeuw to develop a "phenomenology of religion." In every phenomenon that is called "religious," he maintains, one finds the presence of a Power. He treats the unity of religion, that is, the universal characteristic of the fact of religion—the *why* of religion—as well as the plurality of the historical configurations of the phenomenon. Unity and multiplicity are both present and do not contradict one another; rather, they constitute a proof for the validity of a philosophical description of religious experience made possible by the development of philosophical anthropology.

The reflection on religious experience admits a certain circularity in that one moves from anthropology to history and vice versa. One seeks here a characteristic element that is essential, invariable in its qualities, and expressible, especially in a variety of different modes. This element leads one to the search for a divine power. One may keep trying to find this Power, but when one does find it, one is able to grasp and describe the very form of the divine power.

We can call the foregoing historical-philosophical description of religious experience a "phenomenology of religion," which bestows sense to the argument concerning the presence of a particular experience we usually try to label otherwise. Nevertheless, this experience always reemerges and in new ways with its own unique characteristics. The experience of a Power that completely fills us, to borrow from van der Leeuw, is a religious experience: "The meaning of a lived experience of religion refers to a togetherness, to a whole. It can only be grasped from the perspective of eternity."[14] Here, we are treating a particular form of encounter between a human subject and a divine object, but not in an exhaustive manner. This encounter is felt to be a "revelation" because the human being, understood as *capax dei*, knows that the experience comes from an Other. And this is the ground of the revelation, be it natural or supernatural. It is the modality of the revelation that is "extraordinary"; it is hidden, inaccessible yet shown. In this paradox, we find the profound essence of the revelation that allows us to maintain the veritable presence/absence of the divine.

Notes

1. Ludwig Feuerbach, *The Essence of Christianity*, trans. George Elliot (New York: Prometheus Books, 1989), 12.

2. For a detailed discussion of the essential components of the phenomenological method, see Angela Ales Bello, *The Divine in Husserl and Other Explorations*, trans. Antonio Calcagno, in *Analecta Husserliana*, vol. 98 (Dordrecht: Springer, 2008). For the relation between phenomenology and philosophical anthropology, see Angela Ales Bello, *The Sense of Things: Toward a Phenomenological Realism*, trans. Antonio Calcagno, in *Analecta Husserliana*, vol. 118 (Dordrecht: Springer, 2015).

3. See Edith Stein, *Philosophy of Psychology and the Humanities*, trans. Mary Catherine Baseheart and Marianne Sawicki (Washington, DC: ICS Publications, 2000), part 1, section 5.5; *Einführung in die Philosophie*, in *Edith Stein Gesamtausgabe*, ed. Claudia Mariéle Wulf, vol. 8 (Freiburg-im-Breisgau: Herder, 2004), part 2, chap. 2, B 5; *Potency and Act*, trans. Walter Redmond (Washington, DC: ICS Publications, 2009), Kindle ed., chap. 4, 8e.

4. Edith Stein, *Finite and Eternal Being*, trans. Kurt Reinhardt (Washington, DC: ICS Publications, 2002), chap. 8.

5. Stein, *Potency and Act*, 2417–18.

6. Stein, 2301–3.

7. Stein, *Einführung in die Philosophie*, 134 (translation mine).

8. Stein, 144.

9. Stein, *Potency and Act*, 2411–20.

10. Stein, 2597–98.

11. Stein, *Einführung in die Philosophie*, 152–153 (translation mine).

12. Stein, 226.

13. Gerardus van der Leeuw, *Religion in Essence and Manifestation*, trans. Ninian Smart and John Evan Turner (Princeton, NJ: Princeton University Press, 1986).

14. van der Leeuw, 360. I have used part of van der Leeuw's framework in developing my own account of the phenomenology of religion through an investigation of sacroreligious phenomena. See my work, *The Divine in Husserl and Other Explorations* in *Analecta Husserliana*, vol. 98 (Dordrecht: Springer, 2009).

5

"It Is No Longer I Who Do It"
Interiority and the Foreign-Body

BRIAN W. BECKER

> It is in sickness that we are compelled to recognize that we live not alone but are chained to a being from a different realm, from whom we are worlds apart, who has no knowledge of us and by whom it is impossible to make ourselves understood: the body.
>
> —Marcel Proust[1]

Wide-eyed and bewildered, with cannibalistic ferocity, the father gnaws upon the flesh of his adult son's arm, the other arm and head already consumed. Such is the image in Francisco Goya's painting of the Greco-Roman god, Saturn, belonging to his series of *Black Paintings* (c. 1819–1823). It is haunting not merely for its visible spectacle but also for the portrayal of the invisible torment the son endures moments prior to his death. It is reminiscent of another painting, one that possibly inspired Goya's: Peter Paul Ruben's *Saturn Devouring His Infant Son* (1636), depicting, on this occasion, Saturn's infant son, still alive, his left chest being chewed. While disturbing in its own right, Goya's painting displays not only the physical agony of Ruben's infant son but also a psychic suffering; the mature son is acutely aware of what is befalling him as his limbs and his subjectivity are ruthlessly stripped away, bite by bite, by the very one who generated him and the one whom the son may have even loved. We recoil at the

86 | Brian W. Becker

consumption of his humanity as much as, if not more than, the cannibalism of his biological body.

We can say that three bodies are ingested here: first, an extended-body (*le corps étendu*) that is measured and objectified, locatable within specific geometric coordinates and reducible to its caloric intake; second, a lived-body (*le corps vécu*) that feels and feels itself feeling, a body that moves and experiences the possibility of its movements, whose auto-affection gives rise to an *ipseity* accessible to no one else; third, a spread-body (*le corps épandu*), neither fully extended nor lived but spread out, residing as a sort of "frontier zone," expressing a dimension of our depersonalized animality that includes its organic materiality and interior chaos.[2] While each body cannot be considered independent from the other, taken together, the fullness of our embodiment remains elusive, for Goya's painting confronts us with yet another body, one we would not immediately identify as belonging to the son but rather to the father. Nonetheless, this body comes to be incorporated within our own, and upon incorporating it, this body in turn cannibalizes ours—extended, lived, and spread—from the inside out, functioning as an interiorized exteriority whereby "the intimate is Other—like a foreign body, a parasite."[3] Contact with this foreign-body (*le corps aliéné*)[4] exhibits neither the qualities of intercorporeality nor the erotic crossing of flesh but is encountered as an infection living in me as both parasite and symbiote that, like a promethean punishment, feeds off my body and flesh while repeatedly reconstituting me in its image.[5] Can we more rigorously conceptualize and include *this body* among those already identified by phenomenology? And how are we to conceptualize this inner division without retreating from phenomenology's contribution to unifying our interiority with the motility and sensibility of our lived-bodies? These are the questions under consideration in this work, which will turn to medicine, psychoanalysis, and theology to establish the modalities of what Freud called *der Fremdkörper*, the foreign-body, and to draw upon observed convergences, establishing its phenomenological characteristics.

The Limbs of Phenomenology

Among the more notable clinical cases studied phenomenologically is the phantom limb.[6] In this condition, part of the body is absent due to injury or disease and yet, despite this loss, the patient continues to experience, often painfully, the felt presence of that limb.[7] This condition cannot be understood merely in terms of "objective causality," but instead it reveals the intimate relationship between the psychic and physical, forming a lived-body.[8] The phantom limb is no mere mental representation or conscious projection. Rather, this "ambivalent presence of an arm"[9] reveals an inextricable psychosomatic unity, which serves as the very means of *always already* being in a world open to certain spatial possibilities.[10]

Turning to the spread-body, a different medical condition is taken up.[11] Whereas there is a marked presence amidst an absence in the phantom limb, in an anesthetized limb[12] we discover the inverse: an absence amidst a notable presence. This is an absence, not of an extended-body but a lived-body, which no longer feels or feels itself feeling. When part of my body undergoes anesthesia or even when I experience acute suffering, my body can become depersonalized. The anesthetized body "no longer lets through any cries of pain from a particular subjectivity."[13] Consequently, there is an absence of meaning, moving beyond the opposition between sense and nonsense to the absence or limit of sense in the "absence of all self."[14] As such, the spread-body leads to the very limit of the phenomenon, toward the "biological copiousness of a flesh that is profuse and also impossible to subjectify."[15]

Thus, stripped of an extended-body, a lived-body remains (phantom limb); stripped of a lived-body, a spread-body remains (anesthetized limb). But what remains when stripped of my extended- *and* lived-bodies, not by absence through loss but through the *excorporation* of a foreign presence? By excorporation I mean an act that runs counter to an incarnation of the flesh or incorporation of the body. Whereas in the latter I gain something, the former produces a loss, but a loss by addition. At first glance, such a situation appears absurd, for surely if a body persists, it is either the body I have or the body I am. However, in the case of an alien limb, this remarkable medical condition reveals another possibility. Following neurological injury, a bodily limb begins to exhibit a "will of its own." The limb initiates seemingly purposeful activity, independent of the patient's will, exemplified by cases in which one hand buttons a shirt while the other rebelliously unbuttons it, or one hand caresses a beloved while the other violently aggresses against that person. Clinically distinct from reflexes by a limb's purposeful behavior, patients do not report merely unwanted movements (as in the tremors of Parkinsonism or the choreic actions of Huntington's disease) but instead experience a "disobedient" limb, leading patients to personify it, providing it pejorative monikers. On occasion, patients even describe their wayward limbs as being possessed by a demon or spirit. This experience is accompanied by another condition (somatoparaphrenia) in which even ownership of the physical limb is denied, to the point of treating it as a separate being and, on occasion, acquiring the desire to amputate it—its very presence so disturbing and hated (misoplegia). As such, now "the venerated body that appears in phenomenology as 'one's own body' (*le corps propre*) is revealed as infected, not simply with disease and mutilation, but also with division."[16]

The Corporeal Super-Ego

The ambiguous body is claimed to be "phenomenology's closest approximation to the Freudian unconscious"[17] or "the ontic model for any conceivable unconscious."[18] But what kind of ambiguous body is this? One approach has been to situate the unconscious within or alongside the lived-body. Unlike the divided subject usually assumed to be portrayed in psychoanalysis, the unconscious as lived-body constitutes a modality of corporeality as an "undivided being"[19] whose osmotic dimension brings together the body's anonymity and the life of subjectivity that establishes my fundamental openness to the world. The unconscious forms part of a pre-personal, nonlinguistic habitual body that comports itself to its world through perception, feeling, and desire.

Broadening this phenomenology of the body to emphasize the carnal nature of all experience (i.e., the flesh), the unconscious consists of an invisible dehiscence that forms a crossing between the sensing and the sensed, the touching and the touched.[20] Dissolving the divide that separates the "for-itself" from the "for-the-Other," the unconscious points to a fundamental undividedness between embodied consciousness and the other, who is an "echo" in me just as I am in the other. Under this description of the unconscious, psychoanalysis entails a "revelation of intercorporeality, of the Ego-others montage, as it is realized by each one."[21]

A different attempt to consider the unconscious in terms of a body situates it below the personal and beyond the sphere of language.[22] It, too, resides in a frontier between the mental and somatic. However, the manner in which the unconscious resides there diverges greatly from a lived-body, moving away from unity, sensibility, and subjectivity and instead plunging the unconscious into a sphere of chaos and meaninglessness where the light of day cannot be reached by a phenomenological gaze, constituting instead the very limit of sight itself. This dimension of the unconscious, the id more specifically, confronts the ego with a bodily chaos whose "uncontrollable forces" boil over into a kind of powerful violence, driving us to a return to the inorganic lifelessness of a pre-subjectivized materiality.[23] Here, and again in contrast to the other approach, psychoanalysis entails "reaching the limits" and "touching the limits" of discourse and meaning. The practice of psychoanalysis is first and foremost grounded in encountering this limit where our internal chaos is on display in the body spread out on the analyst's couch.

Despite their differences, these two approaches both reject a conditioned unconscious, one in which the signifier dominates. For this reason, it is not surprising that they share an inordinate attention upon the id, sometimes identifying it with the unconscious itself,[24] rarely mentioning the place of the super-ego. However, while the entirety of psychic life begins with and is inevitably tethered to the id, the unconscious, properly speaking, is not present at birth. Rather, the unconscious arrives late, following the formation of the ego from the id's encounter with external reality and incorporating an authority that imposes itself from that reality. This incorporated otherness functions as an agency that represses the id from bubbling to the surface while, at the same time, representing a transformed id to the ego. Termed the "censor" in Freud's early work, it is identified as the super-ego in his later writings, and while we cannot forget the bodily dimension of the id, we would be remiss in continuing to neglect the corporeal super-ego for its place in the formation and ongoing expression of the unconscious.

But how are we to understand the super-ego as corporeal when it is considered to be a kind of "categorical imperative"[25] (Freud) or "a law deprived of meaning, but one which nevertheless only sustains itself by language" (Lacan)?[26] Is this not, as suggested of the "hermeneutic turn," the embracing of "language at the expense of the body"?[27] Indeed, it is not. To quote Lacan: "Language is not immaterial. It is a subtle body, but body it is."[28] But in demonstrating how this is the case, we cannot turn to Aristotle's μεταξύ that "mediates this otherness, crossing back and forth between self and strangeness,"[29] for the corporeal dimension of the super-ego is where such mediation breaks down and crossing is no longer possible. Rather than being exposed to others in the sensitivities of touch, I am infected by a parasitic agency that Freud identifies as a "foreign-body."

Well before developing the central concepts of psychoanalysis, and drawing upon his medical background,[30] Freud employs the term "foreign-body" [*Fremdkörper*] to characterize an intrusive dimension of psychic life.[31] In *Studies in Hysteria* (1895), he describes symptoms produced by prior psychic trauma that "act like a foreign body which after its entry must continue to be regarded as an agent that is still at work."[32] Though continuing to employ this term on several occasions in the same text,[33] he will express ambivalence toward it, clarifying that it is more akin to an infiltration that enters in "relation with the layers of tissue that surround it."[34] In other words, this body is so infused within psychic life as to refuse complete extirpation, there being no clear demarcation between the body I identify with and this body that confronts me and infects me, suggesting that consciousness itself is inextricably linked to and perhaps formed out of it. The difficulty Freud faces at this point in his career is reconciling the medical notion of a foreign-body that arrives externally to infect the surrounding tissue with the analytic experience of it being integral to the functioning of that tissue. Due to this apparent contradiction, he abandons the term, using it only once between 1895 and 1929 when, in his *Five Lectures of Psychoanalysis* (1909), he recalls the earlier comparison of the symptom to a foreign-body, only to reiterate his concerns for its lack of conceptual clarity.[35]

He will be unable to reconcile this apparent contradiction for nearly two decades, until he develops his concept of the super-ego, at which point the term reappears. In *Inhibitions, Symptoms and Anxiety* (1926), the foreign-body is again presented as a symptom that now participates in the ego "to fulfill a requirement of the super-ego," functioning as "a kind of frontier-station with a mixed garrison (*Besetzung*)."[36] To appease the demands of this intrusive force, the ego adapts "to this piece of the internal world which is alien to it," gradually becoming "more and more closely merged with the ego and more and more indispensable to it."[37] He later adds, in *Moses and Monotheism* (1939), that the inherited memories of the past ("memory traces") that the super-ego assumes from the id, function as "foreign bodies" disconnected from consciousness.[38] Freud thus reconciled the apparent contradiction for himself. The foreign-body, as super-ego, arrives as a parasitic agent manifesting as unbidden symptoms and alien memories that, while initially exterior, is eventually incorporated into psychic life, transforming the parasite into a symbiote, but one, as we will see, that never loses its parasitic quality.

Senselessness of the Super-Ego

While Freud's understanding of the foreign-body from *Studies in Hysteria* (1895) to *Moses and Monotheism* (1939) undergoes notable developments, a remarkable consistency remains—namely, its traumatic dimension. This "resurrection of the dead" giving birth to a re-formed past is by no means a welcomed outcome. The original incorporation of the super-ego and persisting agency in the life of the mind remains traumatic, inflicting pain and suffering in the compulsive repetition of a past that relentlessly and violently intrudes upon my present and diminishes my hope in the future. We cannot make sense of this interminable suffering and violence, for it exceeds every possible meaning we can give to it. Nor is it nonsense for I experience it directly as it inflicts a reason that, though viciously circular, appears as anything but contradictory and absurd. Yet, again, it does not offer a sort of limit-experience that goes beyond all sense and nonsense. Rather, the foreign-body confers a nonsensical sense, or a *senselessness* that ruthlessly imposes upon me its perverse "ethical" demand. It reveals itself as a destructive, constricted sense that runs counter to my will and to a self that "has lost everything except . . . reason."[39] This is reason gone mad, and while considered in opposition to each other, madness and reason are intimately linked, deepening that relation as reason becomes increasingly constricted. Whereas the ego is associated with a "reasonability" and the id with an "interminable drive," the super-ego unites these qualities to form an "interminable reason" that respects no limit.

The name offered for this traumatic, repetitive senselessness expressed by the super-ego is the death drive (*Todestrieb*). The death drive is frequently mistaken as a direct expression of the id. However, the id "has no means of showing the ego love or hate. It cannot say what it wants; it has achieved no unity of will."[40] Only the super-ego loves or hates, and most often loves to hate. For while it is true that all drives begin with the id, they only acquire their destructive quality upon the traumatic introduction of another who indeed wills our destruction. As such, the super-ego serves as a "gathering-place for the death-instincts,"[41] "a pure culture of the death-instinct" that "often enough succeeds in driving the ego into death."[42] Upon feeding off the chaotic drives of the id, the super-ego "rages against the ego with merciless violence."[43] Harvester's sickle in hand, Saturn, this agricultural god who represents cyclical time (Father Time) comes to personify death (the Grim Reaper). Paternity, repetition, and death all converge for Saturn as they do with the super-ego, whose parasitic agency feeds off our animality (id) while ruthlessly tearing apart our humanity (conscious ego), bit by bit.

While it has been argued otherwise, it is not in the id's relationship with the ego where we stray from our animality as, according to Freud, "The differentiation between ego and id must be attributed . . . even to much simpler organisms, for it is the inevitable expression of the influence of the external world."[44] The drive of the id in its relationship to the ego is not inherently perverse. If so, we would observe a polymorphous perversity in nonhuman animals as well. Rather, the drive goes "beyond the pleasure principle" only upon the traumatic intervention of a symbolic Other that becomes flesh in excorporating what has been placed there by "biology and the vicissitudes of the human species,"[45] serving as a representative of the id to the ego. Thus, as Freud writes, "We shall have to say that not only what is lowest but also what is highest . . . can be unconscious."[46] The senseless super-ego reflects neither the animality of the id nor the humanity of our ego, but rather it marks a deviant exception to both in introducing the "highest" (the "ethical" imperative) into the lowest (somatic drives) and compelling the ego to accommodate itself to this destructive synthesis.

"Bestiality" is a name given to this "possibility of an animality gone astray,"[47] and it shares remarkable resemblances with the super-ego. To become a beast is to be both less and more at the same time, for in seeking to be more than human, we become less than animal.[48] This pursuit of being more than human reflects a "temptation of angelism" that denies our animality, acting "as though we were totally disincarnate, without passions or drives, without darkness or Chaos."[49] To repeat a quotation of Pascal, "We are neither angels nor beasts, and thus, anyone trying to act the angel acts the beast."[50] And, while this "going beyond our humanity" may be distinguished from "human behavior mimicking an animal world . . . it has never shared," a certain kind of angelism is at play in all forms of bestiality as each reveals a pursuit to transcend our humanity, whether it be a perverse omnipotence (becoming "God") through sadism, voyeurism, and violence, or a perverse *askesis* (submitting to "God") through masochisms of all kinds.

Returning to Goya's painting, Saturn, whose name became associated with the all-consuming lows of melancholy (i.e., to be saturnine), was "the "highest star"—the seventh and most distant of all planets in the ancient universe."[51] The comparison is apt for melancholy is not brought about by what is lowest in us—our animality—but what is highest: "The excessively strong super-ego which has obtained a hold upon consciousness [and] rages against the ego with merciless violence."[52] Herein we find the senseless bestiality of the super-ego. It is also the case that bestiality connects to the experience of another kind of foreign-body—sin.[53] And while we must be cautious not to quickly collapse sin with super-ego or symptom, their parallels direct our attention to a third case of the foreign-body given expression this time by theology.

The Heterocorporeality of Sin

Phenomenology's turn to theology has provided an approach to the body in terms of incarnation (word becoming flesh—starting with the infinite) and incorporation (human becoming God—starting with the finite). Yet, scripture speaks abundantly of another kind of bodily experience captured by neither incarnation of the flesh nor incorporation into the body. Instead, we find a foreignness that claims dominion over us whereby a finitude excorporates another finitude. The body is the site of a warfare being waged between nefarious agents that appear to take possession of our bodies, usurping our will and replacing it with their own.

The New Testament and Paul's letters present a view of the body as fluid and permeable (e.g., Gal. 2:20; 1 Cor. 15:52–53; 2 Cor. 5:4), something never closed off to the outside.[54] Rather, it is a transferable property, to be ruled not by the self but by the mutually exclusive claims of either sin (Rom. 6:6) or Christ (Rom. 7:4).[55] As such, I neither *have* nor *am* a body but rather experience *through* my body a dwelling for other inhabitants who, like Freud's garrison, serve as occupying forces.[56] This "other-directed" dimension of the body is controlled not only by me but "by that reality for which I live, which I serve, and to which I belong."[57] Yet whereas in being ruled by Christ I experience a unity of will through the incorporation of his body, through sin I experience a division not unlike the separation of willing and doing in the alien limb or the compulsive repetition of the super-ego, as expressed in that renowned passage in Rom. 7:

> What I do, I do not understand. For I do not do what I want, but I do what I hate. . . . So now it is no longer I who do it, but sin that dwells in me. . . . For I take delight in the law of God, in my inner self, but I see in my members another principle at war with the law of my mind, taking me captive to the law of sin that dwells in my members. (Rom. 7:15–23)

Sin functions as a foreign-body that infects with a law that leads me to act against my own will and even to will against my will. "Sin leads the sinner by the hand; what the sinner does is to some degree alien to the sinner's own person."[58] In contrast to the differentiated unity of an intercorporeality, we encounter a heterocorporeality that Paul identifies as the sin of the flesh. The descent into bestiality is the descent into plurality reflected by the name of the Gerasene demoniac: Legion. This is a scattering of our embodied being that Augustine in *Confessions* calls "this monstrosity" (*hoc monstrum*), a "sickness of the soul," leading him to proclaim that "there are two wills."[59] We must, of course, be cautious to avoid drawing metaphysical conclusions here. The present concern, as it was for Paul and Augustine, at least in these passages, is the givenness of sin as a dimension of our embodiment, which "is simply to be accepted as it gives itself out to be, though only within the limits in which it then presents itself."[60] We should not let concerns of falling into a kind of Manichaeism prevent us from considering *how* sin gives itself from itself, for in attempting to avoid losing the "metaphysical goodness of creation"[61] we may risk giving limited attention to the phenomenological weight of evil. Our animal body may be "inaccessible through a phenomenological approach,"[62] but the senseless foreign-body does appear in the flesh, even in the expression of evil, for an absence of being does not always entail an absence of phenomenality.

The Thanatonic Phenomenon

In this chapter, I have offered a sketch of the foreign-body as manifested in medicine, psychoanalysis, and theology. Despite clear differences, a certain phenomenality unites the alien limb, super-ego, and sin. Yet this phenomenality, rather than shining by its own light, reveals itself by a borrowed light, one inflected by other phenomena and, above all else, the erotic. For what confronts me, and for which the foreign-body is central, is a possibility that concerns me as much as the question of love and not the least for the parasitic and perverse mimicry of its logic.

Undergoing the erotic phenomenon profoundly reconstitutes my consciousness and possibilities.[63] *Spatiality* is no longer the interchangeable geographical coordinates of my actual world but is heterogeneous and unsubstitutable, defined first and foremost by the place of the beloved. *Temporality* is no longer defined by my present but by the impending arrival of the beloved whom I approach in hopeful expectation for the possible crossing of erotic intentions. It is marked by a distance that, though never collapsed, is traversed. Finally, *identity* is no longer the self-reflexivity of my consciousness. Instead, I am given access to myself in the eroticization of my flesh brought about by the beloved's touch, which, through body and word, awakens me to a self that I could not previously access.

The foreign-body belongs to another logic, which shall be called the *thanatonic phenomenon*.[64] It reveals, like the erotic phenomenon, an alterity that meets me in my bodily existence, but this time in its lived *and* material dimensions where I confront an originary fissure and alienable origin. In the erotic phenomenon, the beloved awakens my flesh, maintaining a distance that makes the traversal of love possible.[65] In the thanatonic phenomenon, the foreign-body that comes from elsewhere collapses all distance in excorporating my body and flesh, consuming my space, my time, and my identity; it is in these three elements, the same three outlined for the erotic phenomenon, where we find its phenomenological characteristics.

First, *spatiality*. Under the logic of the thanatonic phenomenon and in the encounter with the foreign-body, there is a collapse in distance between the "here" that marks my spatiality and the "there" that ordinarily marks my encounter with the other. Now, an "elsewhere" marks my space, not as in the erotic encounter nor as in the natural attitude where a homogeneity of space marks every "there" interchangeable with every "here." Rather, the foreign-body invades me with a "faceless otherness" inaugurating an "absolute and distance-less proximity"[66] that annuls space, revealing to me not another world but the loss of the world I inhabited. In this loss, I undergo a collapse of my possibilities, possibilities that I used to express in the "I can" of the lived-body but now meet with an *apraxia* expressed as the "I cannot" and even the "I cannot not" of a foreign-body.

Next, *temporality*. The future is no longer determined by an expectant hope born from the "elsewhere" of my beloved, nor the present what is made present by the "elsewhere" of the beloved, nor the past of a time that forbids repetition for having been where the beloved was encountered as an event. Rather, "the present is changed into the past."[67] I become marked by melancholic despair as my future disappears and my present is ceaselessly and senselessly intruded upon by the past. Romano, drawing upon Freud, writes that the encounter with the traumatic "frees itself from the limits of this singular experience and invades our whole adventure through its incessant repetition in memory or dreams and, impossible to assimilate, becomes a genuine internal 'foreign body.' "[68] This foreign-body that already invades my space now invades my time, foreshortening my future and producing "an indefinite stagnation of a perpetual present"[69] by its collapse into the past.

Finally, *identity*. When I encounter a foreign-body, I am not given a new knowledge or experience; I am closed off from existing frontiers within me. It reveals itself to me, not as accessible, easy, and apparent, but rather it reveals itself by making me inaccessible, difficult, and obscure to myself. I am rendered *agnostic* as what was previously accessible becomes unknown and cohabitated by a parasitic symbiote living as an intimate exteriority, both alien and inextricable to my identity. My previously unsubstitutable flesh is now lived by another and, in losing part of my flesh, I lose part of myself. There forms in its place a crack where I become exposed to the abyss of my own death, left with only a "shattered self" in which melancholy confronts me in my augmenting nothingness. Thus, my singularity achieved in the erotic encounter is undone as I am rendered a pure *subject*, one who is completely *subjected* to a senseless reason, without means of appropriating any meaning to make sense of this exteriority attacking me from within.

Interiority: Unity and Division

Phenomenology has rightfully drawn our attention to the unity of inner-experience and bodily sense. Such a development served an important corrective to a philosophical current that divided the two in a manner that problematically reverberates throughout a variety of branching disciplines. At the same time, there is a primordial encounter with one's interiority that is at odds with one's body and thus at odds with oneself. The foreign-body is a concept that seeks to address the bodily dimension of this inner foreignness but one distinct from the encounter with the organic body in its depersonalized animality.

Phenomenology's emphasis on our psychosomatic unity has led to a neglect or dismissal of a phenomenology of dividedness. The duality of mind and body was rightfully critiqued as a philosophical abstraction, but might we not ask whether there may be a kernel of phenomenological truth lurking beneath such theorizing? Affirming such is not a denial of the gains made by phenomenology through the notions of the lived-body, affectivity, and flesh. Instead, it is a recognition that an interior unity does not always make an appearance and, instead, marks an achievement of a self that has managed to resist its own dividedness enough to receive its unity more fully. Indeed, this seems to be the path described by many in the mystic tradition. In St. Teresa of Avila, for instance, we are led through a spiritual journey that in the first mansions begins in warfare and temptation, and only upon entrance into the final mansions does this division give way to a unity between the soul and God and thus a unity within the soul itself. Interior unity is to be an accomplishment and not a starting point for thought, and the notion of the foreign-body is the attempt to think through the givenness of our bodies in their diverse modes of manifestation.

Conclusion

The bodily dimension of this foreignness tacitly functions in the ways we find ourselves carried along—speaking, desiring, moving—having the quality of a senseless automaton working behind the scenes, appropriating our actions and beliefs in service of it. It has a life of its own, living in and through me, often seamlessly, until I can no longer maintain the illusion of unity within myself. The foreign-body continues to function and live out through us, penetrating deep within our bodies, functioning as a gravitational force that constrains and directs our activities. The alien automaton goes about its business appropriating and repurposing our considerations, decisions, and actions to conform to its senseless demands. It still lives in and through us, *in* our bodies, masking itself *as* our bodies while also devouring our bodies, as Goya depicts the father, Saturn, devouring his son—a son who was prophesized to usurp him, only to be digested by the body from whence he came.

Admittedly, this analysis leaves us in the melancholy it describes. For in describing it, I perform it, and in performing it, I give witness to it in myself. My every act of love is inevitably tethered to this foreign-body and bears its teeth marks. To deny it is to "pretend to a god or . . . a beast."[70] And as such, its denial is itself the very expression, par excellence, of that bestiality and the condition of possibility for the foreign-body's motility and passage unto others.

Beyond submerging more fully into melancholic despair and beyond a manic pursuit of idols to maintain the imaginary ego, we appear to be offered two additional possibilities in our encounter with the foreign-body and its thanatonic logic—either psychoanalysis or metamorphosis. The former helps us obtain a modicum of satisfaction in coming to terms with the inescapable tragedy of our divided bodies through a repositioning vis-à-vis the signifier; the latter prompts me to ask for another greater than I to "enter under my roof" so I may "put off" this foreign-body and "put on" another body, one that also assumes, rather than consumes, my animality and humanity, not to pervert them but to elevate and transform them. And when I incorporate this body, it lives in me not as infection leading to death but, this time, as *pregnancy*, which, as Plato writes in the *Symposium*, becomes that "kind of everlastingness and immortality for the mortal creature."[71]

Notes

1. *In Search of Lost Time*, trans. C. K. Scott Moncrieff and T. Kilmartin, vol. 3 (New York: Random House, 1993), 404.

2. Each body is associated with its respective philosopher: Rene Descartes with the extended body, Edmund Husserl and Maurice Merleau-Ponty with the lived-body, and more recently Emmanuel Falque with the spread-body, though with forerunners in Nietzsche and Deleuze.

3. Jacques-Alain Miller, "Extimité," in *Lacanian Theory of Discourse: Subject, Structure and Society*, eds. M. Bracher, M. W. Alcorn Jr., R. J. Corthell, and F. Massardier-Kenney (New York: NYU Press, 1994), 76.

4. The translation of foreign-body as "*le corps aliéné*" rather than the closer French equivalent of "*le corps étranger*" is chosen because *aliéné*, while losing the medical connotation, provides a relevant polysemy not found in *étranger*, suggesting qualities such as something being "given up" or "relinquished," the experience of "insanity," and the experience of being "alienated."

5. Does this foreign-body infect me by trauma, language, or even by the mere fact of being born? Each possibility will be suggested in addressing the cases of the alien limb (physical trauma), the super-ego (language, psychic trauma), and sin (birth, language). Yet, for the purpose of focusing on the "how" rather than "why" of the foreign-body, I intend to leave this an open question for now.

6. Maurice Merleau-Ponty, *Phenomenology of Perception*, trans. C. Smith (London: Routledge, 1958; first ed. 1945). See especially "Part I: The Body."

7. Merleau-Ponty, *Phenomenology of Perception*, 88.

8. Merleau-Ponty, 89.

9. Merleau-Ponty, 94.

10. Merleau-Ponty, 94.

11. For an analysis of the spread-body, see Emmanuel Falque, *The Wedding Feast of the Lamb: Eros, the Body, and the Eucharist*, trans. G. Hughes (New York: Fordham University Press, 2016; first ed. 2011). The concept is subsequently developed in his article: "Éthique du Corps Épandu," *Revue d'éthique et de théologie morale* 1, no. 288 (2016), 53–82; and a revised version is found in Emmanuel Falque and Sabine Fos-Falque, *Éthique du corps épandu: Suivi de Une chair épandue sur le divan* (Paris: Cerf, 2018).

12. "We can take as an example the body under anesthetic, something most of us have experienced ourselves and seen in others, both animals and human beings." Falque, *Wedding Feast of the Lamb*, 13.

13. Falque, *Wedding Feast of the Lamb*, 13.
14. Falque, 21
15. Falque, 13.
16. Dylan Trigg, *The Thing: A Phenomenology of Horror* (Alresford, UK: Zero Books, 2014), 90.
17. John Panteleimon Manoussakis, *Ethics of Time: A Phenomenology and Hermeneutics of Change* (London: Bloomsbury Academic, 2017), 107.
18. Paul Ricoeur, *Freud and Philosophy: An Essay on Interpretation*, trans. D. Savage (New Haven, CT: Yale University Press, 1970), 382.
19. Maurice Merleau-Ponty, *Notes sur le corps* (unpublished), cited by Emmanuel de Saint Aubert, "Merleau-Ponty's Conception of the Unconscious in the Late Manuscripts," in *Unconsciousness Between Phenomenology and Psychoanalysis*, eds. D. Legrand and D. Trigg (Cham, CH: Springer International Publishing AG, 2017), 50.
20. Maurice Merleau-Ponty, *The Visible and the Invisible*, ed. C. Lefort, trans. A. Lingis (Evanston, IL: Northwestern University Press, 1968; first ed. 1964).
21. Maurice Merleau-Ponty, *Institution and Passivity: Course Notes from the Collège de France (1954–1955)*, trans. L. Lawlor and H. Massey (Evanston, IL: Northwestern University Press, 2010), 246.
22. See Emmanuel Falque, *'Ça' n'a rien à voir: Lire Freud en philosophie* (Paris: Cerf, 2018).
23. Falque, 109.
24. This is most clearly expressed by Merleau-Ponty where, in the working notes of *The Visible and the Invisible,* he writes: "Hence the philosophy of Freud is not a philosophy of the body but of the flesh—The Id, the unconscious—and the Ego (correlative) to be understood on the basis of the flesh" (270). Paul Ricoeur writes as well that "Freud himself never makes the unconscious think, and in this respect the discovery of the term *Es* or id was a stroke of genius. Unc. is the id and nothing but the id." Ricoeur, "Consciousness and the Unconscious," in *The Conflict of Interpretations: Essays in Hermeneutics*, ed. D. Ihde, trans. W. Domingo (Evanston, IL: Northwestern University Press, 1974; first ed. 1969), 105. It is difficult to make sense of this conclusion upon reading Freud's *The Ego and The Id*, stand. ed., vol. 19, where in the first chapter he clearly writes, "We have come upon something in the ego itself which is also unconscious." Sigmund Freud, *The Standard Edition* [SE], vol. 19 (1923–1925), ed. J. Strachey (London: Hogarth Press, 1961), 17. Falque, to his credit, acknowledges the lack of firm boundaries between the id and ego, showing that the ego is in fact intimately connected to the id. Yet, as of his current writings on the matter, his focus is nearly exclusively on the id. He correctly notes, "Le 'Ça' n'est pas 'moi,' ni même le 'surmoi,' non pas en cela que par lui je connaîtrais mon moi ou mon surmoi . . . mais à l'inverse qu'en raison de lui je ne me connais pas et ne me connaîtrai jamais." Falque, *'Ça' n'a rien à voir*, 43. What this leaves out, however, is that my encounter with the id is only *through* the super-ego, which is its representative to the ego. The id cannot be seen (*Ça' n'a*

rien à voir) but the id's impenetrable depths can be refracted through the perverse prism of the super-ego, allowing a kind of mediated access to the id and, in fact, the only access possible.

25. Freud, *SE*, 19:35.

26. Jacques Lacan, *The Seminar of Jacques Lacan: Book I Freud's Papers on Technique 1953–1954*, ed. J.-A. Miller, trans. J. Forrester (New York: W. W. Norton, 1988; first ed. 1975), 3.

27. Richard Kearney, "The Wager of Carnal Hermeneutics," in *Carnal Hermeneutics*, R. Kearney and B. Treanor (New York: Fordham University Press, 2015), 16.

28. Jacques Lacan, *Écrits: The First Complete Edition in English*, trans. B. Fink (New York: W. W. Norton, 2006; first ed. 1966), 248.

29. Kearney, "The Wager of Carnal Hermeneutics," 20.

30. One earlier recorded occasion in which Freud employs the term is in a letter to Fleiss (March 8, 1895) concerning a medical procedure to remove a half-meter gauze that had been ineptly left in the wound following a previous surgical operation, resulting in an infection and swelling.

31. This analysis of the foreign-body in Freud's work is greatly informed by Rob White's chapter "The Foreign Bodies of Psychoanalysis," in his *Freud's Memory: Psychoanalysis, Mourning and the Foreign Body* (New York: Palgrave Macmillan, 2008).

32. Freud, *SE*, 2:6.

33. At another point, Freud analogizes a patient's disconnected awareness of a love for her brother-in-law with a foreign body, and in this case, it operates as a free-floating ideation disconnected from all affect within psychic life, manifesting itself through unbidden bodily reactions. Freud, *SE II*, 165.

34. Freud, *SE*, 2:290.

35. Freud, *SE*, 11:20.

36. Freud, *SE*, 20:98–99. Freud will more explicitly link this garrison with the super-ego in *New Introductory Lectures*: "The institution of the super-ego which takes over the dangerous aggressive impulses, introduces a garrison (*Besetzung*), as it were, into regions that are inclined to rebellion." Freud, *SE*, 22:110. Important to note is that Freud plays off the polysemy of the German word *Besetzung*, which is translated as either "cathexis" or "garrison" in the *SE* depending on context. This is notable as the super-ego serves as the central cathexis of the psyche, functioning as both an occupying force (of troops) and a charge (of electricity). However, it is debated whether the Greek term *cathexis* (κάθεξις) was the best choice of translation.

37. Freud, *SE*, 20:99.

38. Freud, *SE*, 23:94. Freud will almost always express the foreign-body as either a simile or metaphor, suggesting a step removed from the thing itself. Yet, a simile or metaphor for what? The super-ego, symptom, disconnected idea? Freud, the theoretician, appears at times to make the conceptual more fundamental than any clinical phenomenology.

39. G. K. Chesterton, *Orthodoxy* (New York: Crown, 1991; first ed. 1908), 13.
40. Freud, *SE*, 19:59.
41. Freud, 19:54.
42. Freud, 19:53.
43. Freud, 19:53.
44. Freud, 19:38.
45. Freud, 19:36.
46. Freud, 19:27.
47. Falque, *Wedding Feast of the Lamb*, 69.
48. "Beastiality marks precisely the descent of animality below the animal—a descent of which, paradoxically, only human beings show themselves capable." Falque, 73.
49. Falque, 75.
50. Blaise Pascal, *Pensées*, quoted in Falque, 72.
51. Richard Kearney, *Strangers, Monsters, and Gods: Interpreting Otherness* (London: Routledge, 2003), 171.
52. Freud, *SE*, 19:53.
53. Falque develops this connection between bestiality and sin in section 13, "The Other Side of the Angel," *Wedding Feast of the Lamb*, 79–83.
54. This argument is indebted to the insightful work of Klaus Berger in his *Identity and Experience in the New Testament*, trans. C. Muenchow (Minneapolis, MN: Augsburg Fortress, 2003; first ed.1991).
55. Berger, 61–64. Concerning the image of the body as property, Freud explores a similar image when analyzing a dream:

> The human body is often represented in dreams by the symbol of a house. Carrying this representation further, we found that windows, doors and gates stood for openings in the body and that facades of houses were either smooth or provided with balconies and projections to hold on to. But the same symbolism is found in our linguistic usage—when we greet an acquaintance familiarly as an "*altes Haus*" ["old house"], when we speak of giving someone "*eins aufs Dach*" [a knock on the head, literally, "one on the roof"], or when we say of someone else that "he's not quite right in the upper story." In anatomy the orifices of the body are in so many words termed "*Leibespforten*," [literally, "portals of the body"]. (Freud, *SE*, 15:159)

56. Berger, *Identity and Experience*, 67–68. Elsewhere Berger adds "The self, not being sharply delimited, can be permeated by another 'person.' In effect, another person can become immanent within me" (33).
57. Berger, 69.

58. Berger, 207.

59. Saint Augustine, *Confessions*, trans. Henry Chadwick (Oxford: Oxford University Press, 1998), XIII:IX: 21, 154.

60. Edmund Husserl, *Ideas: General Introduction to Pure Phenomenology*, trans. W. R. Boyce Gibson (London: Routledge, 2012; first ed. 1931), 43. Manoussakis provides an important qualification to what Augustine writes here: "For St. Augustine, ever conscious of the lurking dangers of Manichaeism, the natural capacity to will, though tainted by Adam's sin, could not be anything else but good." Manoussakis, *The Ethics of Time*, 89.

61. Manoussakis, 89.

62. Falque, *Wedding Feast of the Lamb*, 21.

63. Jean-Luc Marion, *The Erotic Phenomenon*, trans. S. E. Lewis (Chicago: University of Chicago Press, 2007). A more recent, concise articulation of the erotic phenomenon is provided in Marion's essay "Thinking Elsewhere," trans. B. W. Becker, *Journal for Continental Philosophy of Religion* 1, no. 1 (2019): 5–26.

64. This essay, written in 2019, marks the first occasion in which this term was deployed, eventually leading to a book that develops the nascent ideas found here. See Brian W. Becker, *Evil and Givenness: The Thanatonic Phenomenon* (Lanham, MD: Lexington Books, 2022).

65. "Loving requires distance and the crossing of distance." Marion, *The Erotic Phenomenon*, 46.

66. Claude Romano, *Event and World*, trans. S. Mackinlay (New York: Fordham University Press, 2009), 109. Many of the phenomenological insights addressed in this section are drawn from Romano's analysis found in the section titled "Despair and Terror," especially part (c) "Terror and Traumatism," 109–114. Here Romano focuses on the traumatic event as what undoes the defining qualities of selfhood as *l'advenant*, including its *passibility*, *singularity*, and *responsibility*, thereby immobilizing the human *adventure*.

67. Freud, *SE*, 23:207. Stated otherwise by Trigg, "This recurrence of the past . . . encroaching upon the present derives from a certain 'demonic character' in mental life, which leads itself toward the compulsion to repeat." Trigg, *The Thing*, 81.

68. Romano, *Event and World*, 109.

69. Romano, 113.

70. Marion, *The Erotic Phenomenon*, 55.

71. Plato, *Symposium*, trans. M. C. Howatson (Cambridge: Cambridge University Press, 2008), 206c–207a, 44.

6

Inner Distance and Surreptitious Patience According to Jean-Louis Chrétien

EMMANUEL HOUSSET
TRANSLATED BY ELODIE BOUBLIL

On August 4, 1942, Sister Teresa Benedicta of the Cross was detained at the Westerbork concentration camp in Holland. She lost everything, and all attempts to escape her persecutors failed. Despite all the violence she endured, she remained peaceful and joyful, even writing these last words: "We [Stein and her sister] are just beginning to experience how one's life can be lived solely from the interior."[1] The words of this philosopher and theologian can be understood only if we grasp prayer as the founding act of an interiority grounded in God. Prayer constitutes an interiority of exodus, which has nothing in common with the philosophical interiority based on the subject's mere act of reflection. It is precisely when we have lost everything, including what is most important—including the "self" in all its social, intellectual, and even personal dimensions—that a genuine interiority can open up a space in which the one to whom this prayer is addressed, namely God, becomes essential. This interiority does not reflect the endurance—even if absolute—of a subject that relies exclusively on itself. Instead, it reveals itself as an inner nudity living from a word other than its own. This Christian conception of interiority offers a path to renew the philosophical understanding of interiority by tearing it away from the myth of an interiority separated from exteriority. Such interiority is more radical than what Nietzsche, Heidegger, or Wittgenstein were able to conceive. Indeed, this conception offers a different philosophical starting point that does not refuse the aforementioned separation. Instead, it starts from another place that allows us to take into account this distinction. Furthermore, this renewed yet old conception of interiority does not lead to a safe haven of peace, which we often seek, quite naively perhaps, while we remain in a cozy home or a similarly safe space. Instead, a Christian philosophical conception of interiority can be viewed as an irreversible dispossession that results from an encounter.

Edith Stein's testimony expresses a conception of interiority that is freed from our common anthropological framework. This interiority goes beyond modern subjectivity and its capacity to represent itself beyond its will to make representation the unique model of our relation to ourselves. However, it also refers to a sense of interiority that was lived through long before the metaphysics of subjectivity reduced our perspective to the sole consideration of the human being. This does not mean that one should think that metaphysical theories of subjectivity are either essential or homogeneous. Instead, one must attempt to conceive, within our historical present, a kind of ipseity that relies neither on the idea of a subject able to create itself nor on a pure will, if we understand the will in the modern sense as an a priori capacity for self-willing.

One could conceivably look into the thought of significant past figures for the possibility of thinking beyond the subject, without worrying about making one's present conception the outcome of teleology or even the result of genealogy, albeit admittedly one can sometimes wonder if such genealogy harbors a hidden teleology. Indeed, it is not the past that points to the present. It is instead from the present, by listening to the past, that one can see a future unfold, one which was not foreseeable, even if it was already on the way. In other words, philosophical reflection can be a *reoccurring question* that finds in the past a conception that pertains to a completely different field than that of an interiority defined by its capacity to produce everything reflexively in representations, including the world that it turned into an image. This philosophical stance also has the advantage of avoiding the pitfall of constructing a fictitious modernity merely so it can be more easily overcome.

In *The Phenomenology of Spirit*, Hegel shows that it is necessary to move out of oneself in order to be oneself. He rejects the claim of a closed and purely reflexive interiority that is opposed to the world. In his treatment of Stoicism, he maintains—earlier than many other philosophers—that the temporality of an interiority that is closed and withdrawn into itself can only be one of boredom and that it is always of ourselves that we are bored.

In the void of boredom, there exists only an ideal time in which nothing happens, in which life is no longer negativity. Hegel thus points out the contradictions of a form of interiority from which one must continuously free oneself to access a living interiority. How can interiority be different from a negation of life? If the unhappy consciousness results from a split, namely, of life, which at the same time always escapes it, this is the case because consciousness wants to make self-control the founding act of its interiority. Moving beyond Hegel, it is then possible to defend the idea that pure interiority consists in being inside-outside, that it is a "distant interior," which requires another form of patience than the perseverance of a will.

Real patience would no longer be an a priori capacity of the subject, which is one of its ways of exercising its power over the world. However, it should be understood as a significant affect in which interiority is not frozen in self-representation so that it never stops listening to the world and others, listening to phenomena in their diversity that is irreducible to the power of constituting consciousness. Before being part of the subject that constitutes or co-constitutes the meaning of the world laboriously in an infinite task of elucidation, patience belongs, first of all, to the respondent, who has to respond only to the event of meaning, which is the founding act of its interiority. Therefore, patience no longer amounts to the calm serenity of the Stoic sage, who is not touched by anything because he has put himself out of reach of the world, or imagines that he has. On the contrary, patience reveals itself in its exposed, chaotic, anarchic, or somewhat stealthy and discreet dimensions insofar as it imposes nothing on phenomena. Such endurance of alterity is what prevents interiority from closing down, from hardening, from becoming inactive, and to be always brought back to what it ought to be.

Therefore, patience is not just one more mood (*Stimmung*). By freeing the notion of mood from any psychological or anthropological dimension, as Heidegger was able to do, one can understand patience as a fundamental mood, one that founds the relationship of the human being to Being and of Being to the human being. It is no longer a question of accessing the truth of Being thanks to the existential categories that are proper to Dasein, as patience in its essence is the renouncement of all mastery of phenomenality in the effort to make it correspond to Being. It is this unintentional expectation that gives dawn the time to rise and, from this birth of the world, human beings can be born to themselves.

In such a correspondence lies the source of true serenity, one that is compatible with being dispossessed of one's world, being chased out of one's place in the world, and also being dispossessed of oneself, of one's manuscripts for the writer, of the power of saying "I." Again, the nature of interiority changes according to the act on which it is founded. If such an act is the "I," we will consider this power to say "I" as what resists, on principle, all destruction, even in the case of the greatest misfortune. If this act is a response to a call, interiority is what is received. In these two understandings of interiority, it is possible to go beyond this representation of an interiority separated from exteriority, either by intentional analysis or by an analysis of transcendence, but the meaning of such questioning will not be the same in both cases. According to these two perspectives, it is also possible to defend the thesis of the inseparability of theoretical questions (the essence of interiority) from ethical questions (what ought to be). However, they can be distinguished in terms of knowing what comes first among the theoretical and the ethical, and on the meaning of what ought-to-be, which is either the endurance of infinite tasks or the responsibility that the respondent receives and carries in its finitude. According to the first path, which is already that of a non-separation of the interior from the exterior, the theoretical from the ethical, it is necessary to refer back to the phenomenon of interiority that lies under its representations. This was the task of Husserl's work, which never ceases to show how phenomenology must distinguish itself from all forms of psychology, which tend to isolate the soul, to close it up in itself, or to cut it off from the world.

The transcendental "I," according to Husserl, from *The Idea of Phenomenology* of 1907 (in which he still speaks of pure *cogitatio* compared to a psychological *cogitatio*) to the *Cartesian Meditations* of 1929, and despite the misunderstandings that his thought encountered, including in his pupils, is precisely not the aforementioned psychological interiority, which is itself nothing but a constituted representation.[2] This attempt to reach pure interiority through a process of reduction that rejects any grounding of consciousness within itself is already found, in a completely different form, in Nietzsche's thought. In Section 355 of *The Gay Science*, Nietzsche shows that what is closest to us, our interiority, is not at all the simplest thing to know and that self-knowledge, far from being a simple and clear starting point of knowledge, must be understood rather as a point of culmination, since it is possible to approach oneself only by discovering one's alterity, one's strangeness, one's distance, in the framework of transcendence.

So we do not have immediate access to interiority, even if it is a reduction, because it is a way of taking part in the world. Here, the second path opens: if I am probably the only one who can answer the question

"Who am I?," this question cannot be asked by myself alone. It follows that it is through the words of others—through the words of the world—that self-knowledge finds the act that founds it. Nevertheless, this is not a recognition, a simple recognition of myself by myself, even when it is mediated by alterity.

Consequently, the distant interior is what the other and the world give me by calling for my word; it is a future that has been given to me. Interiority is no longer a well-defined, reassuring, well-known space, freed from all worries. It is thus animated by a patience that does not require that I see myself in everything, that does not oblige me always to bring the exterior to the interior, what is distant to what is close, what is unknown to what is known. The existential alternative, insofar as it is possible to formulate it, following Nietzsche, is the following: either the fear instinct is the foundation of self-knowledge, and this leads to a state of protective self-enclosure on account of our impatience in the bunker of a closed interiority, or self-knowledge finds its source in a particular trust in the world and in others, which displays a patience that is open to their manifestation.

In this path toward the inside, the one that leads through to the outside and the most intimate aspect of myself, one does not find a "pure I," which ensures the unity of my current and future possible flow of consciousness. It must be understood rather as a pure future, from which I start and from what calls in me, and by which I can become quite different without becoming another, following the existential circle.

It is from our history that we can open up to the unimaginable about ourselves, and yet only a pure future means that I can have a history. It is possible to jump into this circle in which a word always precedes mine and makes it possible, which means that I have neither the first word nor the last since my word gives voice to others. In light of this dialogical essence of interiority, patient interiority is no longer that which I gain against the world through endurance, which could make room for resisting violence. Even locked up in myself, without the outside that allows me to be, I would lose all interiority; there is perhaps no more radical alienation than being isolated with oneself.

Consequently, interiority can disappear in two ways. First, because of the violence of the world, which can prevent me from saying "I," and which can withdraw from me any ground on which I can live, recognize myself, and build myself an identity. Second, interiority can also be in great danger when it is locked up in itself by this process of abstraction in which I isolate myself from the world and, ultimately, from myself by confusing myself with my representation of myself. Thus, interiority can disappear either by an excess or a lack of the world, or even by an excess or a lack of self. In these two situations, the proximity that lives from a distance disappears; the loved one no longer vibrates from a distance.

Since *La Lueur du secret*,[3] Jean-Louis Chrétien has described the patient expectation of another interiority, an interiority that overflows my grasp and calculations, that lives on the proximity of distance as a proximity that reflects a form of trust in which the other gives themselves as inexhaustible. In this interiority, "I am given way more than I can receive."[4] This is why this interiority can never close in on itself and why it reveals itself in the encounter that grounds it. This perspective completely breaks with the philosophies of subjectivity. Here, interiority implies a movement of drawing closer, which is also a way to let oneself be reached.

Consequently, this inner space is a space of meeting, a space of dialogue, and not a space of representation. There is no path leading to this interiority because it is itself the path. My interiority is where it lets itself be reached, hurt; it can only be eccentric. It cannot be unified again by an "I" that will constitute the core of an inner life. It is precisely by bracketing any representations of an ego-center and consciousness, understood as an island, that this interiority based on the encounter reveals itself as a priori capacity. My ability to let myself be met is, in fact, already a gift from the other who exceeds me. From then on, access to human interiority proper is given only to those who have understood that they possesses nothing that they have not received, including interiority. It is always the other who gives me the possibility of opening myself to them, of listening to them, of acting with them. Here lies an originary temporalization, which is no longer the simple development of what was already there because the other makes me other than I was before I met them, and this process is irreversible. The call of my name is the first word. I do not know who I am unless I try constantly to grasp the meaning of this word. My interiority goes beyond the possibilities of my solitude because it is based on an act of dispossession.

In Chrétien's phenomenological elucidation of interior space, patience is also to be understood as the presence of a human being to both what it is and what it is made of or from, which supposes the bracketing of our impatience that is the habitual style of our existence. We can even say that the time of patience is the only real time, the only time that is not a representation,[5] that is not determined by something other than itself. That is why it cannot be the time of instantaneity; rather, it must be understood as the time of a journey, as the time of an expectation filled with hope. The being of a person never immediately reveals itself; rather, it appears during a long relationship in which a person bears witness to who they are and through which we also learn who we are. The patience of trustful listening, then, is that which does not decide beforehand what is allowed to approach; it does not install a bunker on the sands of our fear. It is that by which I can let myself be surprised by what I did not expect. Jean-Louis Chrétien speaks of "surreptitious patience," which is completely withdrawn and restrained, a kind of patience that happens without arranging an appointment with oneself or the other, namely, a hospitable patience that reveals itself in the "trembling of imminence."[6]

According to Jean-Louis Chrétien, the philosophies of presence "make such questions inaccessible. They live to forget them."[7] One can think of a patient interiority as a living afar only if one starts from the idea of an identity broken by what allows it to speak. Therefore, transparency is impossible for such interiority. But this obscurity should not be understood as a deprivation of light because it lives on an entrusted and given secret, which is at the heart of the event and which cannot be absorbed by the infinite work of elucidation. We understand, then, that a new conception of interiority can develop only from a critical reading of the history of metaphysics, understood as a locus of the elaboration of an angelic project of transparency that ends in reducing philosophy to anthropology, defined as the understanding of the world by and for human beings. For Jean-Louis Chrétien, it is more a question of unraveling than destroying, one that aims to shed light on aporias and sometimes on the dead ends of a conception of interiority grounded in the sole act of the subject. Preferring, moreover, the vocabulary of intimacy to that of interiority, which is also linked to the philosophy of subjectivity, he wanted to avoid the dualism of interiority and exteriority as well as the monism of a perfect fusion; he never ceases to defend the idea that the soul is naked only in dialogue. "But . . . its nudity does not form a spectacle there (because), it is by speaking and listening that the person becomes naked and exposes him- or herself."[8] Thus, interiority is what is exposed, that is to say, what manifests and risks, but it is not what is exhibited. Chrétien draws from the idea of "interior nudity" developed by Bérulle in his *Opuscules de piété* in order to develop the thesis of an interiority that is independent from our action and not immediately accessible. Such inner nudity is not understood as a stripping that reduces me to what I am by myself; rather, it lets itself be understood as an uncovered being, without a veil, who stands under the gaze of the other.

Although patient interiority has its possible cracks, this fragility is the ground on which we can stand upright in the world.[9] The founding act of this interiority is not that of subjects reassuring themselves by keeping firmly to their decisions. It is, rather, the act of a fragile and temporal human being constantly having to rethink the meaning of their decisions: "Taking responsibility for one's actions does not mean having to take them on oneself but having to understand oneself in them; it does not mean having to recognize them, but recognizing oneself in them."[10] What is at stake then is being able to think about constancy in terms other than as a habit or an irreversible decision, and, in this other kind of constancy, the meaning of a decision must always be decided. It is a critical interiority, always exposed to the risk of failing, and it is what Jean-Louis Chrétien calls "the luminous insecurity of the promise."[11]

Forgetting fragility amounts to forgetting interiority, for it is from our fragility that we can take responsibility for ourselves and the world. The only true ipseity lies in the good use of one's lapses, failures, and temptations. It is in this patience arising from hope that humans possess an interiority—by being travelers, pilgrims, and exiles. Human beings are traveling railroaders feeling their way through the world clumsily, yet always moving forward, instead of petrifying themselves in a representation of themselves that is, by definition, full of pride: one speaks about oneself from oneself and for oneself. It should even be said that refusing interiority and refusing exteriority are two inseparable moves: to the empty interiority of impatience responds the indifference to exteriority, which is then reduced to a mere representation. True interiority cannot, therefore, be based on the coincidence of a pure and timeless act. I can open myself to another existence when I patiently learn from my sufferings. What exceeds me here urges me to be.

Patient interiority is thus another figure of passivity that escapes the a priori horizon of possibilities since what manifests itself opens up the possibility of responding to it in person. It is Being, the other, or God that gives me the possibility of interiorizing myself, and one of the greatest dangers of doing so comes from myself, from my fear, and even from my fear of fear, which leads me to want to avoid danger and to avoid encountering and being encountered. By thus placing my interiority in an empty, tautological, and out-of-the-world mastery, I put myself out of reach. Jean-Louis Chrétien has never ceased to oppose the autarkic and illusory shelter of an interior citadel and an interiority based on trust living on peril rather than security.[12]

Interiorization is, therefore, not this continuous totalization of oneself, in particular, of one's past, that the philosophies of the subject seek to describe. The "distant interior," according to the deliberately oxymoronic expression of the poet Henri Michaux, is also the impossibility of collecting oneself, of closing all the loopholes of one's existence; it is a matter of consenting to a presence to oneself without coincidence or identity. To suspend any vain project of totalization is to be able to remember what I am called to be and do, by remembering what alone is truly unforgettable: "What is most intimate to the spirit is to be able to turn to what is even more intimate to it than itself; what is highest in it is to be able to turn to what is beyond it."[13] True patience means waiting for the unexpected, which exceeds our expectations and which, in its suddenness, in its radical novelty, always surprises us. The whole of Jean-Louis Chrétien's philosophical work makes interiority a question beyond the pseudo-evidence of self-presence by showing that it cannot be a questioned object—it is the act itself of questioning; this means that questioning is the very act of interiority and that, therefore, there is essentially an inchoative dimension of inner experience. From this new perspective, interiority is nothing other than the patience of our response, and it becomes the place that manifests that to which it responds. What exceeds all expectations is the foundation of surreptitious patience, and this excess of the immemorial and the unexpected is both what divides our present and what gives it its true thickness, one that is much more decisive than the thickness resulting from retention and recollection. Therefore, interiority is not primarily the place where a passive and active subject master meaning and where their presence is loaded by a past and holds no future. On the contrary, it is the place where meaning emerges while confronting alterity, which is not overcome but encountered.

L'appel et la réponse also develops the idea that all human beings live according to a "distant interior," which they cannot open by themselves and which depends on a call that is impossible to anticipate or prevent. The unheard alone, therefore, lets us speak while immediately exceeding any possibility of responding and corresponding, any stammering of speech. This is the true inner voice: one that does not constitute itself, but always responds. The philosophies of subjectivity have often forgotten that what calls me can also exceed me, as well as the idea that the call opens in me the space to listen and thus founds my interiority. It is possible, therefore, to consider the distant interior only by calling into question the thesis that "all inner alterity results from an intimate alteration,"[14] and that ultimately we dialogue with only ourselves. Against such a thesis, the phenomenological task is to show to what extent true interiority is that which is open to what it cannot contain. Returning to oneself presupposes closing oneself off from the world's noise while also moving away from our own incessant internal chatter in order to withdraw into an interiority that is ours only when it is altered by the infinite, by Being, by God. However, "this listening process demands patience," and patience is something other than a hardening of oneself in the face of the world's fury; it is more than standing firm in our resolutions, as it is an expectation devoid of any intent or concern that is opened up by the Unheard itself.

Consequently, if interiority is an interiorization, it is different from the *Erinnerung* of Hegel's *Phenomenology of Spirit*. It is not the recovery of a part of my past by an other that is different from who I was. Chrétien can thus show that the call of the Unheard is the real inner voice because this call is more intimate than my own voice: "What is inner to my voice is what my voice answers by speaking, and it hears only by responding. There is an inner voice only in the ecstasy of a voice that resonates in the world."[15] Another interiorization corresponds to another exteriorization, which is fully responsive, and for which to live is really to be outside. We can only be inside by being outside, by listening and responding. Chrétien demonstrates that the response is not chronologically secondary to listening since the call of the Unheard is truly heard only in the response. Consequently, true patience, which constitutes our interiority, is that which, from our finitude, is open to a presence without image and without representation; it is open to proximity, which will never freeze in possession, and it is open to exposure to what is ungraspable. Such patience, living according to the distant interior, is an act of the whole human being and, therefore, also of the body, which is engaged in the response. In his work, Chrétien continues to defend the idea that there can be no exteriority between my body and all the things I do as a human, namely, as a being that speaks and thinks.[16]

Thus, the body is also of the one who responds to the call of origin. It is also in our bodily existence that we shall not be discouraged, that we shall persevere in listening and responding because our whole being is involved in going out to meet the world. We think hand-to-hand with our bodies. This is why we grow tired, and patience is necessary as an existential. It is, therefore, no longer patience stemming from a will, from our intent, and sedimented in the habit of resistance. Rather, it must be understood as surreptitious patience renewed by Being. This patience awaits the unheard, the unexpected, the unimaginable event that arrives like a thief in the night, according to the biblical expression, and which grounds another way of being oneself: "One is irreplaceable only in ignorance of one's place and in the patience required to support this indispensable nescience. It is there, and only there, where I answer, that my word becomes properly mine, a property crossed by the other, and therefore completely un-substitutable, a property of transit and exodus."[17]

In this interiority, which no longer absorbs alterity and strangeness in order to remain open to the burning of Being, there is a permanent struggle with oneself so as not to impose prior conditions of manifestation on what is given. One can only free oneself from an interiorization by another interiorization, one that is sustained, this time, by recollection: "Recollection is an act of presence: presence to oneself, certainly, but even more presence of the self, which can then be reached, met, touched, grasped."[18] Interiority can then be understood as an act of dilation. Nevertheless, the existential alternative remains that of the illusory dilation of pride or the dilation as enlargement, which liberates us when we welcome the excess that is given to ourselves. An interiority whose recollection is the founding act is therefore essentially distinct from an interiority whose founding act is the recovery of difference in identity.

This patience of recollection is inseparable from compassion, through which we share the suffering of the other without being able to free them from it—a form of compassion that often consists only in journeying with others while they face the unbearable. Patient interiority is also compassionate interiority if we free empathy from any subjective understanding in order to see in it in a way that welcomes the suffering of the other.[19] This claim confirms that interiority is not a remote shelter or back room in which one is finally alone, no longer listening to the suffering of a neighbor. The suffering of the other, because it is not mine, opens my inner space, from which I try to respond from my finitude. In this compassionate interiority, the interior life turns into a sacrifice; it is an offering of oneself, an offering of one's time, of one's listening attention, and of one's actions.

Thus, compassion is also what breaks all representations of interiority, understood as subjectivity's closure upon itself; it is to be understood not only in terms of what opens it up but also in terms of what doesn't—its abyss, that is to say, its space within a horizon that I have not opened myself. It is in this sense that Chrétien concludes his study of the interior temple of the Bible with Saint Augustine: "To live actively in the intimate space which is that of our spirit as in a 'temple,' its core as an altar that is one of the highest thoughts of human dignity, one which cannot be overturned in self-worship."[20] According to this originary spatialization, patience is not one of the possible qualities that interiority is free to develop. On the contrary, it reveals itself as "the stature of the spirit"[21] while being, at the same time, the endurance of the world and the hope that allows for that endurance while unfolding it. It does not deliver us from the sufferings of the world, but it invites us to carry them without letting ourselves be carried away and enclosed within them. Compassion is perhaps nothing more than endurance based on an act of hope. In the act of returning to ourselves, compassion can preserve us from self-worship, which is a pitfall in any conception of interiority.

Any interiority is an interiorization, but it is dependent on its modality and its object: either it reabsorbs the other in itself and works only for the glory of the self, even in cases of bad compassion, or it lets the other open its own interior space from which it can respond and take responsibility. Beyond the too simple opposition between a love of neighbor and a love of the most distant, found in Nietzsche's thought, patient interiority exists only when one is humble enough to stand in the presence of the neighbor, understood as irreducibly other to me. This means we receive interiority only by a force that, in us, opposes dispersion, distraction, and all forms of alienation. This force is received from the object of our encounter, which puts us into infinite debt.

Precisely, in the case of compassion, the other's suffering is not the simple or occasional cause of the deployment of my force, but as I welcome it, I receive a force that I did not have before. So, to refuse to flee from the suffering of the other also enables me to learn to modify my relationship to suffering, to unify myself in it rather than be scattered. Chrétien maintains that "the rise of joy therefore always implies living through our sufferings and remaining patient in the effort."[22] Compassion is what expands the spirit of human beings to the love of neighbor.[23]

The work of Jean-Louis Chrétien highlights the notion that interiority can be thought of without subjectivity, and that this figure of interiority, whose mode of being is patience, is understood to come well before the philosophy of the subject, and does not, by any means, represent its pre-history. This figure of interiority will also outlive the philosophies of the subject and its multiple offshoots. This is not a simple historical fact but a necessity of essence, since a conception of interiority that is only a force of absorption ends up being filled with everything and loses its shape in a radical anonymity. Indeed, the period of thought that identified the person with the subject led to a depersonalization caused by the emptiness of a life whose founding act is a representation and not a response. Conversely, patient interiority overcomes the impossibility humans face when they attempt to unify themselves by making it the foundation of their benevolence and action. It is based, in its constant becoming, on the only act that does not pass, that remains—that of the response—while all other representations, even the highest, disappear. Thus, true interiorization does not fill my lack of being; rather, it leads me far beyond what I imagined to be from my reflection on myself. From this point of view, the help we extend to others teaches us to bear our ills and the violence of the world; we are no longer representatives but respondents, which was also Edith Stein's last lesson as she tried to bring consolation to the detainees in the Westerbork camp.

Interiorization is not primarily a theoretical act but a fight against evil, carried out by the work of our hands; it issues forth from the call of the neighbor who opens in me the inner space of responsibility. It consists in "dwelling in hope," that is to say, "dwelling as we wander on, lurch on sometimes, fall and pick ourselves up again, ever and always frail in a light that we have not and that we are not, but to which we now belong by the tenuous and firm thread of our spiritual gaze, which 'anchors' us in the sky."[24]

Notes

1. Edith Stein, *Correspondance II, 1933–1942*, trans. Cécile Rastouin (Paris: Editions du Cerf, Editions du Carmel—Ad solem, 2012), 715.

2. Without delving here into the Husserlian conception of interiority that I have studied in my other works, we can quote from Husserl's *Zur phänomenologischen Reduktion*:

> If, with such an argument, I lapse into absurdity, reduce myself to my own solitary soul, encysted within itself, and if I confuse the world with my "representation of the world," with my diverse and changing ways of seizing the world, then human life, understood as living within the world in a practical sense, would become an empty appearance. I would have to conclude with the following words: "I am in myself and within my own psychism, and all acting is an internal fiction." All of this is absurd, as is all critical realism. A theory that seeks to grasp exteriority through a deduction from a closed interiority would be terrible. (Edmund Husserl, *Zur phänomenologischen Reduktion: Texte aus dem Nachlass [1926–1935]*, ed. Sebastian Luft [Dordrecht: Springer, 2002], *Husserliana*, vol. 34, 275–76. Translation mine)

3. Jean-Louis Chrétien, *La lueur du secret* (Paris: L'Herne, 1985).

4. Jean-Louis Chrétien, *L'effroi du beau*, 2nd ed. (Paris: Editions du Cerf, 2008; first ed. 1987), 13.

5. You could say that this patience of which the distant is constitutive is anti-modern (or even both pre- and postmodern), if modernity is the time of representation allowing us to be aware of everything, of each rumor of the world, in an immediacy of communication preventing us from any day or night of rest; this "reactivity," a contemporary name for impatience, is the mark of this absence of distant exterior as interior and, therefore, of our alienation as well as our gossip. This instantaneous communication, therefore, has nothing in common with the instant of the event, since everything is there and nothing is present; all messages are transmitted and nothing is said or listened to.

6. Jean-Louis Chrétien, *Promesses furtives* (Paris: Minuit, 2004), 23.
7. Jean-Louis Chrétien, *La voix nue* (Paris: Minuit, 1990), 7.
8. Chrétien, 44.
9. Cf. Chrétien, *Fragilité* (Paris: Minuit, 2017).
10. Chrétien, *La voix nue*, 69.
11. Chrétien, 80.
12. Obviously, for Nietzsche also, according to a famous formula, to live is to be in danger. Nevertheless, if the author of *The Antichrist* is a thinker of the distance, the dichotomy he affirms between distance and proximity prevents him from conceiving the inner distance.
13. Jean-Louis Chrétien, *L'inoubliable et l'inespéré* (Paris: DDB, 1991), 126.
14. Jean-Louis Chrétien, *L'appel et la réponse* (Paris: Minuit, 1992), 68.
15. Chrétien, 95.
16. Cf. Jean-Louis Chrétien, *De la fatigue* (Paris: Minuit, 1996).
17. Chrétien, 155.
18. Jean-Louis Chrétien, *Pour reprendre et perdre haleine* (Paris: Bayard, 2009), 99.
19. Cf. Chrétien, *L'espace intérieur* (Paris: Minuit, 2014), 98.
20. Chrétien, 128.
21. Chrétien, 132.
22. Chrétien, 227.
23. Cf. Jean-Louis Chrétien, *La joie spacieuse* (Paris: Minuit, 2007), 81.
24. Jean-Louis Chretien, *Fragilité* (Paris: Minuit, 2017), 194.

PART THREE
Interiority and World
Metaphysical and Ethical Applications

7

The Self-Awakening (*jikaku* [自覚]) from the Citadel of the Self

Everything is Interconnected with Everything

STEVE G. LOFTS

Introduction

Generally, when we speak of interiority, we speak of what the stoics term the "inner citadel" of the self. We speak, in other words, not only of the interiority of the self but also of the self understood as interiority. The self as interiority finds its classical modern expression in the Cartesian notion of the *cogito*, defined as the thinking substance closed off from both the extended substance of the corporeal world and the infinite substance of God, both of which are understood as radical modes of exteriority. Ultimately, what I want to argue is that there is no interiority per se, no essential interiority, and thus no essential self understood as interiority, at least as it has been conceived in the Western tradition. This chapter critically examines and challenges the Western understanding of interiority and exteriority, and by extension the self as interiority, which is based upon a concept of substance that forms the ontological presupposition about the essence of being: namely that to be is to be self-identical and thus self-relational. Because of this notion of ontological self-identity, the Western tradition has reified interiority and exteriority, and by extension the self and other, into self-identical, autonomous regions. This has resulted in a duality that can never be surmounted or resolved. The abyss that opens between the subject and object, the self

119

and the world, the self and the other, and even between the self and itself, has had grave epistemological, ethical, and socio-political consequences. Implicit in my position are two subsequent points: first, that the regions of interiority and exteriority are cultural constructions, and second, that the ontological presuppositions of a cultural system condition how we understand and, in fact, experience interiority and exteriority. To the degree that we can speak about interiority and exteriority, we must always speak about them as reciprocal and relational notions that exist only in reference to the other. They must not be conceived as autonomous regions that need to be bridged but rather as two relational limits of a single reality. Thus, it is not a question of finding a way out from interiority to the exteriority of the world, to the realm of objects, or to the other self, nor is it a question of explaining how the exteriority of the world enters the interiority of the self.

To develop this position, the chapter will mine the thought of a number of authors. No attempt is made to compare and contrast these authors, nor to exhaustively present their philosophical perspectives, as such a project falls outside the goal and scope of this chapter. In section 1, we more thoroughly frame the problematic of understanding the nature of interiority and exteriority. In section 2, we turn to the work of Ernst Cassirer and examine how interiority and exteriority are posited and configured in and through the various cultural forms, in general and in particular, in and through language as a symbolic form. In section 3, we reflect upon what defines a tradition of thinking and upon the essential characteristic of the Western philosophical tradition and Cassirer's critique of the Western metaphysical tradition in light of the problems that arise from a two-world view of reality. We then consider the problem of interiority and exteriority, and by extension, the nature of the self, from the perspective of the Sōtō school of Zen Buddhism founded by Dōgen Zenji and through the philosophical works of Nishida Kitarō, the founder of the Kyoto School.

1. The Geometrism of Discursive Thinking

In his *Poetics of Space*, Gaston Bachelard draws our attention to the inherent geometrism of thinking and the accompanying "dialectic of division" between inside and outside. The "dialectic of outside and inside" forms the architectonic structure of all intuition and thinking. We are always either on the "inside" or "outside": inside a house or outside, inside a group or outside, in the know or out of the loop. Meaning is either esoteric or exoteric. The self stands over and against the objective world, the immanence of consciousness, and the self is counter-posed to the transcendence of the objects and the world. "Outside and inside form a dialectic of division, the obvious geometry of which blinds us as soon as we bring it into play in metaphorical domains. It has the sharpness of the dialectics of yes and no, which decides everything."[1] The dialectic of outside and inside not only governs our average, everyday modes of thinking but also forms the internal logic of philosophical thought. As Bachelard observes:

> Philosophers, when confronted with outside and inside, think in terms of being and non-being. Thus, profound metaphysics is rooted in an implicit geometry which—whether we will or no—confers spatiality upon thought; if a metaphysician could not draw, what would he think? Open and closed, for him, are thoughts. They are metaphors that he attaches to everything, even to his systems.[2]

In his work, Bachelard goes on to explore poetic experiences in which this geometrism breaks down, where inside and outside can no longer be distinguished. We will not follow Bachelard further but rather return throughout the paper to challenge his position, or certainly qualify it, and in so doing attempt to demonstrate the Western bias of his perspective. We turn now to a brief reading of Ernst Cassirer, who provides us with a transcendental analysis of the construction and reconstruction of interiority and exteriority in and through the symbolic forms of culture, and thus with the *raison d'être* of the geometrism of thinking of which Bachelard speaks.

2. Cassirer, the *Auseinandersetzung*[3] of Interiority and Exteriority and the Function of Language as a Symbolic Form

Cassirer's project of a philosophy of symbolic forms provides a critical, transcendental account of culture and of the various symbolic forms that provide the sense-bestowing horizons that are world-forming. Each symbolic form is a unique mode of symbolic forming possessing its own logic of sense (*Sinn*) that determines its own understanding of objectivity. Each symbolic form thus performs a specific function within the unity of culture as the objective expression of the symbolic function. The symbolic process undertakes the formation, configuration, and structuring of reality in and through which the "I" and the world are separated, opposed, and *interconnectively related*: as Cassirer often puts it, the great process of "the setting asunder (*Auseinandersetzung*) of the I and world."[4] The symbolic is the "in-between" that opens and configures the world, the external world of objects, and the internal world of the subject.

One of the main tenets of Cassirer's philosophy is that neither the world of objects nor the inner world of the subject exists prior to or independently of the symbolic. We are always already in the symbolic, and all intuition, perception, emotion, and thinking are structured and constructed by the symbolic "energies" of objective spirit. There is, therefore, no pre-symbolic reality by which the truth claim of each of the different modes of understanding can be measured. What is more, no one symbolic form possesses a monopoly on the truth; only the systematic totality of the different modes of understanding can serve as the expression of "truth" and "reality." Each symbolic form, therefore, does not portray an objective presence but constitutes a new relation, a genuine and reciprocal correlation between subject and object such that " 'the way toward the outside' becomes at the same time 'the way toward the inside.' "[5] Thus,

> a glance at the development of each individual symbolic form shows us everywhere that their essential achievement does not consist in the fact that they reproduce the outward world in the inward world or that they simply project a finished inner world outward but rather that the two elements of "inside" and "outside," of "I" and "reality," first receive their determination and their mutual demarcation in and through their mediation. If each of these forms includes in itself a spiritual "confrontation" [*Auseinandersetzung*] of the I with reality, then this is by no means to be understood in the sense that the two, the I and reality, are to be taken as given quantities, as finished, existing for themselves as "halves" of being that are only subsequently taken up together into a whole. Rather, the crucial achievement of each symbolic form lies precisely in the fact that it does not have the boundary between I and reality as fixed once and for all but rather first posits this boundary itself, and each basic form posits it differently.[6]

Again: "It is the decisive achievement of every such form that in them the rigid boundary between 'inner' and 'outer,' the 'subjective' and the 'objective,' does not subsist as such but begins, as it were, to grow fluid. Inner does not stand alongside the outer, the outer alongside the inner, as if each were its own separate precinct; rather, both are reflected in the other, and only in this reciprocal reflection does each disclose its own content [*Gehalt*]."⁷

Language and art occupy a privileged place in Cassirer's theory of culture. They are "the basic ways of objectification, of raising consciousness to the level of seeing objects. This raising is, in the end, possible only when 'discursive' thinking in language and the 'intuitive' activity of artistic seeing and creating interact so as together to weave the cloak [*Kleid*] of reality."⁸ For Kant, the term "discursive" thinking designates a mode of cognition by means of concepts—what he often called "thought" (*das Denken*) *tout court*: "Cognition through concepts is called thought (*cogitio discursive*)."⁹ Here, a "concept" is "opposed to intuition, for it is a universal representation, or a representation of what is common in several objects, hence a representation insofar as it can be contained in various ones."¹⁰ In Cassirer's critique of culture, historical linguistic concepts replace the pure and empirical concepts of Kant. It is now language that introduces the internal relations that structure and configure our cognition of the world. It is only through names (concepts) and the sentence (judgment) that things (*Sachen*) are given the consistence existence (*Bestand*) required for them to become the objects of experience.

Let us now return to our question concerning the reason for the geometrism of thinking. In his analysis of language, Cassirer argues that this geometrism stems from the fact that language undertakes the differentiation of the contents of cognition by means of the spatial geometry it employs in configuring cognition and the understanding. Cassirer summarizes his analysis by saying:

> Thus, for language, the precise differentiation of spatial positions [*Sellen*] and spatial distances forms the initial point of departure from which it continues to the construction of objective reality, to the determination of objects. The differentiation [*Differenzierung*] of contents is grounded on the differentiation of places [*Orte*]—the place of the I, you, and he, on the one hand, and the place of the physical object [*Objekt*] sphere, on the other hand. The general critique of cognition teaches that the act of spatial positing and spatial separation is the indispensable precondition for the act of objectivization in general, for the relation of the representation to the object. . . . [As a result] the contraposition of "inner" and "outward," on which the representation of the

empirical I is based, is possible only in that an empirical object is at the same time posited with it: the I can become aware of the changes in its own states only in that it refers to something permanent, to space and to something persistent in space.[11]

It is crucial, however, to emphasize here that within the geometrism of language, interiority and exteriority form reciprocal and even *co-originating* poles of a single, relational reality. Interiority and exteriority are conflicting-opposing elements (*Momente*) of an "originary-relationship" (*Urverhältnis*) that constitutes the logic of the *Aus-ein-ander-setzung* of reality in which things (interiority and exteriority) are understood as the things that they are. It is important to realize that for Cassirer, concept-formation is rooted in ontology; thus, the shift Cassirer makes from substance-concepts to function-concepts marks a transition from an ontology of substance to an ontology of relation. Cassirer effectively inverts the relationship between "relation" (predicate category) and "being" (subject), as it has been understood in the Western tradition, making relation (predicate category) constitutive of being (subject). When Cassirer generalizes this into a theory of the symbolic, each symbolic form constitutes a predicate field in which the subject is differentiated and thus conditioned. The individual element of a relation is nothing other than a point distinguished in a field of relations, a position as a nexus of the infinite possible relational points of that field. The element does not precede the field but is first constituted by its relationship to the field: it is a product of the field that it itself opens. Here, we find the "one in the other" and the "other in the one."[12] As such, the conflicting-opposing elements (*Momente*) cannot be separated without negating the internal unity of the whole that is sense-bestowing of the elements (*Momente*) that exist in the originary-relationship as the expression of that originary-relationship. The originary-relationship of conflicting-opposing elements is the logical structure of what Cassirer calls the symbolic, and it operates within each symbolic form and thus within all symbolic reality—or all reality *tout court*. The "unity of mutual determination forms the absolutely first datum, behind which one can go back no further, and which can only be dissected into the duality of two 'viewpoints' in an artificially isolating process of abstraction."[13] The sense (*Sinn*) of interiority is that it is not exteriority, and the sense (*Sinn*) of exteriority is that it is not interiority. When we speak of interiority or exteriority, we must be cognizant of the dialectical relation of opposition that constitutes them and speak of interiority-*qua*-exteriority and exteriority-*qua*-interiority. For Cassirer, the ontological logic must be a logic of the relational unity of conflicting-opposing elements (*Momente*): a logic of contradictory self-identity. The unity of reality, be it of the symbolic, the world, or the human, is for Cassirer "a dialectic unity, a coexistence of contraries."[14] The symbolic itself, as the whole in which the logic of differentiation takes place, in which the elements (*Momente*) stand in opposition to each other, is itself nothing. Cassirer's thinking is rooted here in the polemos of Heraclitus, not in the dialectical sublation of Hegel. The basic error of all metaphysical epistemologies is that they repeatedly attempt to reinterpret this duality of "elements" (*Momente*) as a duality of "elements" (*Elemente*).[15] We will return to Cassirer's critique of the Western ontological tradition in section 3.

This geometrism is applied to the language that configures our thinking (speaking) of the I and the other. Cassirer illustrates this with an example taken from the Japanese language: "Japanese has coined a word for 'I' from a locative adverb that implies 'focal point' [*Mittelpunkt*] and a word for 'he' from another word that signifies 'there' or 'over-there.' In phenomena of this kind, we immediately see how language draws, as it were, a sensible-spiritual circle around the speaker, and it assigns the 'I' to the center and the 'you' and 'he' to the periphery."[16]

Thus far, we have considered the importance of language only in the configuration of cognition. The differentiation that takes place here produces a cognition of consistently consisting spheres of life; however, it is a cognition of a general and even abstract system of classification. Within discursive thinking one can still make a distinction between the signifier and the signified, to speak in structuralist terms, as well as between the individual and the classification under which the individual is subsumed. However, in mythical thinking we encounter a concrete mode of symbolic configuration in which the signifier and the signified are fused together into an identity. This "identity-thinking" is governed by the "law of the concrescence or coincidence of the members of a relation," in which the members flow together and merge into one another. "The mythical world is not 'concrete' in as much as it has to do only with sensible-objective contents and excludes and repels all merely 'abstract' elements, everything that is simply signification and sign—rather, it is concrete because in it the two elements of thing and of signification merge undifferentiatedly into each other, because they are 'concretized' here into an immediate coalesced unity."[17] This identity-thinking levels down the difference between signification and sign, between the spiritual and the material, and thus leads to "a kind of materialization of spiritual contents."[18] In this mythical-substantial-identity thinking, the names of language and the images of intuition are the thing (*Sache*) itself. Thus, "for original mythical thinking . . . the name . . . expresses the inner, essential being of the person [*Mensch*] and 'is' literally this interiority. Name and personality [*Persönlichkeit*] flow together into one here."[19] In mythical-substantial-identity thinking, we see that the way out is the way in: the objective presence of the god, conditioned as it is by the name and image of the god, is not the expression of an already existing nature but is internalized and forms the inner identity of a life center. "In the external, sensible forms of the cult itself, even if we initially seek to place them before ourselves in their empirical manifold and diversity, there is likewise disclosed a unitary spiritual 'tendency,' a direction toward progressive 'internalization.' Once again, we are entitled here to expect that the relationship between 'inner' and 'outer' forms the guiding principle for the understanding of all spiritual forms of expression."[20] Cassirer follows the gradual working out of interiority as it is discovered and configured through its being thought in mythical concepts (language) and intuited in mythical images. The self comes to its understanding of itself in and through its cognition of the objective presence of the gods and the world. "Once again, the path inward finds here its completion only in that it is united with the seemingly opposite path, with the advance from the inside outward."[21]

In his analysis of language, Cassirer shows that the development of an "inner intuition" is a relatively late product of language.[22] In mythical consciousness there is no strict cognitively posited distinction between interiority and exteriority; the two flow together and meld into a unitary sense of life. The differentiation between the "inner" and "outer" touches and flows immediately into one another in the flesh of the lived body.[23] Thus, language, too, initially persists in a strange indifference toward the separation of the world into two clearly separated spheres, into an "outward" and an "inward" being, but it also almost seems as if this indifference belongs necessarily to its being (*Wesen*).[24] Thus, "a state of indifference precedes the actual sharp working out [*Ausbildung*] of the I-concept in language, a state in which the expression for 'I' and 'mine,' 'you' and 'yours,' etc., have not yet separated."[25] Thus, "the boundaries between the 'objective' and the merely 'subjective' are not rigidly determined from the beginning but instead are formed and determined only in the continuing process of experience and its theoretical foundation."[26]

The separation and establishment of the strict, cognitively recognized opposition between subject and object, interiority and exteriority, that defines the nature of scientific cognitive consciousness, comes about in the

The Self-Awakening (*jikaku* [自覚]) from the Citadel of the Self | 127

moment that the effective activity is mediated by tools. "The opposition between the 'inner' and 'outer' worlds now begins to be more strongly accentuated: the boundary between the world of desire and the world of 'reality' begins to stand out more clearly. One world no longer intervenes directly in the other and no longer transitions into it; rather, through the intuition of the mediating object [*Objekt*] that is given in the tool, a consciousness of mediated doing gradually unfolds."[27] Here the interiority of the will is no longer immediately linked to the exteriority of the world by means of magical-mythical names and images: it is mediated by the tool. In this moment, a spiritual "crisis" occurs, and the exteriority of the world takes on a determinate existence:

> A barrier is now erected between the "inner" and "outer" that prevents any immediate leap over from the sensible drive to its fulfilment, now that every new intermediary stage is interpolated between the drive and that at which it aims, a true "distance" between subject and object is for the first time achieved. It separates off a fixed circle of "objects" that are designated precisely by the fact that they have a distinctive consistent existence (*Bestand*) by which they "oppose" [*entgegenstehen*] immediate longing and desire. The consciousness of the means is indispensable for the attainment of a certain purpose that first teaches the human to comprehend "inner" and "outer" as links in a causal framework [*Gefüges*] and to assign to each of them its own unexchangeable position within this structure—and from this consciousness gradually grows the empirical-concrete intuition of a thing-world with real "properties" and states.[28]

In this moment, we move to an entirely new level of cognition and, subsequently, to an entirely new conception of the self and its relation, for example, to the body:

> The kind of "community" that exists between the lived body and the mind [*Seele*] seems now as a mere "togetherness," and this togetherness includes in itself at the same time a fundamental apartness [*Auseinander*]. The duality has gone from a duality of elements [*Momenten*] to a duality of domains: reality has definitively broken down into an "inner world" and an "outer world." The corporeal no longer appears as the plain expression, as the

immediate manifestation [*Ausprägung*] of the mental [*Seelisch*]. The body does not reveal the mind [*Seele*] but rather is a shell that conceals it. Only when it breaks through this shell in death does the mind [*Seele*] come into its own nature [*Wesen*] as well as its own value and sense.[29]

We have seen that the geometrism of thinking is the consequence of the spatial differentiation and configuration of cognition by language. Because the geometrism of thinking is the consequence of the way language differentiates and configures cognition, we find this geometrism inherent in all human discursive thinking. However, not every tradition understands or navigates the resulting opposition between interiority and exteriority in the same way. There are many layers that must be taken into consideration here. For Cassirer, all seeing takes place by means of the sight of spirit (*Geist*, "mind"). As a symbolic form, language is a transcendental energy of spirit and, as such, possesses a universal function in conditioning and configuring our cognition of the world and ourselves. That said, it is important to distinguish between the worldview of a specific historical language and the mode of sight particular to language as language that distinguishes it from aesthetic sight, religious sight, theoretical sight, and so forth.[30]

The transcendental project determines the nature, source, and limits of specific modes of *sight*, but it cannot determine the facticity of any one concrete mode of *seeing*. To account for the unique form of a historically concrete culture, Cassirer introduces the concept of style. Paradoxically, style forms an idiosyncratic transcendental form that conditions the direction of becoming that takes place in a specific historical culture, and, in fact, *is* the facticity of this historical culture. In this way, one could distinguish the style of Renaissance Italy from that of Baroque Italy. And within a given historical period, for example that of the Baroque, we can distinguish between the styles of Caravaggio and Rembrandt—both would be considered expressions of the Baroque style and examples of the Baroque period. The transcendental form of art, for example, is expressed in the Baroque, and the Baroque is expressed in the works of Caravaggio and Rembrandt, among others. While here we have used art to illustrate the concept of style, Cassirer also speaks of the style of a culture, science, and even philosophy.

What, however, do the Medieval, Renaissance, and Baroque styles share that allows us to speak of them as being European or Western? What determines the style of seeing that defines that mode of seeing that might be identified as Western as opposed to Eastern. Of course, the problem here is what is meant by "West" and "East." Originally, the East and the West designated the relations between the eastern and western parts of the Roman Empire, the *pars orientalis* and the *pars occidentalis* of the unified structure of a single empire. In the medieval period, this continued as a division between the Latin West and the Greek East. That said, just as we can and must speak about different individuals giving expression to a single culture, I think we can and need to speak about the historical unfolding of a unique mode of seeing that continues to operate at the heart of a number of diverse historical cultures and thus conditions them as belonging together despite, or perhaps precisely because of, their many other differences.

Following Nishida, we will define the tradition of the "West" as the thinking of being[31] and, following Cassirer, argue that this thinking of being is grounded in a concept of substance as ontological self-identity. In contrast, the Zen Buddhist tradition that Nishida mines is grounded in what Bret Davis has called "me-ontology, from the Greek *meon* or non-being."[32] In short, the Western tradition, which is grounded in a substantial metaphysics, essentializes this distinction, creating an inherent and resolvable dualism between interiority and exteriority. At the same time, it essentializes the self and identifies the self with interiority. As a result, the self comes to be conceived as essentially itself, absolutely immanent in itself, closed off from the world, others, and ultimately even from itself. The Zen Buddhist tradition on which the philosophy of the Kyoto School is based does not substantialize and reify the inherent geometrism of cognition but seeks to make manifest the *illusory* nature of any distinction between interiority and exteriority, and by extension, the *illusory* nature of what is called the ego-self as a self-identical, autonomous being that can be identified as the true, authentic nature of interiority.

3. The Philosophical Confrontation (*Auseinandersetzung*) with the Geometrism of Thinking

The geometrism of thinking is a consequence of the way language differentiates and configures cognition. It is, however, the ontological presuppositions of a tradition that determine how the relational positions of interiority and exteriority inherent to this geometrism of thinking are to be understood and ultimately experienced.

Bachelard claims that "metaphysics is rooted in an implicit geometry which . . . confers spatiality upon thought." Metaphysics is not, however, rooted in the geometrism of thinking but rather in the ontological framework in which this geometrism is encountered and interpreted. Thus, I agree with Bachelard that "when confronted with outside and inside," philosophers "think in terms of being and non-being," but only if we qualify this claim by saying that it applies to Western philosophers working in the ontological tradition for which the dichotomy of being and non-being operates. This is, however, not true for those philosophers working in the meontological tradition of Zen Buddhism in which the antithetical dichotomy of being and non-being is reconciled in the identity of absolute contradiction. It is, therefore, not true for all philosophers but only for those working in a metaphysical tradition. In the next section, we briefly set out Cassirer's critique of the substantial metaphysics with a special focus on the reification of interiority and exteriority and the identification of the self with interiority. In the final section, we will turn to consider how interiority, exteriority, and the self are treated by Zen Buddhism.

4. The Ontological Interpretation of the Geometrism of Thinking

The geometrism of thinking is clear in Parmenides's claim that "being is a well-rounded sphere." It is, however, the ontological definition he provides for the geometrical image of being that establishes the logic that will operate throughout the Western tradition as a tradition of the thinking of being. For Parmenides, and Greek philosophy in general, something *is* if it is self-identical to itself: "thinking and being are the same" and non-being cannot be thought. Interiority is defined here in terms of thinking-being, whereas exteriority is unthinkable non-being. This principle of self-identity forms the core ontological presupposition that grounds the tradition of thinking of being. Aristotle's theory of οὐσία as the grammatical subject, or ὑποκείμενον, is the classical articulation of the Greek concept of being that functions as the foundation of the Western tradition as the thinking of being. The Greek οὐσία is translated into the Latin *substantia*, which in modern thought constitutes the being of the subject as a thinking substance, the object as an extended substance, and God or the Absolute as an infinite substance. The concept of substance as ontological self-identity, however, not only ends in a series of dualisms but, as a being in-itself, also stands beyond all experience and predicative judgments and so negates the very possibility of knowledge of the world, the other, and ultimately even the self. We are left with an unbridgeable gulf between the predicative concepts of the understanding on the one hand and the individual substances of the real on the other: a rift between abstract universal concepts and concrete reality.[33]

Metaphysical thinking is thus based upon an ontology of substance in which substance means the logical relation of self-identity. As such, "a dialectic unity, a coexistence of contraries" that characterizes the originary-relationship of oppositions that forms the logic of the symbolic is broken asunder, and the opposition relational poles are reified and can be understood only in reference to themselves. In the moment that the two elements of the originary-relationship of the symbolic separate, "the two motives that Heraclitus's metaphysics had seen together and had forced together as one unity . . . experience their independent development."[34]

Dogmatic metaphysics "divides being, for example, into an 'inner' and 'outer,' a 'psychic' [*Seele*] and a 'physical' reality, into a world of 'things' and a world of 'representations.'"[35] For Cassirer, metaphysical systems differ only in terms of which of the two substantial elements (*Elemente*) they privilege—which one they see as the ground of the other. Based upon an ontology of self-identity, and by extension a logic of non-contradiction, metaphysical thought always ends in unresolvable antinomies that can be overcome only through a quasi-mystical transcendence and fusion of the two elements (*Elemente*) or by the negation or sublation of one of the elements (*Elemente*) by the other, as in the case of Hegel. Metaphysics, then, cannot think the originary-relationship of opposition and dialectic unity of coexistence of contraries that form the internal logic of the symbolic that undertakes the *Auseinandersetzung* between the I and the world, interiority and exteriority, and therefore encounter the belonging-together of oppositions that forms the unity of reality. It should be noted that Cassirer, however, resolves this identity through the symbolic originary-relationship that forms the dialectic unity of the coexistence of contraries, which lies beyond all metaphysics. "The symbolic never belongs to the sphere of 'this world' [*Diesseits*] or 'beyond' [*Jenseits*], the region of 'immanence' or of 'transcendence'; its value, rather, consists precisely in its overcoming this opposition, which arises from a metaphysical theory of two worlds. It is not the one or the other; rather, it constitutes the 'one in the other' and the 'other in the one.'"[36]

Thus far we have argued that the inherent geometrism of thinking is the consequence of the symbolic differentiation and configuration of cognition by language. As such, all cognition is inescapably implicated in the relational opposition of interiority and exteriority that functions as the framework for all subsequent cognition. However, because the Western tradition interprets the originary-relationship of opposing elements of the symbolic that differentiate and configure cognition in terms of a logic of self-identity, and thus as self-relational, each of the relational poles of opposition are understood to be a self-existing, closed upon itself region of being standing over against other regions of being between which there can be no interaction. The self becomes a substance, that is to say a self-identical, closed monad that can be understood only in and through itself. Because of the logic of self-identity that determines all Western understanding of the geometrism of thinking, Western philosophy is unable to understand the coexistence of contraries. The project of modern philosophy seeks to navigate the opposition between the private authentic self as the realm of autonomy and the public objective self situated in a realm of determination, between the noumenal self as the self that is conscious and the phenomenal self that is the object self of consciousness. The Cartesian cogito as the thinking substance is closed off from the externality of God as an infinite substance and the external world as an extended substance. As the cogito is a finite closed mind, it is also closed off from all other closed-off finite minds leading to the problem of solipsism. The problem of exteriority is solved in Spinoza by reducing everything to the interiority of one absolute substance. In Leibniz, the infinite monads each reflect the world, but from their own ego-logical perspective they are unable to encounter or confront any other monad. Here again there is ultimately only interiority. And in Kant, the transcendental self, which is the source of knowing, is itself unknowable, as all cognition is conditioned by the categories and concepts of the understanding. Thus, the interiority of the self as a being in-itself cannot ever be the object of cognition, and thus the self is unknowable. Hegel critiques Kant's transcendental philosophy for being based upon the understanding. The understanding, Hegel argues, operates on a binary logic of either/or: either we are inside or out, a subject or an object, free or determined, in-itself or for-itself, and so forth. Reason, Hegel maintains, is able to think of the whole as the unity of the oppositions. It is therefore able to think in and through a concept the dialectical unity of interiority and exteriority, subject and object. This is what Hegel understands by dialectical reason. However, reason thinks the unity (i.e., the true as the whole) of oppositions by transforming them into elements (*Momente*) of a higher ontological reality. In the final analysis, Hegel still operates within the logic of self-identity. The productive difference between identity and difference is sublated into the identity of identity and difference: thus, when "reason speaks of an other, it speaks only of itself."[37] It is often said that nothing escapes the System; there is no outside of the Absolute. Ultimately, there is only differentiated interiority: the Absolute is a being-in-and-for-itself. Once again, we see the closed nature of the Western understanding of the self as interiority.

5. The Meontological Interpretation of the Geometrism of Thinking

We now turn to consider another tradition of philosophical thinking that is rooted in the fundamental experience of Zen Buddhism as it has been understood in the Sōtō school founded by Dōgen. In contrast to the ontological tradition discussed above, we find here a meontological tradition that is inherently unessential, that is based upon a logic of *soku-hi* (即非) ("is and is not"), or, as Nishida calls it, the logic of "absolutely contradictory self-identity" (*zettai mujunteki jikodōitsu* [絶対矛盾的自己同一]).[38] In terms of the geometrism of thinking, Zen Buddhism (and with it the philosophy of Nishida) seeks to free us from a substantialist, and therefore essentialist, understanding of the opposition of interiority and exteriority, and with it, a substantialist understanding of the self as interiority as an essential being closed up on itself.

Central to Dōgen's notion of Zen is the oneness of practice-awakening (*shushō-ittō / shushō-ichinyo* [修證一如]): Zen, then, is not and cannot be a theory. From the perspective of Dōgen and Nishida, just as one cannot understand philosophy without philosophizing, one cannot provide a theoretical account of the experience of Zen without practice: for Dōgen, this is the same as offering a hungry person "a painting of a rice cake [that] does not satisfy hunger."[39] This raises a serious set of problems that we cannot hope to treat here but which must be acknowledged. Is Zen Buddhism a philosophy? Philosophy has always been defined as the thinking of being that operates with the logic of non-contradiction that is the rational expression of an ontology of self-identity. Being is or it is not; nothing cannot be. Philosophy has always been humanistic and scientific. What is philosophy, however, if it is not the thinking of being through concepts? What is philosophy if it is not a rigorous science? At its very core, Zen Buddhism, especially according to Dōgen, seeks to move us beyond a thinking that is entangled in abstract concepts. Is Zen Buddhism then a religion? This begs the question: What is religion? If Western philosophy is scientific philosophy, is Zen Buddhism then a religious philosophy? We cannot hope to address these questions here. I recognize them here only to put them aside for another day.

Let us return one more time to Bachelard: "Philosophers, when confronted with outside and inside, think in terms of being and non-being. Thus, profound metaphysics is rooted in an implicit geometry which—whether we will or no—confers spatiality upon thought; if a metaphysician could not draw, what would he think?"[40] The implicit answer to Bachelard's question is "nothing." What, after all, can be thought without concepts, without the reified images of the geometrism of thinking? And this is precisely the core originary-experience of Zen Buddhism. The practice of Zen is the experience of nonthinking in which "body and mind," and with this all dualism implicated in the geometrism of thinking, "fall off." "To study the way of awakening is to study the self." "To study the Buddha Way is to study the self. To study the self is to forget the self. To forget the self is to be verified by the myriad things [of the world]. To be verified by the myriad things is to let drop off the body-mind of the self and the body-mind of others. There is laying to rest the traces of enlightenment, and one must ever again emerge from resting content with such traces."[41] Zazen, just sitting, is the experience-practice of nonthinking that returns us from the duality and essentialist nature of cognition to the interconnected experience of oneness prior to the subject-object differentiation. Nonthinking is not not-thinking; it is a thinking that has not been differentiated and configured by the geometrism of language, or in which the geometrism of language no longer holds sway or operates. Speaking of the experience-practice of Zazen, Bret Davis writes,

> Thinking is always aimed outward, in other words, it is always "stepping forward." Thinking of not-thinking can be understood as a paradoxical practice that short-circuits this outward orientation of the intentional mind and occasions the "backward step" into the nondual awareness of nonthinking as the ground—or rather empty field—of both thinking and not-thinking. In thinking of not-thinking, we are aiming our intentional mind at its own ground, at nonthinking, and thus turning it into a contentless object of thought, into a kind of relative or privative nothingness. But nonthinking is in truth an "absolute nothingness"[42] in the sense of an essentially indeterminate field of nondual awareness,

a field which underlies or encompasses the determinations of thinking, not-thinking, and thinking of not-thinking.[43]

The nonthinking is a thinking without the geometrism of language: it is what can be thought if one cannot draw, that is, think in the spatial images of language. In *Fukanzazengi*, Dōgen writes, "Sazen is the kōan realized."[44] The aim of the kōan is to frustrate the geometrism of thinking by turning the geometrism of language on itself. "What is the sound of one hand clapping?" "Has the dog Buddha-nature?" The point is not to provide a rational response that solves the kōan, as if there were a solution; rather, the point is to frustrate the rational project of answering, determining, clarifying, and grounding all of which belong to the cognitive faculty of geometric thinking.

Zazen is often thought of as a turn inward; however, this turn inward is not to a substantive ego-self but a turn away from the ego-self to the non-self, or what is called the "original face." Nishida is clear that his philosophy grew out of the originary-experience of zazen, though the precise nature of the relationship between Zen and Nishida's philosophy is a difficult and complex topic that we cannot address here. For our purposes, we will first consider the nature of interiority and exteriority and the self as interiority from the perspective of the experience-practice of zazen before we consider our problematic from the perspective of Nishida's philosophy. To focus our consideration of Dōgen and the zazen practice-experience, we limit ourselves to a commentary on one well-known and often quoted saying of Qingyuan Weixin and follow an analysis of the opening lines of Dōgen's *Genjokoan*, which is the central fascicle of his major work, *Shōbōgenzō* (*Treasury of the True Dharma Eye*).

> Before I had studied Zen for thirty years, I saw mountains as mountains, and waters as waters. When I arrived at a more intimate knowledge, I came to the point where I saw that mountains are not mountains, and waters are not waters. But now that I have got its very substance I am at rest. For it's just that I see mountains once again as mountains, and waters once again as waters.[45]
>
> Before a man studies Zen, to him mountains are mountains and waters are waters; after he gets inside into the truth of Zen through the instruction of a good master, mountains to him are

not mountains and waters are not waters; but after this when he really attains to the abode of rest, mountains are once more mountains and waters are waters.[46]

The first sentence in Qingyuan Weixin's kōan speaks about an unreflective immanence within the natural attitude structured by the geometrism of thinking. The mountains stand present for a subject who sees them and understands them for what they are: mountains. The mountain possesses a consistent existence (*Bestand*) that is given to it by the language of the seer. Suzuki's translation makes clear the subjective intentionality of sense bestowing: "*to* him mountains are mountains and waters are waters." To the businessman, the mountain stands there as something to be exploited; to the tourist, the mountain is the site of a summer vacation; to the Shinto, the towering mountain is the divine spirit, the Shinto Kami of the Shrine. In each case, the mountain is seen as an object whose sense is given it by the language of the speaker. In short, it is to see the mountain from the perspective of the ego-self. The other, the object pole of thinking, is little more than a projected reflection of the subject pole of a self-reflective and thus self-understanding being, a being that is entirely self-referential and thus self-relational. What is more, the object has been transformed into a *Bestand*, a consistent existence that stands present, ready for the subject's use. Of course, the subject too has become a *Bestand*; by seeing the mountain as a place standing there available for the vacation, the subject has become a client within the vacation industry—to speak with Heidegger. This is a state Buddhism calls "ignorance" or "delusion" and is the source of all suffering.

We turn to the first paragraph of Dōgen's *Genjokoan*: "When the various things (*dharmas*) are [seen according to] the Buddha Dharma, there are delusion and enlightenment; there is [transformative] practice; there is birth/life; there is death; there are ordinary sentient beings; and there are Buddhas."[47] What we notice here, I believe, is that Dōgen is pointing out that when one sees the world from the perspective of the *concept* of "Buddha Dharma," one differentiates the world into a geometrical sphere possessing a consistent existence, and so one sees reality in terms of the duality of self-existing elements: "There is birth/life" here, and "there is death" over there; there are "ordinary sentient beings" here, and "there are Buddhas" over there. We clearly see the geometrism of thinking operating in Dōgen's description here. What is more, the paragraph clearly establishes an ego-self perspective: "When the various things are seeing according *to* . . ."

Returning to Qingyuan Weixin, in the second moment—from "a more intimate knowledge"—it is clear that "mountains are not mountains, and waters are not waters." At this stage, we have a nondualistic thinking in which the geometrism of linguistic thinking has been negated, and we are left with an absolute oneness of thinking in which I and object, interiority and exteriority, have ceased to exist. The exteriority of the world of object and the interiority of the self no longer possess an ontological identity. Not only are the mountains not mountains, because there are, ontologically speaking, no such things as mountains, but there is also no I that sees them. Here we overcome the ignorance of the first claim that believes a subject here sees the mountains there, for there is neither a self-identical I that sees, nor a self-identical object that stands there to be seen. This nondualistic thinking is what is meant by enlightenment. However, it is important to remember that as there is no self, no object, no ignorance; there is also no "enlightenment"—there is absolute nothing. Paradoxically, there *is not* even absolute nothing. Thus, not only are the self and all things empty, that is, lacking any essential ontological nature or identity, but emptiness and with it enlightenment, too, are empty. As Dōgen writes: "Just understand that birth-and-death is itself nirvana. There is nothing such as birth and death to be avoided; there is nothing such as nirvana to be sought. Only when you realize this are you free from birth and death."[48] Ignorance or delusion takes place in assuming an ontological stance toward reality as it is differentiated and configured by the geometrism of language. Enlightenment is a state beyond the duality of the interiority and exteriority of life and death. It is not a getting outside of language but a state before there was an inside-outside of language. As Dōgen writes in the second paragraph of the *Genjokoan*: "When the myriad things are each [seen as] without self [i.e., without independent substantiality], there is neither delusion nor enlightenment; there are neither Buddhas nor ordinary sentient beings; and there is neither birth/life nor death."[49] We see here that the geometrism of thinking has been negated, and with it the differentiation between interiority and exteriority, subject and object, and all subsequent dualities: good/evil, life/death, ignorance/enlightenment.

It is in the third moment that the Sōtō school of Zen Buddhism distinguishes itself from other forms of Buddhism: it will posit the dialectical unity of delusion and enlightenment governed by the logic of the *soku-hi* ("is and is not"). In the second movement, not only has the delusion of dualism between subject and object, interiority and exteriority, been surmounted, but the dualism between delusion and enlightenment has also been negated. However, this has not so much freed us from what Buddhism calls the "entangled vines" (*kattō* [葛藤]) of language as negated these entanglements altogether and with them the world. We are thus left with yet another duality between, on the one hand, a delusion so absolute that we do not even realize we are prisoners in and of the inner citadel of the self—even if we create the simulacra of a prison to assure ourselves of the freedom of our inner thoughts—and, on the other hand, an enlightenment so absolute that even enlightenment itself would seem to have been negated by absolute nothing. In the Prajñā texts, it is clear that absolutely nothing exists and is so absolute that even Buddha nature must be negated by it: "The Buddha himself is like an illusion."[50] However, while all phenomena (*dharmas*) are empty (*śūnya*) and therefore lack any essential, substantial ontological identity that would constitute an independent existence, their consistent existence (*Bestand*), the concept of *śūnyatā* itself, is also empty; there is no positive thing called nothing that exists. *Śūnyatā* is not a transcendental state or existence beyond the reality of phenomena (*dharmas*). Phenomena are in their dependent co-origination or inter-relationality and, thus, co-arising.

We return, one last time, to the third moment in Qingyuan Weixin's kōan: "But now that I have got its very substance I am at rest. For it's just that I see mountains once again as mountains, and waters once again as waters." It is only from the standpoint of *śūnyatā*, to speak with Nishitani, from within the field of emptiness, the place of absolute nothingness (*zettai-mu-no-basho* [絶対無の場所]), to speak with Nishida, that each phenomenon (*dharma*) is a unique phenomenon in its co-origination and inter-relationality with all phenomena (*dharmas*). Only from the standpoint of *śūnyatā*, from the place of absolute nothingness, does each and every phenomenon (*dharma*) become manifest in possession of its own "suchness." Each phenomenon, the mountain and the waters, possesses an absolute center, and all things are gathered into a unity that does not level them down into the same, as in Western ontology, but allows them to co-emerge. Dōgen concludes the third moment thus: "Since the Buddha Way originally leaps beyond both plentitude and poverty, there are arising and perishing; there are delusion and enlightenment; and there are ordinary sentient beings and Buddhas."[51] Within the oneness of the field of emptiness, the geometrism of thinking once again manifests itself and we find the differentiation of the field of *śūnyatā* into subject-object, interiority and exteriority. Each is now recognized, however, in its relationality, in its co-originative nature. The world no longer exists outside the self: it is within the self, and the self within the world, the "one *in* the other" and the "other *in* the one," to speak with Cassirer.

The Buddha Way is the awakening way in everyday life that frees itself from the dualism inherent in the geometrism of thinking and understands this geometrism from the standpoint of the field of *śūnyatā*. We thus find the logic of the *soku-hi*, the logic of contradictory self-identity: "plentitude and poverty," "arising and perishing," "delusion and enlightenment" are not separate self-identical regions but co-originating oppositions that open and differentiate the world in which they are within the field of nothingness.

Being and nothing, interiority and exteriority, have lost their absolute and substantial ontological sense. They are now recognized as relative or relational elements of an originary-relationship of oppositions that form a dialectic unity, a coexistence of contraries. The field of *śūnyatā* is the field of absolute nothingness, to speak with Nishida, in which the dialectic unity of the coexistence of contraries between being-nothing, subject-object, interiority-exteriority, life-death, *saṃsāra*-que-*nirvāna*, takes place. Masao Abe writes: "True *Śūnyatā*, as the negation of emptiness and fulness in the relative sense, is an active and creative Emptiness which, precisely in being empty, makes everything and everyone be and work in their particularity. It may be helpful here to mention that *Śūnyatā*, just like *Nirvana*, is not a state but 'realization.' "[52] It is thus not the negation of the Western tradition of ontology that is always the negation of being, a privation of being, a darkness that threatens to annihilate everything that is and with it all possibility. Nor is it the absolute transcendent being, a higher ontological reality, that sublates all oppositions into a synthesis that enfolds yet surpasses them. It is not a great ontological substance that grounds all other ontological substances. Rather, it is the field of absolute nothingness in which being and nothing, life and death, interiority and exteriority emerge in their dependent origination and are what they are by noting being the other, where they co-originate in their opposition, where they form a contradictory self-identity that is the internal logical structure of the world. Thus, to speak with Nishida: "To think the world dialectically is not to think in terms of the opposition of inside and outside. The dialectic resides in thinking what is absolutely opposed as thinking immanence-*qua*-transcendence, transcendence-*qua*-immanence."[53]

Notes

1. Gaston Bachelard, *The Poetics of Space*, trans. Maria Jolas (Boston: Beacon Press, 1964), 211.

2. Bachelard, 212.

3. For Cassirer, the logic of *Auseinandersetzung* marks a fundamental way to view relations and structures of reality. An *Auseinandersetzung* is a complex relational operation in which the oppositions of difference coexist as the mutually defining, opposing limits of each other; each is defined in its being, not through some self-identical essence that it contains in itself but through the strife of opposition as the confrontation with the limit of the other it is not. As such, each element carries within itself the trace of the other, which defines its position in the play of differences, or in Hegelian terminology, it is the determinative negativity that sets apart and yet constitutes the relationship of belonging-together in the opposition of thesis and anti-thesis that operates within the identity-in-difference, but which cannot be sublated into a higher ontological identity. For a discussion of the concept of *Auseinandersetzung* in Cassirer's philosophy, cf. Steve Lofts, "The Symbolic *Auseinandersetzung* of the *Urphänomene* of the Expression of Life," in *Cassirer Studies* 3 (2010): 41–65; and Steve Lofts, "Cassirer and Heidegger: The Cultural-Event" in *The Philosophy of Ernst Cassirer: A Novel Assessment*, eds. Sebastian Luft and J. Tyler Friedman (Berlin: De Gruyter, 2015), 233–58. For a comparison of Cassirer's concept of *Auseinandersetzung* with the logic of absolutely contradictory self-identity, see Steve Lofts, "Toward A Dialogue Between Ernst Cassirer (1874–1945) and Nishida Kitarō (1870–1945) (エルンスト・カッシーラー (1874–1945)と西田幾多郎 (1870–1945)の対話に向けて)," *Journal of Nishida Philosophy Association* 16 (2020): 98–124.

4. Ernst Cassirer, *The Philosophy of Symbolic Forms*, trans. Steve Lofts, vol. 3 (London: Routledge, 2020), 81. All references to Cassirer's *The Philosophy of Symbolic Forms* come from the Routledge edition.

5. Cassirer, 1, 156.

6. Cassirer, 2, 190.

7. Cassirer, 2, 123.

8. Cassirer, 4, 84.

9. Immanuel Kant, *Lectures on Logic*, ed. J. Michael Young, vol. 9 (Cambridge: Cambridge University Press, 2012), § 1, 91. Also cf. Immanuel Kant, *Critique of Pure Reason*, eds. and trans. Paul Guyer and Allen W. Wood (Cambridge: Cambridge University Press, 1998), A19/B34.

10. Kant, 589; see also 309.

11. Cassirer, *The Philosophy of Symbolic Forms*, 1, 147.

12. Cassirer, 3, 447.

13. Ernst Cassirer, "Erkenntnistheorie nebst den Grenzfragen der Logik," in *Ernst Cassirer Gesammelte Werke Hamburger*, vol. 9, Ausgabe (Hamburg: Meiner, 1998–2009), 152ff.

14. Ernst Cassirer, *Essay on Man: An Introduction to a Philosophy of Human Culture* (New Haven, CT: Yale University Press, 1965), 222–23.

15. Cf. Cassirer, *Ernst Cassirer Gesammelte Werke*, 9, 152–53.

16. Cassirer, *The Philosophy of Symbolic Forms*, 1, 158.

17. Cassirer, 2, 28.

18. Cassirer, 2, 67.
19. Cassirer, 2, 51.
20. Cassirer, 2, 270.
21. Cassirer, 2, 238.
22. Cf. Cassirer, 1, 192.
23. Cassirer, 1, 202.
24. Cassirer, 1, 119.
25. Cassirer, 1, 202.
26. Cassirer, 2, 40.
27. Cassirer, 2, 254.
28. Cassirer, 2, 255.
29. Cassirer, 3, 120.
30. Since the linguistic turn, of which Cassirer was a forerunner, it is commonplace to say that language conditions thought. However, few are the studies that demonstrate this concretely through a detailed analysis of a language and its role in the determination of thinking in general and philosophical thought in particular. For exemplary illustration of this, see Rolf Elberfeld's excellent paper "Philosophical Implications of the Japanese Language" in which Elberfeld elucidates the philosophical implications of some distinctive traits of the grammar and word types of both classical and modern Japanese. Rolf Elberfeld, "Philosophical Implications of the Japanese Language" in *The Oxford Handbook of Japanese Philosophy*, ed. Bret W. Davis (Oxford: Oxford University Press, 2020), 665–84.
31. Nishida Kitarō, *Fundamental Problems of Philosophy*, trans. David A. Dilworth (Tokyo: Sophia University, 1970), 237.
32. Bret W. Davis, "The Kyoto School," *Stanford Encyclopedia of Philosophy Archive* (Summer 2019), ed. Edward N. Zalta. https://plato.stanford.edu/archives/sum2019/entries/kyoto-school/.
33. For a comparison of Cassirer's and Nishida's respective critiques of substantial metaphysics in the Western tradition and Nishida, see Steve Lofts, "Toward A Dialogue," 98–124.
34. Cassirer, *The Philosophy of Symbolic Forms*, 1:56.
35. Cassirer, 1, 119.
36. Cassirer, 3, 447.
37. Georg Wilhelm Friedrich Hegel, *Phänomenologie des Geistes* (Hamburg: Felix Meiner, 1952), 389; Georg Wilhelm Friedrich Hegel, *Phenomenology of Spirit*, trans. A. V. Miller (Oxford: Oxford University Press, 1977), 333.
38. Cf. Nishida Kitarō, *Intuition and Reflection in Self-Consciousness*, trans. Valdo H. Viglielmo with Takeuchi Yoshinori and Joseph S. O'Leary (Albany: State University of New York Press, 1987), xxv.
39. Dōgen, *Treasury of the True Dharma Eye: Zen Master Dogen's Shobo Genzo*, ed. K. Tanahashi (Boston: Shambhala Ferguson, 2013), 87.
40. Bachelard, *The Poetics of Space*, 355.

41. Dōgen, "Genjōkōan [Actualizing the Fundamental Point]," in *Treasury of the True Dharma Eye*, 256–57. Here and below, quotations from Dōgen's Genjōkōan will be taken from Bret Davis's translation: "The Presencing of Truth: Dogen's Genjokoan," in *Buddhist Philosophy: Essential Readings*, eds. Jay Garfield and William Edelglass (Oxford: Oxford University Press, 2009), 251–59.

42. It is important to keep in mind that Nishida distinguishes between "nothing" (mu; 無) and "absolute nothingness" (zettai mu; 絶対無). "Nothing" is the opposite of being, the negation of being. "Absolute nothingness" is beyond this relational opposition between being and nothing. Nothing is relational: being is being by not being nothing, life is life by not being death. In the case of "absolute" nothingness, we have the negation of relationality itself and thus the negation of the distinction between being and nothing. The Japanese term for "absolute" (絶対) suggests being beyond or cut off from (絶) the binary oppositions 対 that form the contradictory self-identity of the *Ur-teilung* (originary-division of judgment) of the 対決 or 対立 (confrontation) of antithetical oppositions. The place of absolute nothing, as the absolutely other to ever relational being, is the place whose confrontation renders an individual, individual.

43. Bret Davis, "The Enlightening Practice of Nonthinking: Unfolding Dōgen's Fukanzazengi," in *Engaging Dōgen's Zen: The Philosophy of Practice as Awakening*, ed. Tetsuzen Jason M. Wirth, Shūdō Brian Schroeder, and Kanpū Bret W. Davis (Somerville, MA: Wisdom Publications, 2017), 199–224.

44. Cited in *Engaging Dōgen's Zen*.

45. Alan Watts, *The Way of Zen* (New York: Pantheon Books, 1951), 126.

46. D. T. Suzuki, *Essays in Zen Buddhism*, first series (London: Buddhist Society, 1926), 24.

47. Dōgen, "Genjōkōan," 256.

48. Dōgen, "Shushōgi" ("The Meaning of Practice and Verification"), cited in *Engaging Dōgen's Zen*.

49. Dōgen, "Genjōkōan," 256.

50. *Vinayasūtra, fol 136b*. Cited by Eugène Burnouf, *Introduction to the History of Indian Buddhism* (Chicago: University of Chicago Press, 2010), 509.

51. Dōgen, "Genjōkōan," 256.

52. Masao Abe, *Zen and Western Thought*, ed. William R. LaFleur (Honolulu: University of Hawaii Press, 1985), 182.

53. Nishida, "The Standpoint of Active Intuition," in *Ontology of Production: Three Essays*, trans. William Haver (Durham, NC: Duke University Press, 2012), 75.

8

Ultima Ratio Decisions and Absolute Interiority
From Hegel to Bonhoeffer

CHRISTIAN LOTZ

Introduction

The resistance and objection to, and even the total rejection of, existing laws, rules, customs, power, and social and moral norms has been, from the beginning of Western philosophy, not only a problem for real existing societies, groups, and nations but also a problem for the philosophical reflection that emerges when members of these societies find themselves living in opposition to their own societies. The possibility of resistance, in all of its forms, makes us aware of the fragility of all political and moral orders established by humans and leads to the question of how individuals in their capacity to give themselves moral norms can be brought into harmony with social orders, which are always *found* but never *created* by the individual. We belong to families, groups, cultures, political constitutions, and histories before we are able to discover ourselves with the capacity to conceive ourselves outside of those orders. Indeed, the latter is itself a historically constituted possibility and belongs to modern societies.

The claims of individuals to know what is right and wrong solely within themselves usually remain hidden behind everyday practices and everyday lives. Inasmuch as we go along with what "most people do," almost all of our actions do not have much to do with genuine autonomy or self-determination, nor with acts of opposition or total rejection. The "they"—"das Man," as Heidegger puts it—is the social form of the self. Yet in exceptional situations the individual can be in total opposition to what is established as a valid order for the society or even for the world. More complicated than this, an individual may desire to be part of that order while at the same time feeling forced to stand against it. Consequently, if the order is total, as it is in totalitarian societies, the rejection must be total too.

In order to move the issue away from abstraction, let us consider two examples. On July 13, 1943, Kurt Huber, a professor of philosophy at the University of Munich, received the death penalty for his resistance against Nazi Germany. Huber belonged to the Munich group called "Weisse Rose," a group that produced and distributed political flyers calling for a political change in Germany. In the face of extreme risk, the Munich group had begun to work against the state. In Huber's last written statement, which he prepared before his final trial, he writes:

> My actions and my will will be justified in the inevitable course of history; such is my absolutely firm faith [trust]. I hope to God that the inner strength [*geistigen Kräfte*] that will justify my deeds will just in time be released from my own people. I have acted as I had to do on an inner voice. I take the consequences upon myself in the way expressed in the beautiful words of Johann Gottlieb Fichte: "And you should act as if on you and on your deed depended the fate of all German affairs and the responsibility were solely your own."[1]

Huber was executed "in the name of the German people" and by (Nazi) German law, together with the main members of this student-run group, Hans Scholl, twenty-five, and his sister, Sophie Scholl, a twenty-two-year-old student of biology and philosophy at the University of Munich. Both received the death penalty and were executed on February 22, 1943. Sophie recounted a dream in her diary the morning before her execution: "It was a sunny day and I was carrying a child in a long, white dress to its baptism. The path to the church led up a steep mountain. But I was carrying the infant safely in my arms. Suddenly a crevasse was gaping before me. I had just enough time to put the child safely down on the other side, before I fell into the abyss." She added the following explanation of her own dream: "That child is our idea; it will persevere despite all obstructions. We were permitted to pave the way, but we have to die for it first."[2]

Let us look at a second example, namely the words of the Protestant theologian Dietrich Bonhoeffer. Bonhoeffer, who, alongside Barth and

Bultmann, was one of the most famous Protestant theologians of the last century and was connected to one of the groups who tried to kill Hitler in 1944, was hanged in the name of the German people and by German law on April 9, 1945, three weeks before Germany was liberated by the Allies. In his *Ethics,* which remains unfinished, Bonhoeffer writes, "The responsible human being who is placed between commitment and freedom, who must risk in her being committed to act autonomously, neither finds her justification in her commitment nor in her freedom, but solely in the one who has placed her in this—humanly impossible—situation and demands the deed. The responsible human being delivers herself and her deed over to God."[3]

I will come back to these two examples later. For now, I would like to point out the following three observations: First, all of the aforementioned political figures died for their deeds, and they knew that what they had decided to do would most likely lead to their deaths. Second, all of them were religious persons, but more specifically, they were theoretically trained and well-educated Protestants. And third, all of them stated that they resisted the political principles and the legal system, as well as most of their social environment *because of* what they understood their consciences to be telling them; since their consciences pushed them into horrifying internal conflicts and prompted their opposition to what they still conceived as their own society, they acted as the final authorities on their actions. The concept of conscience enters the scene at this point since the individual suddenly finds herself in a situation within which she is unable to operate, and she cannot justify and act on the grounds of something that is established as valid *in* the order. To use Hegel's terminology here, the individual is no longer recognized, and what she believes about the order no longer *counts.* Consequently, the individual's consciousness in this specific configuration is not allowed to *exist* in its social-political environment. The self-realization, the reality of what is taken to be "right," the *Dasein* and reality of what is taken to be moral, is somehow blocked, limited, or—in extreme situations—even negated. It is as if the self-consciousness of this individual is disconnected from its external existence and is now pushed back into its inner world. Consequently, this person can no longer act and create the social environment, as she perceives the social environment as external to herself. Put differently, the individual can no longer exist outside herself in *her* own social reality and, accordingly, she is thrown back to herself and must try to find the recognition of what it takes for something to be right in herself. It is precisely at this point that the concept of conscience comes into play.

Several philosophical questions arise out of this bundle of observations: What is conscience, and to what do we refer when we refer to our conscience, philosophically or otherwise? How is conscience related to resisting action? Why does conscience lead to what Bonhoeffer—reminding us of Kierkegaard—called the "humanly impossible" situation?

In what follows, I will try to outline—in dialogue with Hegel and Bonhoeffer—that the concept of conscience demarcates what I would like to call the "a-rationality of moral agency." Put briefly, I will propose—with Hegel—that conscience should be understood as the very form of practical self-consciousness, which a moral agent must adopt in order to generate certain lines of action. This moment of adoption is the condition of the reality of practical self-consciousness and, since it is the condition, it cannot itself be based on a higher form of moral consciousness since this would lead to an infinite circle. Consequently, this moment of nontransparency and absolute interiority highlights the moment at which an agent loses any rational standard for her decision to act in certain ways (assuming that all normal social-political standards have receded into the background). Conscience is then necessarily opaque and can be further characterized as a form of conviction and faith. This faith, though blind, makes us see. The main point is this: conscience is a specific formation of self-consciousness in which the agent is related to itself as being moral. As conscience, moral consciousness has faith in itself *as* moral consciousness.

From here, I shall proceed in two steps. Using Hegel, I will first reconstruct conscience as a form of self-relation. In a second step I will sketch how these reflections can be "translated" into an existential theory horizon, by appealing to Bonhoeffer's *Ethics* as my aspiration. As such, I am here not so much concerned with normative questions as I am interested in the answer to the question of what conscience is and what role it plays in regard to individuals. I am interested in the ontology of action and the agent, or if you wish, with the existential dimension of the concept.

What is Conscience?

As few people know, Hegel did not open a bottle of red wine on Christmas Day; rather, he opened a bottle of red wine on every annual celebration of Reformation Day (on other days he drank beer). This can be explained by recourse to Hegel's claim that with the advent of Protestantism in the modern world, modern subjectivity and the modern conception of reason was born and came to the forefront in the form of reason, morality, and culture. This "event of Protestantism" is taken to be an exceptional historical shift and rupture for Hegel (and presumably others), since it gives birth to modern subjectivity, as well as to its theoretical grasp within German Idealism. In this connection, in his famous response at the *Diet of Worms*, Luther said the following:

> Since then your serene majesty and your lordships seek a simple answer, I will give it in this manner, neither horned nor toothed: Unless I am convinced by the testimony of the Scriptures or by clear reason (for I do not trust either in the pope or in councils alone, since it is well known that they have often erred and contradicted themselves) I am bound by the Scriptures I have quoted and my conscience is captive to the Word of God. I cannot and will not retract anything, since it is neither safe nor right to go against conscience.[4]

In this quote three aspects are important: First, the individual (here, of course, still conceived as in relation to God) takes himself to be the *source of* morality, and by doing this tries to be an autonomous being; second, the consequence of the first aspect is that the individual appears to be *in opposition to* external authority or to societal norms; and third, the new form, according to which this consciousness is related to itself, namely conscience, is born out of the first and second aspects. Finally, conscience as a form of consciousness is itself the result of *resistance*, in this case, Luther's resistance to the Church. Conscience and resistance—if we take Luther as an example—have been closely connected since their modern formulation. Let us turn our present attention to the aforementioned points by considering the internal structure of the modern moral subject, as we find it exemplified by Luther.

The core conception of the modern moral subject (or moral consciousness) is (at least) characterized by the following three criteria: First, the subject knows she has to fulfill certain duties and tasks in relation to herself and in relation to others; second, the subject knows that as a moral subject she does not need to follow specific norms or rules *just because* these rules are part of a given society, a specific peer group, or a historical moment; and third, she knows that the main source of her attempt to be good must be located and found in herself, that is, in her rational will, her rationality and inwardness. Out of these aspects three consequences follow.

The first one is that this subject takes the world to be world that should be overcome, since fulfilling tasks implies that those tasks have not yet been realized. The second consequence is that—in the projected possibility of being *moral*—the subject must place herself in her consideration, deliberation, and reflection, at a *distance* from the social-political environment in which this deliberation takes place, given that the relation between individual and social environment is a *negative* relation—"negative" because the individual taken as a moral subject is not what she is in her everyday social existence. Furthermore, if rationality is no longer found in external authorities, this individual is confronted with a type of rationality that is split: one side is to be found in abstract thought, while the other side is to be found in "concrete" (for Hegel "abstract") reality, which in this context means social reality. In addition, if morality is supposed to be rational, the individual cannot take even this morality to be *her own* morality; rather, she must take herself to be a universally determined consciousness. Consequently, this moral individual not only takes reality as external to herself, but she also takes her own individuality as external to herself. Hence, she is alienated both from herself and from her world because, taken as moral consciousness, she is understood neither as an individual nor as reality.

Both the relation to the social reality and the relation to herself come together and are united in a new form of self-relation, namely, the *action* or acting consciousness. Let me explain this structure. The consciousness of an individual who takes her own morality as a task knows that rationality is not simply in the world, but rather that rationality must be *realized* in this world. The split between moral rationality and the reality is experienced as a lack that must be overcome by the individual. This consciousness of overcoming the gap is precisely the agent's consciousness. I am outlining here only two aspects of Hegel's analysis of morality and the moral world view, which is offered in his *Phenomenology*. Accordingly, we would do well to briefly examine the important structures of moral consciousness, social reality, and acting consciousness, as this will lead us to the complex concept of conscience as it was developed in German Idealism, and to the concept that I would like to use in my attempt to understand the situation as outlined in my introductory remarks.

The acting consciousness is the individual hinge between abstract moral consciousness on the one hand and realized moral consciousness on the other hand. Social norms, duties, rules, and laws, for example, as we all know, are virtually nothing without their *existence* (Dasein) in a social-political reality. Accordingly, the internal problem for moral consciousness, or for the moral subject, is precisely its own existence and its own reality. Consequently, moral consciousness is characterized not only by a gap between its own universality and the social reality but also by the attempt to appropriate this gap, which can only be done by the individual alone. The reality and existence of moral consciousness is what Hegel calls "recognition," since the reality of a law, norm, or rule depends upon whether it counts and is valid (*gelten*) in its externality.[5] In Hegel's words, moral consciousness, once it goes beyond its immediate certainty and abstract identity, must be recognized outside of itself in order to relate itself to itself, and in order to find itself in externality. Self-consciousness is here understood as a dialectical relation between moral consciousness in its abstract form and moral consciousness in its realized or external form. Both are one in self-consciousness. Consequently, if moral consciousness is unable to see itself in its own external form, it must remain within itself and must take the reality as a foreign and hostile environment. In other words, it must take its own externality and reality as abstract as its own abstractly defined moral status. To simplify, if the moral subject (moral consciousness) finds itself in a situation in which this external recognition is not present, it must regress into itself and remain in its own inner world with its own emptiness. Seen from this perspective, moral consciousness remains abstract and alienated because its obligations, tasks, and oughts remain unrealized and hence do not exist in the actual world. For Hegel, this means that moral consciousness, as such, is one-sided and remains without content; it is empty and does not *exist*.[6] Modern moral subjectivity is permanently forced to define itself in relation to its being as an agent. It is torn between its abstract knowledge of what "one"—as a universally determined, willing entity—ought to do, and the realization of this abstract level *for* "itself." In this connection, Hegel writes: "Moral consciousness does not possess this moment of recognition by others, of *pure consciousness* which has *real existence*; and consequently does not act, or actualize anything at all."[7] Moral subjectivity, therefore, leads to a *negative* relation to what makes itself possible, namely to the social-historical and political world, within which this consciousness finds itself and within which it must live its life. This is to say that a moral subject is a subject that positions itself in *opposition* to the social-political reality in which it grew up and lives. Put briefly, this negative relation between consciousness and reality is first and foremost expressed in the gap between knowledge of what one's duties, tasks, and obligations are, and the not-yet-existing realization of these tasks through action.

The real center of action, as I pointed out above, is individuality, for moral consciousness taken to be an agent is abstractly defined neither in its inner universality nor in its outer reality. Hence, we find here in the agent's consciousness a new form of self-relation. As an agent, the moral subject constitutes itself on a new level, inasmuch as it acknowledges that it must realize itself in this world if it wants to take itself as what it is, namely a moral agent. Moral consciousness, taken to be realizable, is forced to constitute itself as being more than just an abstract and empty disposition. Instead, it should *do* the good and not only *think* of it. It is not sufficient that moral consciousness takes itself to be the consciousness of moral considerations, moral intentions, or moral maxims; rather, it must take itself to be a consciousness that has to become a reality in the world to which it is opposed. *Acting* consciousness, therefore, is a transformed mode of abstract moral consciousness, which according to Hegel, must be understood as a second-order self-consciousness. In this second-order self-consciousness, which is the agent's consciousness, moral consciousness becomes an object for itself.

It is precisely at this point that the concept of conscience enters the stage, for *conscience* is the name for this second-order consciousness, according to which the principles, maxims, rules, obligations, or duties in the form of intentions, universally determined goodwill, or a good disposition, are *adopted by* the individual. In Kantian language we could say that conscience is a practically conceived transcendental apperception. In this connection, Hegel writes: "Looking more closely at the unity of the moral consciousness and at the significance of its moments, we see that it regards itself as the *in-itself* or *essence*; but as *conscience*, it apprehends its *being-for-self* or its self."[8]

Let me repeat this point: the abstract consciousness and abstract knowledge of what one's duties are and of what should be done, essentially and for everyone, become a moment of a specific, practical form of self-consciousness. As such, acting consciousness is a new form of self-consciousness, and in this form of acting consciousness, moral subjectivity is, to put it in Hegel's language, *for itself*. It is immediately related to itself in this form of consciousness. Moreover, in adopting its *own* consciousness (as *universally* determined), the moral subject appropriates and transforms what it takes to be right into something of its own. This specific "having of oneself" is, according to Hegel (and according to Fichte, too), *conscience*. Through this act of being certain of itself, moral consciousness transforms itself into an agent and overcomes its own abstractness.

Hegel's reconstruction of the dialectical movement in this form of consciousness is complicated to be sure. But for the purpose of this essay it is sufficient to see the main point, namely that conscience is the form of self-consciousness within which moral subjectivity is the object of itself, the immediate identity of which is expressed in a simple form of confirmation ("witness"), which he also calls *conviction* (*Überzeugung*; "self-witnessing").

At this point a remark about language is necessary, for some semantic differentiations that are immediately clear to French and German speakers are lost in English. These aspects are important: "conscience" originally comes from the Latin word *con-scientia*, which literally means "with-knowing." In French this meaning is preserved, for "conscience" in French means "consciousness." The German word for "conscience" is *Gewissen*. The word *Wissen* means "knowledge." Hegel also preserves this sense of the word. Moreover, *Gewissen* is related to *Gewissheit*, which means "certainty." Finally, *Mitwisser*, the German word for "with-knower," refers to a *witness* who shares a secret with someone else. A witness, *Zeuge*, is a person who confirms and attests to the truth of an event or a claim about an event. *Überzeugung* ("conviction") also expresses the second-order level that I just introduced, for in my being convinced, I am a "witness" to myself and to what I take to be true. It is not surprising that the word "witness" in Old English means "knowledge," which is derived from *wizzan*, the Old German form of *Wissen*. These semantic considerations are interesting as such, but for our purposes we should keep in mind that all four horizons—knowing, certainty, consciousness, and conviction—are preserved in the everyday use of the German word for "conscience." It follows naturally then that conscience is interrelated with self-consciousness in the German philosophical tradition.

Conscience is a form of self-consciousness and—in Fichte's terminology—a form of "harmony" because it unifies and synthesizes the difference between knowing and reality in one form of self-consciousness. Conscience is a simple form of identity and certainty because principle and reality are no longer taken in separation from each other. Instead, they fall into each other. It is imperative to note that, according to this view, we must—from now on—give up naive concepts of conscience, such as "God's voice," or an inner judge for good and bad, given that conscience is here laid out as the very *condition* of moral action. As such, "conscience" refers to the moment in which all deliberations are cut off and instead united in a simple form of certainty, in which the agent takes her abstract and moral consciousness to be the "truth."[9]

Conscience and the Extraordinary Situation [*Grenzsituation*]

I believe that the gap and wound between moral consciousness and its reality cannot be healed by philosophical rationalism. Indeed, this irreducibly problematic moment cannot be reached by theory, which explains why the concept of conscience plays such an important role in the thought of Kierkegaard, Jaspers, and Heidegger. As should be rather clear by now, I am not interested in the "usual" use of the term conscience, by which we typically indicate a voice, or either a "bad" or "good" conscience; rather, I am trying to reveal that conscience should be understood as a specific mode in which we encounter ourselves, a form of "with-knowing" (*con-scientia*) and a mode of self-relation in which our own existence and our own being is an issue for us. It seems to me that on this view we can easily translate the transcendental analysis of practical consciousness into existential philosophy.

Here is how: conscience is, in terms that Heidegger uses in his early *Jaspers-Review*, "a historically defined 'how' of self-encounter,"[10] by which he means the "having" of oneself as something that is at stake, especially in situations that are experienced by the agent as historically decisive. It is obvious that we are usually not confronted with ourselves in the *explicit* mode of conscience, which is to say that we are typically not related to ourselves in the mode of a crisis. Usually, in our everyday lives and situations, we are carried along as part of a larger collection of actions, deeds, and behaviors. Writing this essay is certainly not a situation I encounter in which I feel forced "to do" something or in which I feel "displaced." Everything is in order and I recognize myself as part of the normative network that is in place, which involves rules for writing, publishing, and reading, and rules that grant institutionally guaranteed rights, such as, for example, free speech. However, as we know, from time to time, under special existential and political conditions our being part of our social environment can break down, the consequence of which is that recognition and social reality may be destroyed. The most extreme and extraordinary situation occurs when one faces one's own death. It is clear immediately that in such a situation, one encounters the *impossibility* of realizing oneself morally and politically, and turns not only to resistance, or if no action follows, to ethical isolation and inwardness, but also back to oneself *as* an individual. The concreteness of these extraordinary situations and their historical dimensions force us to understand them as *exceptional*, leading one ultimately to a confrontation with oneself. It is precisely at this point that we appear in this world *as* individuals.

Bonhoeffer: Conscience and the Exception

We are now at a point in our reflection where we can come back to what I introduced at the beginning of this essay, namely the resistance in Nazi

Germany during World War II, given in the examples of Kurt Huber, Sophie Scholl, and Dietrich Bonhoeffer.[11] All of them, as I mentioned, struggled with their situations in terms of their consciences, insofar as they found themselves placed in an extreme tension between what they deemed right and what they could do to realize themselves as moral agents. This tension was based on the total breakdown of legal recognition and the dissociation of state and law in Germany at that time. As all tensions do, it included two moments. On the one hand, given they took themselves to be moral, these agents had to act out of certainty; on the other hand, given there was no *present* recognition of what they took to be moral, they had to act out of uncertainty. The moment they began to do what they did they had to presuppose four things: One, they had to have faith that there would be a point in time in which their actions would be fruitful, would be recognized as moral, and would turn from absurdity into meaningfulness. Two, this point in time was taken to be beyond their own individual lives. Three, they had to believe that their actions were justified in a world beyond their own social-political reality, and consequently had to act out of the future, which is to say, out of blindness. And four, they were forced to turn into their own inward world and try to make themselves certain of what they did, especially when faced with the horrifying reality of the German police and legal system. Kurt Huber's words, which I quoted in my introduction to this chapter, are a perfect expression of these points and, given what I have developed with the help of Hegel, true acts of conscience.

Huber and Bonhoeffer were fully aware at that point that they acted in the face of the German catastrophe and put themselves in total opposition to their own country. Each, confronted with himself *acting solely out of himself*, was unified in a form of self-having that was determined by pure faith—a faith that was based on pure, subjective conviction and directed toward a point in time beyond his life and beyond his own society.

Huber, Bonhoeffer, and the Scholls, were just four of more than two thousand individuals who received the death penalty in 1944, which was enforced by the so-called people's court (*Volksgerichtshof*), primarily targeting groups and individuals who were involved in the German resistance movement. Of approximately eighteen thousand rulings issued by the court, more than five thousand were death penalties.[12] Given this, we should note that conscience is not a form of hope in the mundane sense, since hope in the mundane sense lacks the element of certainty. Everyone who remembers or has seen documentary material about the demonic Freisler knows that in this situation death was almost certain.

Conscience is then a specific formation of self-consciousness, in which the agent is related to itself as possibly being moral. As conscience, moral consciousness has faith in itself *as* moral consciousness, that is, in its existence and reality. We see immediately that it is precisely this conflict that is the problem for agents such as Huber, Bonhoeffer, and the Scholls. Put briefly, Huber and Bonhoeffer were able to take their own actions to be moral because they had to assume the existence of a world *beyond* their own in which everything would be justified and would make their actions possible. They acted in total darkness, and I find it more and more astonishing that it is precisely this blindness that made them see. We can see that in these radical cases, moral philosophy and moral theology are extremely close to each other insofar as this type of action requires a leap of faith, that is, action without knowledge and certainty without certainty.

Bonhoeffer's thinking was, from the beginning, torn apart by the attempt to synthesize his theological thought with his existential reflections on the role of individuals who identified themselves as Christians. Early on, he was connected to the Protestant resistance against Hitler, but he later decided to become part of a group that tried to kill Hitler. In his *Ethics*, he argues (in a central chapter) that the structures of what he calls a "responsible life" and the "enterprise of concrete decisions"[13] find their ground in a form of a-rationality in which the individual is unable to generate moral right and wrong out of herself although she is *forced* to find this grounding in herself. In order to overcome this tension, Bonhoeffer claims, one must give oneself over to a higher "ground," namely God, which—in the context of this lecture—means that one is certain about being right *without* immediate recognition. In this connection, Bonhoeffer writes: "The deed, which occurs with responsible deliberation of all personal and non-personal circumstances . . . is *in the moment of its execution* delivered over to God. The ignorance in regard to one's personal good and evil and, hence, the dependency on grace belong *essentially* to responsible historical action."[14]

Though written using Christian language, I believe we can translate Bonhoeffer's words back into philosophical language, as I presented it in my reconstruction of Hegel's position. Bonhoeffer follows a moral theology that claims that in certain situations, which we cannot determine in advance, actions are not justifiable by the agent and require a form of certainty that is not the *result* but rather the *condition* of this type of consciousness. This conditional self-consciousness has the form of an unshakable faith that the action will be recognized in a not yet existing world. Moral actions are for these agents in these situations generated out of a loss of any rule and law, which in the words of Bonhoeffer, delivers the agent over "in her own decision and deed to the divine steering of history."[15] These types of actions, in other words, cannot be foreseen or calculated in advance. Instead, they are grounded purely in their situatedness.

As Bonhoeffer himself points out, an acceptance of this *ultima ratio* theory implies an a-rational moment, since the grounds on which the agent acts can be neither justified nor transformed into a normative claim at the moment of its realization. It is precisely this structure that allows us to speak of acts of conscience. Consequently, what we are faced with here is the exceptional moment in which, as Bonhoeffer puts it, agents find themselves above every law precisely because the individual is forced to *posit* the law.[16] Positing the law is itself not bound to the law. It is the exception. Here we also find the explanation for Bonhoeffer's characterization of this type of responsibility as "humanly impossible." The possibility of acting in total resistance—that is, without recognition—is "humanly impossible" because the agent, as we have said, must trust in her own standards as belonging to a world that does not exist and might never exist. In this way, the agent must trust solely herself that her actions in history will be right beyond history. "We believe in the future," as Bonhoeffer puts it, "no matter what."

Conclusion: The Unavoidability of Irrationality

I shall finish with one last remark. I was astonished when I discovered that in Adorno's *Lectures on Moral Philosophy*, which he held at the University of Frankfurt during the 1960s after his return from the US, he pointed to a similar structure for moral philosophy. In his first lecture course Adorno points out that moral theory is based on a tension that it cannot overcome since, as theory and as an ideal reconstruction of moral action, it never truly reaches the *real* acting agent and her situation. Put differently, the motivation and source of ethical reflection is found in what this reflection can never fully grasp, though it is compelled to return to it, namely, life. In this spirit, during the very first hour of this lecture course, Adorno refers to the German resistance against Hitler, reminding his students of the real motivation for philosophical ethics. He writes: "I believe that this act of resistance—the fact that things may be so intolerable that you feel compelled to make the attempt to change them, regardless of the consequences for yourself and others, and in circumstances in which you may also predict the possible consequences—is the precise point at which the irrationality, or better, the irrational aspect of moral action is to be sought."[17]

What can we conclude from this? Perhaps the following: there is something paradoxical about these cases. On the one hand, individuals like Bonhoeffer, the Scholls, and Huber act in total uncertainty; on the other hand, what makes them act is precisely the opposite, namely, absolutely certainty. We might wonder, then, to put it in Derrida's words, whether the possibility of these actions is precisely their impossibility.

Notes

1. Inge Scholl, *Die Weiße Rose* (Frankfurt am Main: Fischer, 1993), 66–67. If not indicated otherwise, the translations are my own.

2. Scholl, 60.

3. Dietrich Bonhoeffer, *Werke: Sonderausgabe*, eds. Eberhard Bethge and others, vol. 6 (Gütersloh: Gütersloher Verlagshaus, 2015), 289.

4. Martin Luther, *Luther at the Diet of Worms* (1521), in *Luther's Works*, vol. 32 (Philadelphia, PA: Fortress Press, 1986), 112.

5. See Georg Wilhelm Friedrich Hegel, *Gesammelte Werke*, vol. 8 (Hamberg: Meiner, 1980), 215, 220, 227.

6. Many commentators misunderstand Hegel's critique of Kant's categorical imperative, insofar as they overlook that "empty" for Hegel means that something is without existence (*Dasein*).

7. G. W. F. Hegel, *Phenomenology of Spirit*, trans. A. V. Miller (Oxford: Oxford University Press, 1977), 640; G. W. F. Hegel, *Gesammelte Werke*, vol. 9 (Hamburg: Meiner, 1980), 344. For the connection of conscience, language, and existence, see Karen S. Feldmann, *Binding Words: Conscience and Rhetoric in Hobbes, Hegel, and Heidegger* (Evanston, IL: Northwestern University Press, 2006), 62–63.

8. Hegel, *Phenomenolgy of Spirit*, 638; Hegel, *Gesammelte Werke*, 9:344.

9. Although in his *Phenomenology* Hegel reconstructs the problem of the relation between the moral worldview and conscience without referring explicitly to other philosophers, it is clear that he refers to what Fichte had worked out in much more detail in his *System of Ethics* (1798) and in his *Vocation of Man* (1800). Fichte develops the problem further since, according to Fichte, we must ask the following question: How does a subject know that the possibility of acting is not a mere chimera and, in Fichte's words, a mere appearance? How does the subject know that she is able to *realize* herself as moral consciousness and that her self-determination is not an illusion and something that only belongs to her "inner" world? Fichte's answer is the following: we *never* know in a *propositional form* whether we can act or not, and we will never find a theoretical proof for the reality of morality and moral action;

rather, something must lead and force us to *believe*—as a presupposition for every moral action we take—that moral self-realization is more than a theoretical concept. The argument for this thesis is clear: propositional "knowledge" of whether we are able to realize ourselves as moral consciousness *in* this world is only possible *after* the action is done. In German there is only one word for belief and faith, which is "*Glaube.*" Accordingly, if we are to follow Fichte up to this point, "faith" is identical with the agent's *conviction* that morality is not a mere illusion or inner appearance. To be sure, the line from Hegel to Bonhoeffer needs to take into account not only Fichte as a "mediator" but also Kierkegaard. I have dealt with Fichte in more detail in Christian Lotz, "Certainty of Oneself: On Fichte's Conception of Conscience as Non-epistemic Self-Understanding," *Southwest Philosophy Review* 20, no. 1, 2004); and Christian Lotz, "Faith, Freedom, Conscience: Luther, Fichte, and the Principle of Inwardness," in *The Devil's Whore: Reason and Philosophy in the Lutheran Tradition*, ed. Jennifer Hockanbery Dragseth (Minneapolis, MN: Fortress Press, 2011).

10. Martin Heidegger, *Supplements: From the Earliest Essays to Being and Time and Beyond*, ed. John van Buren (New York: State University of New York Press, 2002), 95 (translation altered).

11. In the following I will leave this path of moral theory, about which one could certainly reflect much more, since it would lead us to a next step of how Kant and Fichte reconstruct the aforementioned faith as a transcendental condition of moral action and in terms of moral theology. As Dieter Henrich, in his two-thousand-page reconstruction of the four-year period between Kant and Fichte, has shown, the birth of Post-Kantian German philosophy should be seen in the tension between moral theory and moral theology. Dieter Henrich, *Grundlegung aus dem Ich: Untersuchungen zur Vorgeschichte des Idealismus; Tübingen–Jena 1790–1794* (Berlin: Suhrkamp, 2004), 1467–1550.

12. It took until 1985 for the German constitutional court to declare *all* judgments of Freisler's court illegal, on the basis of which it was declared an instrument of political terror.

13. Bonhoeffer, *Werke*, 6:256.

14. Bonhoeffer, 6:268 (emphasis added).

15. Bonhoeffer, 6:256

16. Bonhoeffer, 6:274.

17. Theodor W. Adorno, *Problems of Moral Philosophy*, trans. Rodney Livingstone (Stanford: Stanford University Press, 2001), 8 (translation altered).

9

Critical Phenomenology and the Rehabilitation of Interiority

Ann V. Murphy

Critical phenomenology has emerged as a noteworthy, transdisciplinary methodology in the early twenty-first century. Without going so far as to claim there has been a critical "turn" or a radical alteration of the phenomenological method, it is nonetheless possible to locate a body of contemporary work that hones some version of the phenomenological method as ethicopolitical critique.[1] In the main, critical phenomenology is phenomenology that is meticulously attentive to the operation of power; its methodological self-understanding foregrounds the necessity of taking seriously the institutional, structural, and systemic architectures of power, as well as historical and cultural context.[2] While not all critical phenomenologists employ the phenomenological reduction (at least in its orthodox form), the method is marked by the suspension of everyday beliefs and convictions in order to illuminate, describe, and analyze the structures that underwrite what Lisa Guenther has called "commonsense accounts of reality."[3] The structures that phenomenology brings into view count as transcendental to the degree that they serve as the condition for the possibility of lived experience as such. As the phenomenological method has evolved, a reflexive and transcendental move has arguably remained in place, albeit one with a different scope and purpose. The method now brings into relief structures that are not ideal but historical; following Guenther, they are quasi-transcendental and not strictly transcendental.[4] In this sense, the purview of critical phenomenology is not delineated in reference to a priori structures that are categorically binding irrespective of context, but rather to quasi-transcendental, historical structures (patriarchy, white supremacy, and heteronormativity) that inform how we see and make the world.[5] This attentiveness to context has required that the focus on the first-person perspective, generally axiomatic in phenomenology, be understood in light of exteriority and those historical and cultural forces that coalesce to produce the subject itself and inform every description of the world undertaken from the first-person perspective.[6] Of course, this pivot toward the outside is in no way singular to phenomenology among continental methodologies; it is characteristic of many of the methodological orientations in twentieth- and twenty-first-century continental philosophy.[7]

Interiority and Phenomenology

The historical association of interiority with transcendental philosophy, and in particular with the notion of a constituting consciousness, has motivated critique in both methodological and ethical registers. The philosophical lineage that runs from Hegel through Nietzsche to Foucault understands interiority as the residuum of subjectivation and an artifact of power's social and cultural machinations. Foucault's criticisms of phenomenology in *The Order of Things* and the *Archaeology of Knowledge* concern what he takes to be phenomenology's naivete regarding the possibility of describing transcendental structures from a first-person vantage point that is always already saturated with power.[8] Further still, criticisms of philosophical, epistemological, and methodological figures of interiority have extended into the ethical and political realms via the understanding of interiority as a totalizing motif, one insufficiently engaged with questions of alterity, exteriority, and difference.[9] The critique of transcendental philosophy that dominates the French philosophy of the 1960s, for instance, often understands thought, consciousness, and sense as violent to some degree. The early Foucault warns that thought can "liberate and enslave"; thought is haunted by violence in this regard.[10] However, while these criticisms target particular models of consciousness and cognition, they do not indict the principle of interiority per se. An understanding of consciousness that conceives it either as constituting the world in an act of sovereign meaning-making, or as a possessive gesture of cognition or recognition, differs from the more modest conviction that there is a phenomenologically salient sense of inner life. The former concerns a specific understanding of cognition or recognition, while the latter concerns a ubiquitous domain of lived experience that informs sense itself.

Criticism of phenomenology's presumptive subjectivism and methodological naivete does not undercut the axiomatic methodological conviction that my own experience, as lived by me, is known in its interior textures by me alone. This is not to deny that inner life is radically shaped by those institutional, social, and intersubjective structures that both generate and determine it. It is, rather, to acknowledge a necessary feature of human experience: it is not available to others from a first-person perspective. Indeed, it is impossible to understand the human experience of love, joy, fear, shame, or grief without appeal to an inner world. That said, interiority need not be aligned with the idea of a constituting consciousness that determines the phenomenal world in some strong sense, nor should it be understood as a disavowal of the ties that bind inner life to one's being with others and being in the world. This much is clear given Merleau-Ponty's descriptions of inner life in *Phenomenology of Perception*: "The true *Cogito* does not define the existence of the subject through the thought that the subject has of existing, does not convert the certainty of the world into a certainty of the thought about the world, and finally, does not replace the world itself with the signification 'world.' Rather, it recognizes my thought as an inalienable fact that eliminates all forms of idealism by revealing me as 'being in the world.'"[11]

The appeal to a phenomenologically salient sense of interiority does not require that the world collapse into the self or that phenomenological inquiry be reduced to solipsistic descriptions of a world that is little more than a subjective projection. Indeed, criticisms of phenomenology's recourse to interiority often conflate phenomenological, epistemological, ontological, and metaphysical understandings of the binary between inside and outside, but it is possible to read interiority more modestly. Interiority is not necessarily tethered to any particular metaphysical mooring. Indeed, to acknowledge a phenomenologically meaningful sense of interiority is not necessarily to endorse any specific metaphysics at all. The sense of an inner life remains phenomenologically salient irrespective of metaphysical and epistemological considerations.[12] Moreover, interiority—necessarily but perhaps paradoxically—opens onto questions of reflexivity that have always been at the heart of phenomenological method and continue to animate critical phenomenology today. Essentially, interiority gestures beyond itself; as a felt sense (and not a metaphysical postulate), it is a constitutive feature of psychic life, one that ceaselessly opens to what lies outside or beyond the subject.

As a reflexive inquiry into the systems of power that inform the basic structures of experience, critical phenomenology's methodological commitments necessarily contest the legitimacy of the distinction between interiority and exteriority. In her essay "What Makes Critical Phenomenology Critical?" Gayle Salamon cites Foucault's description of critique as an effort "to move beyond the inside-outside alternative."[13] This understanding of critique productively problematizes the continued recourse to interiority in contemporary phenomenology and motivates several important methodological questions. If the very understanding of critique refuses the binary of interiority and exteriority, or more modestly calls it into question, then of what worth or relevance is the continued appeal to interiority itself? Moreover, as phenomenology is increasingly employed as a critical form of inquiry, and part of what identifies the inquiry as *critical* is the rigor of its engagement with historical and institutional exteriorities, how can the principle of interiority be rehabilitated for a critical phenomenology? This chapter argues that it is worthwhile to consider the possibilities for this rehabilitation beyond the retrograde gesture of a return and in a more expansive and contemporary frame. What does it mean to consult interiority in the context of a critical project, particularly when critique is itself understood as a contestation of the boundary between inside and outside? Does interiority remain relevant in the context of critical phenomenology?

What is Critical Phenomenology?

Critical phenomenology is a work in progress, a methodological orientation that is still coming into its own. There will be debates regarding the degree of fidelity it does or does not bear to classical phenomenology, and whether a break with the classical method is definitive, or whether, in recent decades, a "critical turn" in the tradition of phenomenology is even evident. At present, these questions remain open. While some thinkers have endorsed the trope of a "critical turn," others view trends in contemporary phenomenology as a reawakening of tendencies that have marked phenomenology from the start.[14] To the extent that phenomenological inquiry relies upon a bracketing of the natural attitude in order to bring into view the transcendental structures that condition experience, such that they can be described and analyzed with greater precision, it has always performed a reflexive, critical gesture. For this reason, there may be no radical break, no manifest "turn," that marks the move from classical to critical phenomenology.[15] Indeed if, as Robert Bernasconi has argued, "Phenomenology cannot be passed down like a possession; it must be reactivated, renewed," phenomenology's current moment may count as a moment of renewal, more so than a rupture or break.[16] Husserl himself doubtless understood the critical force of phenomenology: "What is clearly necessary," he writes, "is that we *reflect back*, in a thorough *historical* and *critical* fashion, in order to provide, before all decisions, for a radical self-understanding."[17] The historical evolution of phenomenology has long been informed by a concern with crisis and its amelioration. From its inception, phenomenology's self-understanding as a primarily descriptive method has been braided with variable degrees of recognition regarding its role as a philosophy that responds to crisis and its role in observing and understanding the movement of history.

The moniker "critical phenomenology" gained traction following the publication of Lisa Guenther's groundbreaking book *Solitary Confinement: Social Death and its Afterlives*, in which she links phenomenology's critical capacity to enhanced recognition of the intertwining of subjectivity and intersubjectivity: "I have sought to develop a method of critical phenomenology that both continues the phenomenological tradition of taking first person experience as starting point for philosophical reflection and also resists the tendency of phenomenologists to privilege transcendental *subjectivity* over transcendental *intersubjectivity*."[18] If this initial formulation of critical phenomenology spotlights intersubjectivity, more recent articulations of the method—including Guenther's own—have privileged considerations of power. In her essay "Critical Phenomenology," Guenther narrows the lens to consider not only intersubjective structures more broadly but also the specific role of "quasi-transcendental" structures such as patriarchy, white supremacy, and heteronormativity in structuring perception. "Structures like patriarchy, white supremacy, and heteronormativity permeate, organize, and reproduce the natural attitude in ways that go beyond any particular object of thought. These are not things to be seen, but ways of seeing, and even ways of *making the world* that go unnoticed without a sustained practice of critical reflection."[19] Guenther's movement from the transcendental to the quasi-transcendental brings together the reflexivity of phenomenological method (or the fact that phenomenology is concerned with the illumination of the basic structures of lived experience) with the imperative that this reflexive endeavor be historically situated. Absent here are classical phenomenology's presumptive aspirations to a purely transcendental inquiry that would grant philosophy the rigor of a science.[20] Presumably, what contemporary phenomenology loses in terms of the apodictic and universal reach of its inquiry, it gains in terms of its sensitivity to the milieu in which it finds itself.

In ways that vary, and are more and less pronounced in different instances, phenomenology has always endorsed a constitutively reflexive, and thus critical, turn of consciousness. Resisting, to some degree, the trope of a "critical turn" in phenomenology—one that would mark a salient shift in phenomenology's methodological self-understanding—Salamon suggests a more abiding sense of critique that has informed phenomenology from the start: "When asking what a critical phenomenology is, we might maintain that it reflects on the structural conditions of its own emergence, and in this it is following an imperative that is both critical in its reflexivity and phenomenological in its taking-up of the imperative to describe what it sees in order to see it anew. In this, what is critical about critical phenomenology turns out to have been there all along."[21]

Yet even as she understands the critical potential of phenomenology to have "been there all along," Salamon notes the more recent methodological supplementation of phenomenology with resources drawn from critical theory, a supplementation or hybridization that has rendered phenomenology more critically robust and incisive.[22] Critical theory, for its part, brings into play "questions of violence, racial injustice, gender inequality, and a host of other urgent political issues" that have all too often fallen by the wayside in phenomenological inquiry.[23] While acknowledging points of manifest methodological divergence and incompossibility, Salamon nonetheless notes "fundamentally significant resonances" between the critical and phenomenological enterprises.[24] One of these is cited above in reference to Foucault, namely the idea that critique endeavors to "move beyond the outside-inside alternative."[25] Salamon also highlights a productive understanding of limits in both phenomenology and critical theory, one that refuses the idea that critique is merely a negative gesture and instead asserts the generative, productive, and potentially liberatory aspects of critical thought and practice.[26] Finally, Salamon aligns critique and phenomenology to the degree that both involve the work of description. To be sure, the work of description has taken many forms and charted many courses as phenomenology has continued to evolve.

In a similar vein, Robert Bernasconi charts an especially open-ended course for phenomenology in a particularly prescient essay written two decades ago, "Almost Always More Than Philosophy Proper," in which he asks:

> What is the future of phenomenology? What will become of it? Or rather, what will it become? If phenomenology were a set of doctrines, one might ask about its current status, and the challenges, philosophical and institutional, that await it on the

horizon. The same would be true if philosophy were a uniform method. But, as Herbert Spiegelberg explained, phenomenology is a movement. There is a common point of departure but no homogeneity. . . . There is still no basis for defining it. That much has not changed. A lot else has changed and will continue to change about phenomenology as it continues to change in response to the changing world, and perhaps, helps to set the agenda for philosophy more generally.[27]

With his description of phenomenology as "almost always more than philosophy proper," Bernasconi puts his finger on phenomenology's singular methodological indeterminacy, nominating it as a point of promise. Neither a philosophical method fixed in time nor a set of doctrines, "phenomenology has never merely been one philosophical movement amongst others."[28] Phenomenology, on Bernasconi's reading, may loosely signal a shared canon or lexicon, but more importantly it signals a "readiness to be open to whatever kinds of evidence seem appropriate to the matter at hand."[29] Contrary to strands of philosophical orthodoxy that recognize the legitimacy of a method only on the basis of preordained criteria, phenomenology operates in a mode of perpetual self-invention. Because phenomenology, Bernasconi writes, "Exceeds philosophy, future phenomenologists have at their disposal a way of thinking that has resources not only to challenge the reigning conception of philosophy, but also to enrich philosophy from what—for the moment at least—is still considered outside it."[30] Phenomenology is here rendered as a bit of a methodological troublemaker to the degree that it refuses to be defined once and for all by any list of axioms. As a method that is constitutively relational (or "improper," in Bernasconi's account), phenomenology's methodological investments, subject matter, and transdisciplinary trafficking are necessarily expansive. In a similar vein, Michael Marder has described phenomenology as a method that must be renewed and reanimated in the living present through a process of perpetual "self-rejuvenation."[31] The upshot, he argues, is that one cannot do phenomenology without changing what it is: "All worthwhile work in phenomenology necessarily puts in question the meaning of phenomenology itself."[32] Phenomenology is an expansive and capacious method—what Bernasconi calls a "broad church."[33] Indeed, it is hard to debate the precise parameters of a philosophical methodology whose evolutionary course calls the very idea of methodological orthodoxy into question. Given this, there is very little that is surprising about the emergence and naming of critical phenomenology in the early decades of the twenty-first century.

For Bernasconi, the transcendental and reflexive movement of phenomenology is bound to phenomenology's preoccupation with the inaccessible, inexpressible, and invisible: "Phenomenology is concerned with questions of access and particularly questions of gaining access to what is largely inaccessible,"[34] a formulation that mirrors Guenther's more recent description of critique as "a capacity and willingness to question what might otherwise seem unquestionable."[35] In this, "phenomenology situates itself at the margins not just of philosophy, but of what can be thought and said at all. It exceeds the boundaries of what is recognized as philosophy."[36] This claim anticipates the inter-, multi-, and trans-disciplinary lives to which phenomenology now lays claim.

Still and always, phenomenologists have been at pains to describe how their method yields descriptions of lived experience that are distinct from ethnography, autobiography, and other forms of first-person narrative.[37] What requisite criteria must be in place in order for inquiry to count as phenomenological? One response is that phenomenology's transcendental (or quasi-transcendental) aspirations make this method singular among other methods that consult the first-person perspective. While there is presently some ambiguity surrounding the degree to which phenomenologists understand the reduction as a requisite feature of any phenomenological inquiry that would nominate itself as such, generally speaking there continues to be a transcendental move that is endorsed as phenomenological method, past and present. While the early Merleau-Ponty continued to endorse the idea of a reduction, he famously insisted in the preface to *Phenomenology of Perception* that it could never be complete; the natural attitude can never be wholly bracketed, and the retreat to the transcendental can never be entire.[38] Critical phenomenology, by and large, endorses this insight into the incomplete nature of the reduction and so operates with a looser conception of the transcendental nature of phenomenological inquiry.[39] No longer tightly tethered to the steps of the reduction as rendered in Husserl's work, this reflexivity in critical phenomenology is understood in ever-widening ways. What, then, marks critical phenomenological descriptions as such, and what role does inner life continue to play in these descriptions?

Interiority and Critique

Critical phenomenology is not simply a methodology that understands phenomenology to be importantly, indeed necessarily, situated amid considerations of historicity, structural injustice, and power. The methodological aspirations of critical phenomenologists also rest firmly on the conviction that the critique itself is not fully critical without a substantial reckoning of the psychic life of oppression or violence. O'Byrne aptly captures this double inflection in her description of critical phenomenology as "an approach to the world that will be critically phenomenological, and phenomenologically critical."[40] The latter element is just as important as the former. Critical phenomenology is not only a particular kind of phenomenology; it is also a particular kind of critique. Here phenomenology's interrogation of inner life is not so much a liability but a locus of critical insight. In contrast to critics who understand phenomenology's investment in first-person perspective as a cut against its critical efficacy, critical phenomenologists understand the consultation of experience as a vital component of critique. Phenomenology's grounding in lived experience is narrated in reference to a constellation of features, interiority among them. Indeed, the principle of interiority remains of interest precisely because it is the phenomenological locus of the subject's undoing in others and the world. What if interiority were conceived as a privileged site of exploration, one in which we explore that which binds us to others? What if interiority were conceived not as that over which I am most proprietary but instead as the site of my dispossession and vulnerability? What if psychic life were understood not over and against a world but as the realization of the world in a vulnerable and open self? What would it mean to truly acknowledge, in the context of ethical and political critique, that perception is not private but participatory and indeed may serve as the foundation of care?[41]

Interiority, as the felt sense of an inner life, is fundamentally and absolutely relational. Inasmuch as interiority is a requisite and constitutive dimension of experience, it has never been understood as a cloistered or insulated domain of lived experience, but rather as a domain in which the subject's dispossession in the world and in others is consolidated in the phenomenologically salient sense of inner life. Read in this light, interiority is not so much proprietary as it is a site of dispossession. Or perhaps it is both at once. When one considers the contours of inner life, one is immediately called to recognize the always already ethical resonance of phenomenology to the degree that the principle of interiority and psychic life is one place in which the enworlding of the self is made manifest.[42] My own-most existence is necessarily a coexistence. Every phenomenologist since Husserl has thought as much.[43] Critical phenomenology, for its part, simply refuses the myth of innocent coexistence in favor of a more complex, power-laden, and historically nuanced understanding of what it means to claim, as Guenther has recently put it, that transcendental subjectivity and intersubjectivity are equiprimordial.[44]

To some degree, this insight echoes Judith Butler's account in *Psychic Life of Power*, in which she critiques the conception of power understood as pressing on the subject from the outside, as a mechanism of relegation and subordination.[45] While this application of force may be one way in which to understand the myriad ways that power moves in, through, and on the subject, Butler emphasizes a more expansive view that takes seriously the formative force of power in a broad sense: "But if, following Foucault, we understand power as forming the subject as well, as providing the very condition of its existence and the trajectory of its desire, then power is not simply what we oppose but also, in a strong sense, what we depend on for our existence and what we harbor and preserve in the beings that we are."[46]

Because critical phenomenologists focus the lens on the historical structures that frame lived experience, they recognize what Butler describes as the "harboring and preservation" of historicity and power in psychic life. This movement of power within the self is not the ontological residuum of a discreet event or instant in which power was internalized; rather, the subject is "repeatedly constituted in subjection, and it is in the possibility of a repetition that repeats against its origin that subjection might be understood to draw its inadvertently enabling power."[47] For Butler, as for Foucault, power inaugurates the subject; it does not impose itself after the fact. For these reasons, Butler understands the subject to be initiated through a primary submission to power, a submission that belies the distinction between interiority and exteriority, and returns attention to the domain of interiority as a felt sense that is born of dispossession in the other. "In each case," she writes, "power that appears at first external, pressed upon the subject, pressing the subject into subordination, assumes a psychic form that constitutes the subject's self-identity."[48] The psychic form that power takes "is relentlessly marked by a figure of a turning, a turning back upon oneself or even a turning on oneself."[49] Even as the ontological status of this founding moment, this twisting, remains uncertain, it is clear that the figure of turning is evoked to capture the generative co-implication of the psyche and power.

History moves forward, institutions change and evolve, and the normative architecture through which we make meaning is in perpetual flux. What is distinctive about critical phenomenology as a form of social critique is not only the consideration of power or history, which most forms of social critique necessarily share, but also the reflexive nature of the inquiry into lived experience itself, which necessarily entails the exploration of inner life. If it is reasonable to claim phenomenology has gained more critical traction in recent decades, this gain is not only a function of heightened attention to institutional, cultural, or historical structures; the architecture of the subject does not, after all, remain static, simply narrated at different times in different contexts. The subject of phenomenological inquiry also radically changes, obviating the abiding critical force of first-person narration.

The suspicion surrounding phenomenology's recourse to interiority has often been at the heart of broader reservations about phenomenology as a method. The principle concern is typically phenomenology's alleged naivete, to the degree that meaning and truth remain tethered to the first-person perspective.[50] At first blush, phenomenology seems insufficiently critical in this regard, issuing descriptions of lived experience that are unsatisfactorily grounded in historical, institutional, and cultural architectures of power. Surely, recent work in critical phenomenology should be understood as redressing this concern in both the methodological and ethical registers. It's a fair guess that the evolution of phenomenological method will continue to be charted, at least in part, in reference to its critical capacity and acumen, and that its critical capacity will itself be understood in reference to its willingness to describe, explicate, and analyze the institutional and historical context that breathes life (or death) into lived experience. But this rendering of critical phenomenology risks emphasizing the greater contextualization of lived experience in a way that may veil the question of how the principle of interiority—and the question of how interiority is even understood—also evolves, and will continue to evolve, as phenomenology charts its critical afterlives. As phenomenology evolves, more than its context changes. Interiority should not be understood as a static or formal feature of lived experience as such, one that simply absorbs or accommodates the differential ebb and flow of experience and the institutional and historical structures that give it shape. The critical edge of critical phenomenology does not concern only a more fine-grained engagement with the problem of power.

Critical phenomenology's emphasis on the felt textures of lived experience is crucial for understanding historically specific instances of injustice *as they are lived*. Furthermore, the ontological injuries and prejudices that critical phenomenology brings into relief are often, if not always, incomprehensible without appeal to an inner life. Indeed, to consider the breakdown of subjectivity in different instances of deprivation or torture, an appeal is often made to the dichotomy between inside and outside.[51] Injury can be the consequence of a loss of the felt integrity of the boundary between self and world—a sense that there is no beginning or end to the self. So, too, there is injury when this binary becomes reified to the point of prohibiting the relationality and expressive commerce that are requisite for psychic life. In either case, the ontological status of these violations is unintelligible without reference to interiority as a salient register of phenomenological description.

The idea that social critique must attend to what critical phenomenologists have understood as *ontological* injury, distortion, or deprivation can be nominated as one of critical phenomenology's most important insights. When Fanon claims that "any ontology is rendered unrealizable in a colonized and civilized society," the indictment of colonialism transcends preoccupation with the overtly white supremacist imaginary that mobilizes colonial life in every register.[52] The structure of being, then, is radically perverted under colonialism, and ontological structures are pushed to the point of collapse. The psychic fallout of this collapse is described in reference to ontology, and in this case the unrealizability of ontology, to signal a breakdown in being. Phenomenology is particularly well-suited to speak not only to the circuitry of interiority and exteriority that is psychic life itself but also to the devastation that results when the institutional, political, and historical frame to which critical phenomenology attends manifests as a breakdown of subjectivity itself. This privation, injury, or even social death is not fully intelligible without reference to the distortions of inner life under colonialism. This is also the case for Guenther's more recent examination of the breakdown of subjectivity and selfhood in solitary confinement.[53] Indeed, critical phenomenology, in seeking to reflexively account for architectures of power that operate as the condition for the possibility of lived experience, persistently narrates the harm they enact as an *ontological* injury. An account of this injury that refused its psychic dimensions and inner life would no doubt be an impoverished one.

Notes

1. The argument for a "critical turn" in phenomenology is not necessary for an investigation into the relevance of the figure of interiority for critical phenomenology today. Gayle Salamon and Anne O'Byrne note that phenomenology has been critical, in some sense, all along, and that the body of work that currently self-identifies as "critical phenomenology" has no single point of origin. See Gayle Salamon, "What's Critical about Critical Phenomenology?," *Puncta: Journal of Critical Phenomenology* 1, no. 1 (2018); Anne O'Byrne, review of *50 Concepts for*

a Critical Phenomenology," eds. Gail Weiss, Ann V. Murphy, and Gayle Salamon, *Puncta: Journal of Critical Phenomenology* 3, no. 1 (2020).

2. According to Lisa Guenther, "The main difference between classical and critical phenomenology turns on a methodological and ethical commitment to pay attention to the way power and history shape lived experience." Lisa Guenther, "Six Senses of Critique for a Critical Phenomenology," *Puncta: Journal of Critical Phenomenology* 4, no. 2 (2021).

3. Lisa Guenther, "Critical Phenomenology," in *50 Concepts for a Critical Phenomenology*, eds. Gail Weiss, Ann V. Murphy, and Gayle Salamon (Evanston, IL: Northwestern University Press, 2020), 15. The reduction in Husserl's early work entails the transcendental and eidetic reductions, in which our naive faith in the natural attitude is bracketed in order that we may discern the transcendental structures that condition knowledge and experience. This discernment entails the recognition of essences that lend the phenomenal world intelligibility for us. Authors writing in contemporary phenomenology do not always perform the reduction in ways that would be recognizable to Husserl, but phenomenology remains marked by a reflexive turn back to the conditions for the possibility of experience, even if this turn may appear inchoate in comparison to the precision with which Husserl describes the reduction in his early work.

4. All of the structures that Guenther nominates as "quasi-transcendental"—white supremacy, heteropatriarchy, ableism, and so forth—concern identity, but presumably the category of the quasi-transcendental includes both structures and institutions that are oriented around identity and some that are not.

5. Guenther, "Critical Phenomenology," 12.

6. Because the focus of this chapter is interiority in the context of critical phenomenology, the first-person perspective is front and center. Critical phenomenology, however, occasionally expands its purview to consider second- and third-person perspectives. It does not remain dogmatically fixated on first-person accounts.

7. Certainly poststructuralism and various strains of dialectical and historical materialism have focused the critical lens on the forces—both psychic and material—that bear down on and produce the subject as we know it.

8. The transcendental status of phenomenological investigation is undermined by the fact that man is not only the transcendental ground of the empirical sciences but also their proper object. For this reason, the subject's knowledge of that world can never be clear or entire as it finds itself implicated in the appearance of the world in ways that obscure certain kinds of knowledge even as others emerge. This point would not be foreign to most phenomenologists, but for Foucault it posed devastating problems for the phenomenological enterprise.

9. One can think of Levinas's critique of Heidegger, for example, which indicts ontology as a kind of "imperialism" or tyranny when it is conceived as first philosophy. Emmanuel Levinas, *Totality and Infinity: An Essay on Exteriority*, trans. Alphonso Lingis (Pittsburgh, PA: Duquesne University Press, 1969), 44.

10. Michel Foucault, *The Order of Things* (New York: Random House, 1994), 328.

11. Maurice Merleau-Ponty, *Phenomenology of Perception*, trans. Donald A. Landes (London: Routledge, 2012), lxxvii.

12. This is not to claim that metaphysical and epistemological concerns are unimportant or irrelevant, but one can address the phenomenological salience of interiority without having to justify it metaphysically. Here I am understanding metaphysics as a domain of philosophical inquiry to which phenomenology does not necessarily speak.

13. Gayle Salamon, "What's Critical about Critical Phenomenology?," 14.

14. See, for example, Salamon, "What's Critical about Critical Phenomenology?"; and O'Byrne, review of *50 Concepts*.

15. For decades, authors including Iris Marion Young, Linda Martin Alcoff, and Lewis Gordon have been writing in the vein of what is now called critical phenomenology without it having been named as such.

16. Robert Bernasconi, "Almost Always More Than Philosophy Proper," *Research in Phenomenology* 30, no. 1 (2001): 6. Bernasconi's claim that phenomenology must be reactivated and renewed differs from Husserl's claim that the philosopher is a perpetual beginner. To renew a method is not to begin again but to take up what has come before, in order to alter and reinvigorate it.

17. Edmund Husserl, *Crisis of the European Sciences and Transcendental Phenomenology*, trans. David Carr (Evanston, IL: Northwestern University Press, 1970), 17.

18. Lisa Guenther, *Solitary Confinement: Social Death and Its Afterlives* (Minneapolis: University of Minnesota Press, 2013), xv.

19. Guenther, "Critical Phenomenology," 12.

20. In *Crisis of the European Sciences*, Husserl understands phenomenology both as a response to an historical moment that poses clear dangers in need of address and as a method capable of illuminating a transcendental science of essences that could ground other modes of inquiry, preventing pernicious instantiations of relativism. There are tendencies in the work that pull for and against the evolution of phenomenology into critical phenomenology as we know it today.

21. Salamon, "What's Critical About Critical Phenomenology?," 12.

22. Guenther makes a similar claim when she notes that critical phenomenology is a "hybrid" method.

23. Salamon, "What's Critical About Critical Phenomenology?," 14.

24. Salamon, "What's Critical About Critical Phenomenology?," 13.

25. Michel Foucault, "What Is Enlightenment?" in *Ethics, Subjectivity, and Truth*, ed. Paul Rabinow, trans. Robert Hurley (New York: New Press, 1997), 315.

26. Salamon, "What's Critical About Critical Phenomenology?," 13.

27. Bernasconi, "Almost Always More Than Philosophy Proper," 1.

28. Bernasconi, 1.

29. Bernasconi, 2.

30. Bernasconi, 2.
31. Michael Marder, *Phenomena-Critique-Logos: The Project of Critical Phenomenology* (London: Rowman and Littlefield, 2014), 10.
32. Marder, 2.
33. Bernasconi, "Almost Always More Than Philosophy Proper," 4.
34. Bernasconi, 3.
35. Lisa Guenther, "Six Senses of Critique for Critical Phenomenology," *Puncta: Journal of Critical Phenomenology*, special vol., *Critical Phenomenology at the Collegium* (2021).
36. Bernasconi, "Almost Always More Than Philosophy Proper," 5.
37. Anne O'Byrne astutely questions phenomenology's aversion to being cast as "merely" autobiographical in her review of *50 Concepts for a Critical Phenomenology* in *Puncta*, 30.
38. Merleau-Ponty, *Phenomenology of Perception*, lxxvii.
39. This may be apparent in the move from the transcendental to the quasi-transcendental, as in Guenther's work or more broadly in the variable ways in which contemporary phenomenologists understand the reflexive nature of the method.
40. O'Byrne, review of *50 Concepts*, 28.
41. See Emmanuel de Saint Aubert, "The Perceptual Foundation of Care," in *Transforming Politics with Merleau-Ponty: Thinking Beyond the State*, ed. Jérôme Melançon (New York: Rowman and Littlefield, 2021).
42. This is why phenomenology can never be a purely descriptive method. Its descriptions always bear normative weight insofar as first-person attestations are necessarily situated in perpetual dialogue with the world and with others.
43. Generally speaking, a line of inheritance may be traced from Husserl's conviction that transcendental subjectivity is intersubjectivity to Merleau-Ponty's claim in *Signs* that "I borrow myself from others" and to subsequent articulations of the co-implication of self and other. This co-implication is axiomatic in phenomenology since its inception. Maurice Merleau-Ponty, *Signs*, trans. Richard McCleary (Evanston, IL: Northwestern University Press, 1964), 159.
44. See Guenther, "Six Senses of Critique."
45. Judith Butler, *The Psychic Life of Power: Theories in Subjection* (Palo Alto, CA: Stanford University Press, 1997), 2.
46. Butler, *The Psychic Life*, 2.
47. Butler, 94.
48. Butler, 3.
49. Butler, 3.
50. The accusation that phenomenology is a naive methodology is complicated, given that phenomenology aims at a critical contestation of naive faith in the natural attitude, only to endorse a naive and astonished, even awestruck surveying of the world once the natural attitude has been (however imperfectly) put out of play. In this sense, one might argue that phenomenology interrogates one naivete

and celebrates another. Withal, the relationship of phenomenological method to naivete is complex. Critical phenomenology, for its part, is grounded in a faith that the naivete celebrated in philosophical method can turn critical.

51. See Guenther, *Solitary Confinement*.

52. Frantz Fanon, *Black Skin, White Masks*, trans. Richard Philcox (New York: Grove Press, 2008), 88.

53. See Guenther, *Solitary Confinement*.

10

Joy, Interiority, and Individuation
A Steinian Account

Elodie Boublil

References to interiority and a person's inner life often point to an emotional life, conscience, the deeper layers of motivations, or the existential and affective source of a will to live. Since Plato, Western philosophical ethics has been struggling with the troublesome features of passions and how they would disturb and even disrupt the tranquility and activity of rational thinking. Breaks, impairments, nonsense, traumas, and what Nietzsche would call the Dionysian activity of life cast doubt on the harmonious illusion of Apollonian individuation characterized by self-mastery. Philosophical thinking seems to be stretched into these two opposite faces. For instance, contemporary works in the phenomenology of emotions have paid specific attention to negative or hostile emotions.[1] Indeed, drawing on Max Scheler's or Edmund Husserl's analysis of empathy and on their respective understanding of the structures and layers of affective life, current philosophical debates revolve around the essence and understanding of pain, suffering, hate, trauma, existential despair, vulnerability, or contempt.[2] In other philosophical traditions, such as virtue ethics, happiness studies flourish quite independently from their negative counterparts.[3] Recent publications in continental philosophy offer a phenomenological analysis of love in its relation to embodiment and empathy—or an ethical understanding of it—under the form of a revaluation of compassion.[4] While these philosophical trajectories rightly portray the complexity of our affective life and the human condition, this chapter will focus on Edith Stein's analysis of joy to sketch out how her reflection offers new perspectives on interiority that depict a phenomenological conception of the inner life, at the crossroads of philosophical anthropology, ethics, and metaphysics. Indeed, the phenomenon of joy offers Edith Stein the opportunity to unfold a phenomenological conception of interiority. The latter is built on an original understanding of individuation that overcomes the dichotomy between the inside and the outside, self and world. It offers a glimpse into the very possibility of becoming *coherent* in and through our breaks and failures thanks to a proper understanding of the dynamics of the heart, which diastolic and systolic rhythms echo the attentive yet vulnerable engagement one may have with oneself and others.

Apart from a specific section in *Finite and Eternal Being*,[5] which focuses on the definition of essence and uses the concept of joy to engage in a discussion with Aquinas,[6] Stein has provided us with neither an explicit theoretical analysis of joy as such nor another treatise of passions. Nevertheless, throughout her collected works, joy serves as a critical concept that helps her contrast her understanding of classical, phenomenological, or metaphysical notions (e.g., essence, empathy, intentionality, feeling, act-feeling, the core of the person, education, grace, freedom, and God) with her own innovative and personal philosophy of the human person and interiority. Indeed, we find occurrences of and discussions involving joy (*Freude, Heiterkeit*) in almost all of her writings, from her phenomenology of empathy to her theological and mystical writings inspired by St. John of the Cross. As a sign of apparent contradiction, her philosophy of the person and her theology of the cross reveal a quest for joy and fulfillment. This fulfillment does not rely on the self-centered sense of fullness that we may tentatively experience during times of satisfaction or contentment, but rather it stems from the decentered and scattered yet genuinely individuated perspective one may have on life once the depth and orientation of its interior movement are revealed (*Sinn*).

Consequently, this chapter will argue that the concept of joy in Stein's writings, which articulates several philosophical differentiations and interconnections, can be considered critical to reframe existential and philosophical questions related to personal individuation and interiority. This philosophical revaluation stems from, first, a refutation of existentialist accounts of individuation (notably Heidegger's); second, an overcoming of traditional phenomenological accounts of interiority (Husserl's and Heidegger's); and third, a spiritual appropriation of the experience of joy that has its own philosophical value to rethink interiority. By differentiating the various layers of our experience and understanding of joy (satisfaction, enjoyment, empathic joy, deep joy, rejoicing, divine joy, etc.), Stein progressively unfolds an innovative conception of personhood and singularity, ultimately grounded in a renewed approach to philosophical anthropology and Trinitarian ontology. The phenomenon of joy becomes the revealing and expressive phenomenon of a shattered transcendence that roots and stirs up from within our desire to love.

This chapter starts by contextualizing the specificity of Stein's phenomenological approach regarding traditional accounts of happiness. Then it analyzes the passion of joy in the history of philosophy as a revealing phenomenon of the subject's inner life. An examination of Husserl's analysis of the intentional structure of joy related to the ego-constitution follows in the third part. Stein's analysis of joy, notably in *Finite and Eternal Being*, demonstrates a genetic analysis of this feeling and its crucial role in the phenomenological description of personal individuation. However, by referring to the notions of "lifeforce" and "transcendent depth," Stein designs a new framework for individuation, discussed in the fourth part, that avoids the metaphysical difficulties of both ontological realism (Aquinas) and vitalism. From an existential standpoint, she also argues, against Heidegger, that personal and collective individuation are intertwined and that Dasein's individualization, based on the experience of anxiety, may contradict the relational and open structure of the human person. In the fifth part, we move from "aversion" to "conversion" as Stein elaborates a hermeneutic understanding of the phenomenological *epoché* in which "deep joy" plays the role of a grounding existential feeling that reveals an inalienable interiority. Ultimately, her reading of Bergson may have influenced her final understanding of mystical joy and love, as inner yet other-oriented phenomena, discussed in the last section, and their decisive roles in individuation processes and intersubjective experiences.

Interiority and the Quest of the Good Life

From Aristotelian ethics to contemporary hedonism, the quest for happiness remains a trait of our human condition and a common thread in philosophy, spirituality, and religion. In this sense, as Adam Potkay explains in the opening lines of *The Story of Joy*, considerations of happiness and the analysis of positive emotions reflect the good life and, consequently, a connection between ethics and philosophical anthropology.

Joy is often reduced to happiness or described as an emotional criterion to indicate the righteousness of our decisions.[7] In classical treatises, joy is considered a positive passion that brings about ethical behavior such as compassion, kindness, patience, and dedication. As Potkay summarizes, "Joy is a delight of the mind from the consideration of a present or approaching good, and while this good may just be one's own good, it generally involves beliefs about the good more generally. The discourse of joy thus involves us in shifting and competing interpretations of human ends. The story of joy is, in one light, the history of the good pursued by affective means."[8]

Nonetheless, happiness generally refers to the final state of being and living in the good. In contrast, joy implies a kind of lived intensity related to our inner experience and consciousness of time, as if joy breaks through our pre-reflective experience of time-consciousness to offer us a precise glimpse of the authenticity and fullness of the living present (*lebendige Gegenwart*) and interiority.

This sense of duration associated with joy has been studied by, among others, Spinoza, for whom joy reveals an increase in power and a passage from a lesser to greater perfection; Nietzsche, for whom joy expresses the freedom of the spirit able to turn suffering into self-mastery; and Bergson, who relates joy also to creativity and a living sense of achievement. According to these authors, the fundamental aspect of our experience of joy makes it a specific passion that reveals the desire and capacity for self-transformation lying at the core of the human being.

In brief, one may say that philosophical investigations of joy uncover the following characterizations: an ethical quest, an anthropological disposition, and a metaphysical understanding of the relations between the finite (human beings) and the infinite (God or Nature). Moreover, genuine joy arises—it is welcomed and received rather than self-produced or created by our efforts. In this sense, it also entails a sense of alterity (joy for the other, before the other, with the other, from another field or place in me, etc.).

Husserl's discussion of affective life takes place in dialogue with Brentano's philosophy and descriptive psychology. His analysis of emotions, feelings, and moods is strongly connected with a reflection on their relations to values and volitions. In this context, Husserl introduces further distinctions between joy, enjoyment (as related to the feeling of pleasure and displeasure), and the subsequent denomination that will be attached as a "value" to the experienced object. What I perceive as enjoyable becomes simultaneously valuable.[9] Sensory pleasure or displeasure is a primary state (sense feelings), whereas enjoyment is intentional. Indeed, emotions imply a value judgment on the object itself that is presented and experienced. As Husserl writes in his recently published manuscripts on the structure of consciousness: "It is manifest that the joy about the beautiful, the relation that it elicits, is not joy about the mere being of the object, but joy about the being of the object of value."[10]

Consequently, due to a new philosophy of consciousness and the ego, the Husserlian approach to affective life revises our traditional analysis of human passions and interiority. Phenomenological psychology describes the various layers of affective life (sense feeling, emotion, moods, etc.) and the complexity of their relations with the other components of the human mind (cognition and the will). Stein inherits such methodology, as evidenced by her doctoral dissertation on empathy,[11] and carries it further in her later works, as shown by her analysis of joy in *Finite and Eternal Being*. In this context, Stein uses joy as a key concept to question the structure of intentional consciousness and the status of the transcendental ego, in order to provide us with an innovative understanding of individuation in its relation to the inner life of the person.

Joy, Intentionality, and the Ego

Throughout his texts on affective life and phenomenological psychology, Husserl elaborates a typology of joy based on the intentional structure of consciousness and the modes of experience of joy (and enjoyment) in various contexts. As Mariano Crespo explains,[12] according to Husserl, first "joy arises, when the object of desire is realized"; when "desire is fulfilled," joy is an intentional feeling that can be expressed in several ways. Second, joy can be defined as "a reaction"—the apprehension of a pleasant object causes joy in the subject. And third, joy can be grasped as a "state of mind"—one may remain "joyful" long after the original source or occasion of joy disappears. Stein does remember this aspect of Husserlian analysis while reflecting on empathy and memory, yet her reading of Bergson and the evolution of her considerations on the vital force (*Lebenskraft*) transform that conception and her analysis of the primary characteristics identified by Husserl (fulfillment, reaction, state of mind, or coloration of the inner life). The way in which she progressively questions Husserl's analysis and, notably, the role of the transcendental ego in the unification of our inner life shapes and transforms her approach to joy, interiority, and individuation.

Her discussion of joy in *Finite and Eternal Being* shows that she remains partly faithful to the Husserlian framework. Indeed, using the example of the "good news," she writes:

The experiential content is essential for the unity of the structure. Such a unity or unit, for example, is the joy that one experiences upon the arrival of good news. This joy presupposes my appreciative listening to the news and my knowing comprehension of its gratifying nature. Nevertheless, these presuppositions are not part of the joy unit (*Einheit der Freude*) as such. It may well be that I have known this news for some time prior to my experiencing joy over its content. I may either not have fully grasped its significance right in the beginning, or, having understood the gratifying nature of the news, I may not have been able to experience joy over it owing to my preoccupation with other matters. We may say then that the experience of the content "joy" is conditioned by the object and by the ego (*Ich*). The object—in our example, the content of the news—is not itself a part of joy as experiential content, whereas the tending toward (*Richtung*) that object is indeed a part of the experiential content. (Phenomenology uses the term intention to designate this tending toward.) The characteristic which makes this experience joy with respect to this particular object is a constitutive part of the joy, and the same is true of the intentional object (i.e., the object "toward which joy tends"). The entire *Erlebniseinheit*, "this particular joy," is closed or completed at the moment when I no longer experience this joy or at the moment when I may "again experience" joy but not concerning the same object.[13]

In this paragraph, Stein defines joy as an intentional feeling depending on the object's apprehension ("tending toward") and the value attached to it. Nevertheless, she takes a step further by mentioning the case in which I can recognize something, or an event, as objectively joyful based on my previous experience or a moral understanding of it, but I cannot feel and experience that joy. In this case, she identifies a kind of resistance that she attributes to the self:

But what kind of a self or ego is it that we have in mind here? When I try to give an account of why I cannot experience joy, I may discover that I am so engrossed by some profound grief that there is no room left for joy. Or I may simply find that I cannot experience joy without naming any specific reason. But I am convinced, nonetheless, that the reason for not being able to experience joy "lies in me" even if I find it impossible to track it down. I must conclude, therefore, that there are things hidden—"within me"—all kinds of things—which are unknown to me. And in this sense, it may be said that the ego is not part of the experiential content: The ego transcends my experience, as does the object in a similar and yet not identical manner. This is why Husserl applies the term transcendent to both the object and the "psychological ego."[14]

Two elements seem important here. First, there is a lack of self-transparency, a kind of inner opaqueness that prevents both self-mastery and self-creation. The subject cannot—literally—decide to be joyful in the genuine sense of the term. And second, the subject encounters an emotional resistance that she cannot break by itself, even if the subject is free to consent (or not) to the finitude and limitations of her affective experience since the "ego transcends the experience." Joy appears here as a pivotal concept because it allows Stein to move from a Husserlian understanding of the transcendental ego to her account of the human person, a person whose self is shaped by what could be termed transcendental affectivity. Indeed, Stein gives flesh and consistency to Husserl's pure ego in her account of the subject's inner life while redefining the sense of personal individuation and freedom and the deeper layer of the soul unveiled by her analysis of joy. In *The Problem of Empathy*, Stein already stressed that "the depth of a feeling of value determines the depth of a feeling based on the comprehension of the existence of this value."[15] Accordingly, she will bridge the genesis of our inner life with the awareness of our values and motivations, as revealed in and through our emotional life and relations.

Joy and the Inner Life of the Subject: Stein on the Genesis of the Interiority

Several features characterize the originality and legacy of Stein's analysis of joy, each one of which contributes to rethinking interiority as a dynamic and individuating experience of self-dispossession and self-transformation. First, Stein converses with *Lebensphilosophie* and vitalism through her concept of "vital force" and thereby follows up on the metaphysical tradition that links joy with desire and perfection. She reconnects the philosophical discussion on emotions with the conceptualization of the vital force. In this context, joy contributes to sustaining the dynamic of personal and collective individuation and to the flourishing of one's personal note. Indeed, joy feeds the vital force, whereas fear or a hostile attitude diminishes its power. She describes the relation between the vital force and interiority as follows:

> All these inner movements of the soul have a curious relation to its power. On the one hand, every act consumes power, and the greater the power, the more the soul is involved. On the other hand, the emotions are marked by polarity in the specific content that divides them into "negative" and "positive" emotions. These are not only stances for or against something approaching from outside, but also contrary kinds of feedback affecting the soul's very being, increasing or decreasing its power. Anger, annoyance, grief, etc. sap the soul, while enthusiasm, joy, etc. enhance its life.[16]

Second, the vital force may explain the intensity of the experience, but it does not exhaust its reality and presence:

> Joy, for example, which filled my heart a moment ago but which is now "fading away" can no longer be called fully alive, but neither is it entirely extinguished and forgotten as if it had never been real. It is still there, but—as compared with its full vitality—it is in a weakened state of being. This is, in varying degrees, true of all that exists in the present but is not fully alive; it is true of everything which at one time was but no longer is fully alive, inasmuch as it can pass over again from its present mode of being into a state of full vitality; and it is true of everything that will be fully alive in the future, provided it once possessed that seminal mode of being in a preceding span of time.[17]

Third, this lived-through experience and the precariousness or fragility of our experience of joy leads Stein to reflect on temporality—from the temporality of our inner experience to the finitude of our temporal being. She builds on Husserl's analysis of time consciousness and the living present to assert the contemporaneity of our experiences and their intertwining within the living present. In other words, we do not "move on," we "move through" emotional experiences.

Joy, Interiority, and Individuation | 183

> After all, we really do experience joy, fear, and so on, and, moreover, we experience these as units which are construed in a time-consuming movement. This movement is my life or my living being. Whatever structure "arises" within this movement, I encompass (each individually) from the vantage point of this present moment in which I am alive. Nothing of all this "stands" in the past. Whatever of all that I have been is still alive, is within me, and with me in the present moment.[18]

And Stein observes further,

> My existence is a continuous movement, a fleeting and, in the strictest sense, a transitory kind of being and thus the extreme opposite of eternal and immutable being. . . . The being of the ego is alive only from moment to moment. It cannot be quiescent because it is restlessly in flight. It thus never attains true self-possession. And we are therefore forced to conclude that the being of the ego, as a constantly changing living present, is not autonomous but received being. It has been placed into existence and is sustained in existence from moment to moment. This, however, implies the possibility that this being may have a beginning and an end and that it may suffer a break.[19]

Consequently, authenticity and self-transformation do not arise solely from a decision of the will. However, they occur through a continuous yet opaque movement provided the subject lets herself be guided by the deeper layer of her soul—which unfolds her personal note—and pays specific attention to the truthfulness of her experience. In other words, it is not the subject who *constitutes* her own inner life but the inner life of the subject that *stretches* the self to the point she can welcome and encompass all experiences as hers. Therefore, joy signals here genuine individuation and appropriation.

Fourth, indeed, joy emerges as well in Stein's reflections on authenticity. The greater "perfection" brought about by true and deep joy has to do with its original modes of presentation. In several passages, Stein analyzes and questions the truthfulness of our experience. Like many other authors, she denounces, for instance, *Schadenfreude*, the rejoicing in the other's pain and misfortune, but also "fake joy," which is unable to lead the subject to self-transformation and growth. She often calls for "intellectual honesty" in the way we look at our own emotions and feelings: "No one can make me understand what joy is unless I have experienced joy. But once I have experienced joy, then I also understand what 'joy as such' is."[20]

Finally, authentic and deep joy does not arise from a reactive attitude (reaction to something or someone) but from a receptive attitude. In a sense, deep joy precedes the subject. The subject welcomes it, and joy radiates throughout the layers of her person. True joy arises from the inner life of the person. It is first-personally given and spreads out of the "transcendent depth" of the soul: "Does the joy originate in the pure ego? If by pure ego we understand with Husserl only that self which is alive in every 'I think,' 'I know,' 'I desire,' etc. and which is conscious of itself as a thinking, knowing, desiring ego, then we must conclude that this joy originates in a transcendent depth which discloses itself in the conscious experience of joy, without, however, becoming transparent."[21]

Sixth, and finally, Stein's mystical understanding of the soul and its ontological darkness and depth allows Stein to reframe the phenomenological categories and descriptions provided by Husserl—notably his concept of the pure ego and its emphasis on self-transparency—into an ontological understanding of the human person: "Ego and soul are not merely juxtaposed but inseparably linked. To the human soul, there belongs a personal ego that dwells in the soul, embraces the soul, and in whose life the being of the soul becomes a living and conscious presence. And the human ego is so constituted that its life rises out of the dark depth of the soul."[22]

Stein departs from Aquinas's theory of joy as a "passion of the appetitive faculty" that results from "an expansion of the heart" (joy as Laetitia)[23] to reflect on how joy manifests the correlation between a dynamic sense of individuation and the deepening of one's own interiority as one moves through life experiences. Consequently, her phenomenological reframing of the heart will also entail a new sense of interiority inspired by spiritual writings. Theresa of Avila's approach to subjectivity has influenced Stein in her critical refutation of Heidegger's understanding of Dasein's individuation and interiority.

From Aversion to Conversion: Stein's Response to Heidegger's Concept of Anxiety

Soon after the publication of *Being and Time*, Stein published a critical analysis of Heidegger's philosophy in which she assesses his philosophical argumentation and the validity of the concept of Dasein to account for human experience.²⁴ While she acknowledges the phenomenological and existential value of Heidegger's emphasis on the central role of temporality in individuation, she nonetheless argues three points. First, that a philosophical understanding of individuation does not limit itself to a comprehensive investigation of individualization (*Vereinzelung*); second, that consequently, anxiety is not Dasein's ultimate experience as Dasein, in the sense that Dasein's is less thrown than welcome and supported by Being; and third, that Heidegger's ontology leaves out our human concrete experience of alterity and the role played by the community in individuation and the constitution of the person. Ultimately, she would rather root genuine individuation in a growing conversion process to alterity and inner depth—a process that still allows for the unfolding of one's personal note through its encounter with others—rather than in a movement of aversion from the world, as displayed by Heidegger.

Indeed, Heidegger's approach to Dasein leads us to understand individuation in terms of appropriation and self-interpretation. Heidegger radicalizes the Husserlian phenomenological gesture by providing a strong criticism of the principle of sufficient reason and rehabilitating a sense of contingency that makes Dasein responsible for its individuation in and through its projects and the possibilities she appropriates. His analysis of anxiety demonstrates a new interpretation of singularity and ipseity that insists on one's ability to synthesize meanings while projecting worldly possibilities in an appropriate configuration.

"Being-toward-death" becomes an existential principle of individuation. Anxiety confronts the subject with the contingency of her existence, emptiness, and the ultimate possibility of death. Anxiety reveals individuation as a hermeneutic process of singularization, resolutely rooted in existence and conceived as a liberation from the rawest vital facticity. Heidegger explains: "In what anxiety is about, the 'it is nothing and nowhere' becomes manifest. The recalcitrance of the inner-worldly nothing and nowhere means phenomenally that what anxiety is about is the world as such. . . . Anxiety individuates Dasein to its own most being-in-the-world, which, as understanding, projects itself essentially upon possibilities."²⁵

Anxiety thus appears as a form of epoché that highlights a process of constitution that is no longer the proof of objective intentionality but the test of intentionality fomenting the existential structure of Dasein—in other words, the proper movement of its individuation and separation from the world itself. Like the epoché, anxiety neutralizes meanings while admitting that they are coextensive with the phenomena it brought to light.

Anxiety separates the subject from the world and from the anonymity of the "they." Stein describes Heidegger's analysis, in this sense, as a movement of aversion, that is, a movement that could be characterized as the exact opposite of empathy. Instead of empathizing with the world and others, Dasein expresses, literally, an antipathy toward the environment from which it differentiates itself. Through this differentiation, it might then conquer new possibilities of existence to be mastered and appropriated.

According to Stein, such a view leads Dasein back to a situation of mastery in which the individual's will to power makes her think she might have control over her world and others. Heidegger's Dasein reveals itself as a Faustian character. As Stein explains, "The human being, however, is conceived as a little god insofar as it is claimed to be the being distinguished among all beings as that being from which alone information about the meaning of being is to be hoped for. God is spoken of only now and then in footnotes, and then only in a dismissive fashion: that divine being is something which could have significance for the meaning of being remains completely excluded."[26]

To this view, Stein opposes and proposes a movement of conversion that she sees at stake in the epoché, understood as "metanoeite (conversion)."[27] She does not deny the value of retreating from the natural attitude to be self-conscious of one's own individuation. Rather, she demonstrates the value of individuating oneself through one's existence with others to fully accomplish the relational dimension that makes individuation authentic in and through the awareness and appropriation of our inner yet worldly experiences. In her *Lectures on the Human Person*, she criticizes the existential dead end to which Heideggerian and Sartrean philosophies may lead if they disconnect the philosophizing subject from the world and others in an overhanging position. As she writes, "The philosophy of existence presents us with the human being in the finitude and nothingness of her existence. It fixes its gaze on what the human being is not, which prevents it from paying attention to what, positively, she is despite everything, and to the absolute, that arises behind this conditioned being."[28]

The relational dimension of the person and the call to become a full member of a community are to Stein as important as Dasein's understanding of her finitude. Indeed, she contends that intersubjective experience and the structure of "being with" are not fundamentally inauthentic experiences. Rather, they contribute to the development of the person and the unfolding of her personal note, whose flourishing also enriches the community as a whole:

> The person is just as much called to being a member as to be an individual; but to be able to be both in its own particular way, "from within," it must first step out of the imitating mode in which it lives and is bound to live at first. Its own innermost being needs the preparation provided by the being-with others to be, in its turn, guiding and fruitful for others. This must be ignored if one does not want to acknowledge development as an essential feature of the human way of being, and one must ignore development if one denies human beings an essence different from their Dasein, the temporal unfolding of which is its existence.[29]

This analysis of Heidegger's ontology concludes that the intertwining of the collective and personal dimensions of individuation stems from "within," that is, from the symbolic locus in which our singularized, lived-through experience meets the personal values and conscience constituted in and through the life of the community to which we belong. Stein here articulates individuation with a renewed sense of interiority inspired by Augustine and Avila yet informed by the Husserlian analysis of intersubjective experience and the lifeworld's constitution. Her understanding and evaluation of peace, joy, or love as positive feelings that may contribute to the flourishing of the community draw on such a phenomenological and anthropological picture of individuation.

In her lectures on *The Philosophy of Psychology and the Humanities*, Stein defines, for instance, the phenomenon of "resting in God" as a form of recollection that does not result from exhaustion but, rather, helps nourish the person with a spiritual force needed to rebuild her motivations:

> Compared to the cessation of activeness from the lack of life power, resting in God is something completely new and unique. The former was dead silence. Now its place is taken by the feeling of being safe, of being exempted from all anxiety and responsibility and duty to act. And as I surrender myself to this feeling, new life begins to fill me up, little by little, and impel me—without any voluntary exertion—toward new activation. This reviving infusion appears as an emanation of a functionality and a power that is not my emanation and becomes operative within me without my asking for it. The sole prerequisite for such a mental rebirth seems to be a certain receptivity, like the

receptivity supporting the structure of the person, a structure exempted from the sensate mechanism.[30]

This reconstitution of the vital force through its relationship with a spiritual force attributed to God illustrates the role played by interiority, transcendence, and affectivity in individuation processes.[31] The relational dimension of the person urges her not only to find deep within herself—in her heart, the "soul of the soul"—the genuine source of transcendence but also to be aware that she is open to others and in an inevitable relation with them through empathy: "Something similar may be possible in the communications of one person with another. The love with which I embrace a human being may be sufficient to fill him with new life power if he breaks down. Indeed, the mere contact with human beings of more intense aliveness may exert an enlivening effect upon those who are jaded or exhausted, who have no activeness as a presupposition on their side."[32] Stein's conception of the heart and communal experiences and feelings reflect this view of interiority and its powers. The heart for Stein is not a new dimension within the structure of the person (body-soul-spirit). However, it is the lived space and organ through which the unification of the person reveals itself and makes itself sensible through its capacity to love. It expresses the inner depth of the soul in its intimate relation with the body and the spirit and the point of contact with transcendence.[33]

In this framework, joy may appear as an existential/ontological feeling that discloses the source of personal and collective individuation—as a new form of epoché that reveals the relational and dynamic dimension of Being as it gives itself through love and vitality—through the expressivity of the heart. The qualitative dimension of joy and its phenomenological importance for exploring interiority has been explored by Stein in dialogue with the philosophy of Henri Bergson.

Mystical Joy and the Constitution of the Self: Stein and Bergson on Interiority

In her lectures on psychology and the humanities, which followed the end of her collaboration with Husserl, Edith Stein undertakes a phenomenological analysis of human emotions and feelings to elucidate why they are experienced differently by individuals and how they shape their intersubjective experiences. In a very original manner, Edith Stein continues to endorse most of the claims she made in her earlier dissertation on empathy and seems to remain faithful to Husserl's theories as developed in *Ideas II*, a text we now know she helped him write. Yet she also addresses issues discussed by Scheler and Bergson at that time, namely the relation between the emotional sphere and objective values (Scheler) and the qualitative aspect of our experience of inner time (Bergson). Both authors also reflected and wrote on joy and mysticism. In this final section, I would like to compare Bergson's and Stein's analyses of inner experience and joy to bring to light the relation between joy, the subject's individuation, and the dynamic ontology of life that Stein would ultimately portray as the truth of Trinitarian ontology.

Stein explicitly refers to Bergson's philosophy of consciousness in her lessons on psychology and the humanities. In the early 1920s, she remains faithful to Husserlian phenomenology and does not give up on the transcendental ego. As she wants to endow the subject with a sense of absolute freedom, her Husserlian account of the ego helps her build a concept of "motivation" that allows the subject to escape the determinations of the sentient life and physiological mechanisms. She nonetheless agrees with Bergson on two essential aspects that will be elaborated further in her later metaphysical and mystical writings: one, according to Stein, Bergson has rightly articulated the qualitative aspect of our lived-through experience, its intensity, and its sense of duration; two, individuation operates through the dynamism of a spiritual force that informs and sustains the development of one's personal note or singularity.

> In any event, it seems as though wherever the requisite objective foundations are available, but any life power emanating from them is lacking, the resolve of the will itself can produce itself in the same way it generates other free acts. This marvelous capability of generating "impulse powers" out of itself obviously indicates a power source lying beyond the mechanism of the individual personality, which flows into the willing ego and in which the ego is anchored. The closer explorations of these relationships, which we cannot pursue here, lead into the field of philosophy of religion.[34]

Stein agrees with Bergson's claim that some actions come out from the depth of our inner life with some urging necessity that presses us to act, as if the decision were unconsciously made and emanating from "the elan vital" that imprints on the world the irreducible marks of our creativity. But she refuses to merge the ego with the flow of consciousness and to deny any value to consciously and rationally elaborated decisions that entail "the realization of a state of affairs as something that's demanded by conscious motives."[35] According to Stein, it "would certainly be absurd if—as Bergson believes—the ego coincided with the total lifestream. That thesis certainly is to be rejected. The willing ego that we have in view, the subject of the resolve, is a pure ego, which Bergson regards as a mere construct of the intellect. All past experiences, as well as the present experiences, belong to the pure ego, but it does not arise from them."[36]

Nonetheless, as Stein became more acquainted with and influenced by Christian mysticism and ontological realism, she put aside progressively, as we have seen, Husserl's concept of the pure ego. To "move beyond the pure experiential science of the psyche," one needs to delve into the notion of "transcendent depth" that seems to be inherited from her readings of Carmelite mystics such as St. Theresa of Avila or St. John of the Cross but that we may also trace back to her readings of Bergson. Moreover, even if Stein does not refer to Bergson in her later writings, it is worth noting that *Les Deux Sources de la Morale et de la Religion*, in which Bergson develops his theory of mysticism, was published in 1932. Stein came to France that same year to participate in a conference in Juvisy on Thomism and phenomenology. Even if there is no explicit engagement with Bergson's account of mysticism in Stein's work, we can presume she continued to read his works; in her letter to Ingarden, dated October 3, 1918, she claims to be enthusiastic about his philosophy. In any case, it seems that the analysis of joy and mysticism in *Les Deux Sources* matches Stein's similar efforts to reconnect the subject's freedom with love and concern for the community.

It seems, indeed, that Stein and Bergson shared a common interest in rehabilitating the figure of the mystic as a paradigmatic case of personal individuation, revealing the irreducibility of life to mechanism and determinations, whether scientific, political, or social. Nietzsche already considered the saint as the paradigm of genuine individuation—able to integrate and overcome the contradictions and breaks of our existence. Stein and Bergson saw personal and collective individuation, in relation to cultivating one's inner depth, as a solution to counteract the deadly future offered by closed societies. As Bergson writes about the mystic, "She felt the truth flowing into her from her source as an acting force. She would not help but spread it any more than the sun would pour out its light. However, it is no longer by simple speeches that she will propagate it. For the love that consumes her is no longer simply a man's love for God. It is God's love for humankind. Through God, she loves all humanity with divine love."[37]

To Bergson, joy is the outward manifestation of that deep love and the way it radiates and allows itself to be communicated to other people.[38] Bergson insists on the mystic's humanity and sense of action, just as Teresa of Avila did while describing the inner castle. Genuine mysticism is not about supernatural experiences, but rather about a sense of inner experience and union with the divine that expresses the soul's conversion into a transcendent depth able to welcome others and circulate love around itself.[39]

In her discussion of Heidegger's concept of anxiety and its existential function in the life of Dasein, Stein shows us that anxiety (as understood by Heidegger) reveals our finitude in a gnostic manner. Anxiety reveals to us our experience of being thrown in the world, resolutely condemned to death. I contend that the way she understands joy—upsurging from that transcendent depth—replaces anxiety in her framework and helps her understand "finitude"—and, consequently, individuation—in a completely different way: the paradoxical coincidence of self and alterity, activity, and passivity, within the subject, reintegrates affective life—flesh and blood, incarnation—in our understanding of the person's interiority, while bringing to light the underlying dynamics or *dunamis* (force) that sustains it. In this sense, Stein's final understanding of joy in its relation to suffering also conveys an ethical dimension, traceable to her reading of St. John of the Cross. This ethical standpoint echoes her ultimate legacy to the world: the science of the Cross is not about suffering; it is about love.

Notes

1. The author acknowledges the support of the Alexander von Humboldt Foundation for the research carried out during her fellowship (2018–2020) at the University of Cologne. The research results presented in this chapter are the sole responsibility of the author.

2. See, for instance, Saulius Geniusas, *The Phenomenology of Pain* (Athens: Ohio University Press, 2020); Ingrid Vendrell Ferran, "Contempt: The Experience and Intersubjective Dynamics of Nasty Emotion," in *Emotional Experiences: Ethical and Social Significance*, eds. John J. Drummond and Sonja Rinofner Kreidl (London: Rowman and Littlefield, 2017); Erinn Gilson, *The Ethics of Vulnerability: A Feminist Analysis of Social Life and Practice* (New York: Routledge, 2014).

3. See Michela Summa, "Joy and Happiness," in *The Routledge Handbook of Phenomenology of Emotion*, eds. Thomas Szanto and Hilge Landweer (New York: Routledge, 2020).

4. See Sara Heinamaa, "Values of Love: Two Forms of Infinity Characteristic of the Human Persons," *Phenomenology and the Cognitive Sciences* 19, no. 3 (2020): 1–20; Sara Heinamaa, *Thinking about Love: Essays in Contemporary Continental Philosophy*, eds. Antonio Calcagno and Diane Enns (Philadelphia: Penn State University Press, 2015); Anthony J. Steinbock, *Knowing by Heart: Loving as Participation and Critique* (Evanston, IL: Northwestern University Press, 2021).

5. Edith Stein, *Finite and Eternal Being: An Attempt at an Ascent to the Meaning of Being*, trans. Kurt F. Reinhardt (Washington, DC: ICS Publications, 2002), 62–85.

6. See Thomas Gricoski, "Essential Being and Existential Metaphysics," in *Edith Stein: Women, Social Political Philosophy, Theology, Metaphysics, and Public History; New Approaches and Applications*, ed. Antonio Calcagno (Dordrecht: Springer, 2016).

7. As Michela Summa summarizes: "Considering recent work, the discrepancy between a large amount of research on happiness and the comparatively little one on joy is remarkable (cf. Christoph Demmerling and Hilge Landweer, *Philosophie der Gefühle* [Berlin: Springer, 2007], 111–25; Adam Potkay, *The Story of Joy: From the Bible to Late Romanticism* [Cambridge: Cambridge University Press, 2007], 1–29). Interdisciplinary research on happiness has flourished in the last decades, and research fields called 'happiness studies' or 'the science of happiness' have developed (cf. Sara Ahmed, The Promise of Happiness [Durham: Duke University Press 2010], 2–20; Dan Haybron, "Happiness," in *The Stanford Encyclopedia of Philosophy* [2011]). Several attempts have been made to establish more or less standardized criteria for the evaluation of individual and social happiness. This interest for happiness and happiness standards concerns not only scientific research but also social discourses: we read articles about the happiest country in Europe, about how to keep a happy relationship, about being happy with what you are, etc. There seems to be nothing similar concerning joy." Summa, "Joy and Happiness," 416.

8. Potkay, *The Story of Joy*, viii.

9. Denis Fisette, "Emotions and Moods in Husserl's Phenomenology," in *The Husserlian Mind*, ed. Hanne Jacobs (New York: Routledge, 2021), 222.

10. *Studien zur Struktur des Bewusstseins: Teilband II. Gefühl und Wert* (Texte aus dem Nachlass 1896–1925), ed. U. Melle and T. Vongehr (Dordrecht: Springer, 2020), 94–95, quoted by Denis Fisette, "Emotions and Moods," 222.

11. Edith Stein, *On the Problem of Empathy* (Dordrecht: Springer, 1989).

12. Mariano Crespo, "Fenomenología de la alegría: Un caso de intencionalidad afectiva," Anuario Filosofico 53, no. 3 (2020): 471–94.

13. Stein, *Finite and Eternal Being*, 47.

14. Stein, 47.

15. Edith Stein, *On the Problem of Empathy*, 102.

16. Edith Stein, *Potency and Act: Studies toward a Philosophy of Being*, vol. 11, in *The Collected Works of Edith Stein*, trans. Walter Redmond (Washington, DC: ICS Publications, 2009), 388.

17. Stein, *Finite and Eternal Being*, 39.
18. Stein, 45.
19. Stein, 54–55.
20. Stein, 68.
21. Stein, 54.
22. Stein, *Potency and Act*, 431.
23. See Stein's discussion of Aquinas and the essence of joy in *Finite and Eternal Being*, 69 and sq.
24. See Edith Stein, "Martin Heidegger's Existential Philosophy," trans. Mette Lebech and "Martin Heideggers Existentialphilosophie," in *Edith Stein, Endliches und Ewiges Sein: Versuch eines Aufstiegs zum Sinn des Seins, Edith Stein Gesamtausgabe*, vol. 11/12 (Freiburg: Herder, 2006), "Anhang," 445–500.
25. Martin Heidegger, *Being and Time*, trans. Joan Stambaugh (New York: State University of New York Press, 2010), 181–82.
26. Edith Stein, "Martin Heidegger's Existentialphilosophie," in *Endliches und Ewiges Sein, Versuch eines Aufstegs zum Sinn der Seins, Gesamtausga*be, no. 11/12 (Freiburg: Herder, 2006), 445–500. Trans. Mette Lebech *in Maynooth Philosophical Papers* 4 (2007): 55–98.
27. "The call to reflect on true being, as it resonates for us in Heidegger's metaphysics with radical acuity, is a fundamentally Christian call, an echo of the *metanoeite* by which John the Baptist was called to prepare the ways of the Lord. Of all the Christian philosophers, none made this call his own with more passionate energy than St. Augustine." Edith Stein, *Der Aufbau der menschlichen Person* (Freiburg: Herder, 1994), 29.
28. Stein, 29.
29. Stein, "Heidegger's Existential Philosophy" (Lebech translation), 73.
30. Edith Stein, *Philosophy of Psychology and the Humanities*, vol. 7, in *The Collected Works of Edith Stein*, trans. Mary Catharine Baseheart and Marianne Sawicki (Washington, DC: ICS Publications, 2000), 84–85.
31. As Angela Ales Bello explains:

Through spiritual force, the *psyche* opens itself to the objective world and can acquire new impulses; the nourishment of the spiritual strength of the individual psyche can come from an 'objective' spiritual world, a world of values, or the spiritual strength of other subjects and from the divine spirit. In any case, it is necessary to identify a nucleus, *Kern*, above all physical and psychic conditionings, different, therefore, from the same vital, sensitive, and spiritual force, and constituted by the capacity to want, by the sphere of free acts. (Angela Ales Bello, *Fenomenologia dell'essere umano: Lineamenti di una filosofia al femminile* [Rome: Città Nuova, 1992], 113)

32. Stein, *Psychology and the Humanities*, 85.

33. See Elodie Boublil, "Stein's Perspectives on the Heart at the Crossroads of Phenomenology, Anthropology and Carmelite Mysticism," in *Edith Stein's Itinerary: Phenomenology, Christian Philosophy, and Carmelite Spirituality*, eds. H. Klueting and E. Klueting (Münster: Aschendorff Verlag, 2021).

34. Stein, *Psychology and the Humanities*, 89.

35. Stein, 96.

36. Stein, 96.

37. Henri Bergson, *Les deux sources de la morale et de la religion* (Paris: PUF, 1965), 247.

38. Such a description of joy echoes the one proposed by Stephan Strasser:

> We do not find the joyful emotion in the animal, but only in man. Only in man's case does joy lead him to an inner being-apprehended. Only man can become so overpowered by the joy that he no longer grasps the condition of things. Only he can shed tears of joy. He experiences that which brings joy as a gift that removes him from the everyday. The bodily bearing of rising becomes for him a jubilant sursum corda; to the external movements of self-opening corresponds a being-opened of the heart. He can translate his inner release into the language of kindness and affection toward other men. (Stephan Strasser, *Phenomenology of Feeling* [Pittsburgh, PA: Duquesne University Press, 1977], 336)

39. As Antonio Calcagno explains, commenting on Stein's later works: "Depth becomes not only a way of describing the nature of certain relationships, in that depth is viewed as a quale of the soul, quality of the nature of its existence, but also a place—a place of poignant encounter. The soul has become depth, an infinite space where the human person can encounter the divine persons." Antonio Calcagno, "Assistant and/or Collaborator? Edith Stein's Relationship to Edmund Husserl's *Ideen II*," in *Contemplating Edith Stein*, ed. Joyce Avrech Berkman (Notre Dame, IN: University of Notre Dame Press, 2004), 262.

11

Gerda Walther's Phenomenology of Interiority and the Idea of a Fundamental Essence

Antonio Calcagno

Philosophers have long justified the possibility of an inner life or interiority. From Aristotle's *bios theoretikos* to Augustine's *in te redi* to Hannah Arendt's life of the mind, thinkers have defended the distinction between an interior realm and an external or outer one by speaking about the difference between internal and external perception (e.g., Edmund Husserl's first version of the *Logical Investigations*, as well as Edith Stein's early works in phenomenology); the existence of the "I" of consciousness that has its own realm of ownness and self-relation (e.g., the reflexive philosophy of Jean Nabert); a place of encounter where one encounters the divine (e.g., Thomas Aquinas); or simply the act of thinking (understood as Plato's *dianoia*). Hardcore materialists will often speak of the idea of an inner world as a projection of the brain. Gerda Walther, a member of the early phenomenological movement, also contributes a rich and developed understanding of interiority in her two major phenomenological works, *Ein Beitrag zur Ontologie der sozialen Gemeinschaften*[1] and *Zur Phänomenologie der Mystik*.[2]

To date, there exists no comprehensive scholarly account of her concept of interiority, and this is due to various reasons. First, Walther's work has been largely neglected by scholars of phenomenology as the tendency has been to focus on Edmund Husserl and Martin Heidegger as representing two dominant streams of phenomenological investigation. Figures in the early phenomenological movement (e.g., Edith Stein, Roman Ingarden, Adolf Reinach, Dietrich von Hildebrand), as well as philosophers from the Munich

Circle (e.g., Hedwig Conrad-Martius, Johannes Daubert, and Alexander Pfänder), are now being studied by a new generation of scholars whose investigations will expand phenomenology beyond its two canonical poles of Husserl and Heidegger. Second, Walther could never obtain habilitation as a woman in the German university system; women in philosophy were systematically denied this possibility, though in other disciplines they could habilitate, for example, in mathematics. Her work, therefore, never circulated or had the same status as the writings of her male professor counterparts. Finally, there is a lingering prejudice that surrounds Walther's work, namely that she abandoned phenomenology to pursue work on the fringes of parapsychology, a field of inquiry that is largely considered unscientific. Walther has inadvertently been identified as focusing exclusively on the paranormal, and her own admission to having experienced telepathic and mystical revelations has tarnished her reputation as a philosopher. While it is true that Walther was deeply interested in parapsychology, one must read this research as informed by both phenomenology and psychology, and as ultimately motivated by an attempt to bring to presence aspects of consciousness and the unconscious that fall within the realm of documented human experience. One finds in her *Nachlass* many essays and articles that bring phenomenology into dialogue with psychology and parapsychology.[3]

This chapter focuses on Gerda Walther's concept of interiority. I argue that one finds in Walther's two major phenomenological works mentioned above a developed eidetic description of interiority. In the first part of the chapter, I reconstruct her idea of interiority. In the second, I explore a provocative phenomenological claim made by Walther, namely that though there exists a unity between the three important constitutive elements of interiority (I, self, *Grundwesen*, or fundamental essence), the unity between these different elements is looser and more flexible than one would find in the account of the human person given by her teacher, Edith Stein, for example. Walther allows for breaks in the unity that allow for important dissociations from the self and one's person that serve various functions that include: providing a space for the unconscious and what she calls the embedment of passive structures of mental life (e.g., habits) that have a deep influence upon and connection to consciousness and its capacity to experience the world; locating a space in which certain forms of mental illness and pathology unfold; and finally, explaining how these breaks and dissociations permit other experiences of consciousnesses that lie outside the scope of traditional phenomenological understandings, for example telepathy and mystical, religious experiences.

A Phenomenology of Interiority

Before we can proceed to sketch out Walther's idea of interiority, I would like to address two important questions: Why use the phenomenological method as a means to access interiority? Where does this method begin and what comes to presence initially in Walther's phenomenological investigation? Both of these questions deal with beginnings. Concerning the first question, Walther maintains that phenomenology is a rigorous philosophical method for obtaining eidetic descriptions of real phenomena. She was deeply shaped by her teachers Alexander Pfänder and Edith Stein, both of whom introduced her to the phenomenological method, albeit in two different forms. And though Walther came to Freiburg to study with Husserl, she did not adopt his transcendental method, at least as he conceived of it in his *Ideen I*. Walther had a deep background in psychology and was attracted to the Munich School's approach to it, which distinguished itself from the prevailing experimental and positivist schools that dominated many German universities of her time. She, like many of her phenomenological counterparts, was very weary of psychologism and its attempts to reduce all mental life to psychological processes. Mental life, she claimed, consists of more than the life of psyche; it also includes the rich life of spirit, largely understood as the domain of reason, will, motivation, and valuing, which produces objective realities like politics, art, socialities, religions, and culture.

For Walther, phenomenology can make present aspects of mental life that cannot be adequately represented by empirical or psychological study alone, for these aspects cannot be reduced merely to their partial, external, quantifiable expressions. Interiority, then, is one of the unique phenomenological objects that can be adequately obtained only through phenomenological study. Though interiority can express itself externally and present certain signs or effects of its existence, for example movements or reactions to stimuli of the body; expressions of emotion or thinking, speech, mood; and even works of art or the imagination, it would be wrong to say that these objective expressions are identical with, or reducible to, the interiority that produces them. What does not appear externally are the processes and structures that give rise to the aforementioned external expressions themselves. Furthermore, interiority is not simply the projection of the brain.[4] Interiority is not reducible to the work of neurons—electric and chemical impulses—for the phenomenological object of the interior realm has a discrete existence, which is not merely an extension of the brain. It can affect the brain in ways it does not intend or foresee, especially when this realm of interiority becomes communal or suprapersonal. For example, the rich and varied phenomenon of love, understood not only as a value but also as a series of deep relations with objects or other persons, can shape the chemical functions of the brain: the externalized and spiritual phenomenon of love bends back to condition the physical, bodily conditions of the brain, which are, in part, located in the brain.

If phenomenology can explore objects that are not purely representable by the quantifying sciences, how does it presume to capture its objects? Walther follows the Husserlian argument that objects grasped by phenomenological investigation manifest or give a sense or meaning (*Sinn*): when adequately or fully obtained in and through eidetic variation, the sense of the object reveals the essence or structure of the thing in its reality. In this case, interiority presents a sense that is grasped and recorded by the phenomenologist. What this sense of interiority is, I will present in due course. In terms of identifying a contextualizing starting point for Walther's own approach to interiority, we must situate her work within the phenomenological framework of sense-making and sense-grasping offered by the analysis of both noesis and noema. This being said, we must also isolate another important starting point of Walther's investigation of interiority, namely the pure I or zero-point of orientation. She begins her analysis by adopting a phenomenological stance, that is, she decides to bracket from her mind all possible naturally occurring prejudices and attitudes she may have about her object of inquiry. She follows the phenomenon as it unfolds, distinguishing it from other phenomena that may be similar but are nonetheless different than interiority. The phenomenologist, for Walther, begins by observing what the pure I reveals,[5] and it is from the pure I that our own study begins.

When one brackets one's natural attitude and assumes the phenomenological stance, one becomes aware of one's own consciousness and a zero-point of orientation or a pure I around which consciousness appears to move. The I can consciously see that there is a foreground and background. To borrow Husserl's language, there is a horizon of consciousness. This consciousness also has specific content, and the I can pause to examine the content in order to try and understand what is presenting itself to consciousness. Fascinating for Walther is the fact that the I can select which content it will focus on while ignoring the rest. This power or capacity to select content, to direct consciousness from the zero-point of orientation, is the manifestation of freedom (*Keim der Freiheit*).[6] Like all phenomenological investigations, Walther asserts three important givens: the real existence of consciousness with its specific content, the existence and activity of an orienting pure I, and the capacity of this I to make free choices (the I can move—*Ich kann*). These phenomenological givens launch Gerda Walther into the analysis of the interior realm.

The three givens are experienced in ways different from other mental acts. The aforementioned givens are experienced neither as external perceptions nor as acts of the imagination or remembering. Walther distinguishes between inner and outer perceptions, a distinction accepted by Scheler, Stein, and Husserl (of the first version of the *Logical Investigations*). In outer perception, the object of the act of perception lies outside or stands before the object as a separate, real flesh-and-blood object distinct from the perceiver. In internal perception, the object appears within the subject, and there is no necessarily corresponding external object. For example, the feeling of sensuous pleasure is experienced from within—it is real—but there is no object called pleasure that stands before the subject as a distinct separate unit. The very act of inner perception is a requirement to do phenomenological analysis, and it signifies the distinction between an internal and an external realm of experience.

But how do we know if inner experience is not simply the work of the imagination and/or memory? In inner perception, the content or the *perceptum* is distinct from the perceiver, that is, the *perceptum* has its own independent reality that is dependent neither on the perceiver for its coming to present itself nor on its being. When there is no distinction between what is imagined and the imaginer, we usually encounter cases of hallucination or psychotic breaks. The I becomes the same as the imagined.[7] Acts of memory are distinguished from acts of inner perception in that past content of experiences is brought forward and can be represented, and even altered or modified, by the now consciousness in which the memory appears. In inner perception, an object stands before us that is not a representational object of something that once was; rather, an object stands before us, upon which we can fix our gaze, that does not appear as a recollection or representation. The object of inner perception gives itself and is not dependent upon a prior act of a subject's remembering.[8]

So far, Walther has justified the reality of inner perception that reveals a free I, a pure ego. But what more can be said about this I? More is disclosed about the pure I when we read Walther's two major phenomenological texts mentioned above. In the *Phenomenology of Mysticism*, she focuses her phenomenological gaze on the essence of mystical experience, generally understood as a religious encounter with a divine being/reality.[9] The work is not interested in explaining the accounts of these experiences that exist in various religious traditions, for example, in Islam or Roman Catholicism; rather, Walther wishes to understand the conditions that make possible mystical experience, which include a real outside Other or divinity and its encounter with a human being. The encounter is experienced largely from within the life of a human being and is phenomenologically graspable as an *Urphänomen* (originary experience) much like a tone, color, or value.[10] Walther spends a large part of her work on mysticism uncovering the essence of a human being, a being who has the capacity for a religious encounter with the divine.

What is the human being that is capable of mystical experience? The fundamental essence (*Grundwesen*) of the human being is described by Walther as a lived unity of body, psyche, and spirit. Turning to reports of mystical experience, including some of her own, Walther claims that all mystical experience is localized within human bodies. The lived body, the body that is experienced from within inner experience, is described by Walther as a living, sensate organism that is animated by psyche and displays embryonic signs of the life of spirit,[11] for example *kalokagathia*, or the transfiguration of the body by the good and the beautiful of the spirit.[12] Her description *ab initio* notes the intimate connection between body, psyche, and spirit. Though the body remains distinct, it does not function separately from psyche and spirit. All three aspects are interwoven into one another, confirming the existence of a fundamental unity that marks the essence of the human person. Walther also remarks that the two dominant philosophical views of the body, either as the prison of the soul and spirit or whose brain generates epiphenomena like the lived experience of the body, as well as the experience of psyche and spirit,[13] must be rejected, for the former position does not give full recognition to the real lived experience of being embodied and its crucial role for the life of psyche and spirit, especially in terms of expression, and the latter view is materially reductive and does not acknowledge the distinct lives of spirit and psyche, in particular the force of the will, which Walther stresses as fundamental for the constitution of human personhood, more so than reason or intellect. She describes the flow of psyche and spirit through the body as a kind of canalization.[14] The unique lived experience of the body is described as living the flow of the life force within one's being; one feels the energy of a life force flowing within and animating one's physical being.[15]

Unlike Stein and Husserl, who describe the body not only in vitalistic terms but also as a field of sensations, indexicality, and movement, Walther emphasizes not only a pulsating life force or vitality within being but also sexual differentiation.[16] She notes that one of the principal ways that one experiences one's body is through the male-female binary. One feels and lives the body most intimately in physical, sexual union,[17] especially given the fact that this union may result in the generation of a new person. Husserl struggles in his account of the sexuality of the other's role in empathy as he complains that the *Analogieschluss*[18] necessary for empathy to occur does not work when the individuals involved are of different sexes. Husserl acknowledges the importance of sexual difference, but he does not develop his insight, whereas Walther recognizes the fundamental importance of sexuality and sex for understanding ourselves as lived bodies. One not only perceives and feels sexual differences of others, but these very differences are constitutive of a lived experience of embodiment. Though Walther is a binary thinker of gender, a position that is challenged by more contemporary gender-fluid models of sexuality, she, like Scheler,[19] recognizes the importance of sexuality for embodiment: sexuality is a fundamental aspect of our personhood as it allows us to experience our bodies in unique ways.

Psyche or soul is identified as a distinct realm of human being in which one lives feelings and affects such as love, hate, and desire. The content of the experience of one's own psyche flows in a particular fashion: not from top to bottom but from the bottom up or from the back forward, all directed to an I-center.[20] One lives this experience of psychic flow, Walther says, as if it were a flow from the "heart," from the depth of one's being.[21] Psyche is described as the psychic source of feeling:

> This is well observed in lived experiences of telepathy in which non-essential but supplementary elements are lacking. In these cases, an aversion, sympathy, or any other feeling of the heart (including, wonder, surprise, etc.) comes to be lived as stemming from a one who transmits the experience. Likewise, a current of love is perceived by the receiver as coming from the transmitter within the region of "heart." Often, the receiver responds in a similar manner with an analogous personal experience in which his or her I-center is immediately immersed. Both experiences of the transmitter and sender live . . . simultaneously one's own and the other's experience of love, pain, etc. up to the point they do not merge and the I of the receiver lives contemporaneously the love of the other and his or her own in that intimate region of the heart out of which sentiments arise.[22]

The "interior region"[23] of the heart is vital for mystical experience, and one finds reference to it in various cultural and historical traditions, from Christianity to yoga.[24] The sentiment of the heart can be experienced as distinct from the cause or object of a certain emotion. One can experience an emotion or feeling in and of itself, says Walther, and this can only be grasped internally through the life of psyche.

Citing Simmel,[25] Walther notes that psyche also gives or manifests another unique experience of itself, namely, a "feeling of oneself."[26] Walther claims that the feeling of a self undergoing emotional experiences or feelings marks the interiority of psyche. One experiences this self as having its own coloratura, depending on what is being felt. For example, intense feelings of joy accentuate the feeling of oneself as undergoing and being affected by joy. Likewise, painful or emotionally distressing experiences diminish the feeling of oneself: the self is suffused with pain or distress, and the self is not felt as strongly. Walther notes that psyche will express itself in and through the body, and this coloratura of the self may be observed in others. We can see and understand the emotions or feelings of others: we can see the heart of another[27] by the intensities of the emotions expressed by the other to us. It is the manifestation of the inner life of psyche that grants us access into the psychic life of another. In her earlier text on the social ontology of communities, Walther notes that empathy is the key that allows us to grasp the psychic life of others.[28] In the *Phenomenology of Mysticism*, Walther concentrates on telepathy and not on empathy.[29]

Spirit (*Geist*) is identified by Walther as the most unique aspect of our humanity, vital for the very possibility of an encounter with the divine in mystical experience. It is deeply interconnected with body and psyche, but it also possesses uniquely distinguishing features. How does Walther phenomenologically justify the existence of spirit as a unique realm of interiority? If the body is lived as a site of sensation marked by sexuality and the flow of life power, and if psyche is lived as a site of deep feeling and a sense of the self—a reflexive self-awareness—spirit comes to manifest itself in the experience of an inner voice, a voice that guides the human being: one sees the depth of the heart and one seeks truth. In spirit, the inner voice guides one to carry out meaningful actions. Walther writes,

> When I am conscious of being fully drowsy, I think with the spirit alone, from *the well of my heart*. The spirit can see more, whereas the psyche sees otherwise. In this earthly life, we can only see what is here (we cannot see the great beyond, the

realm of fundamental being). . . . The interior life lies dormant principally in persons who dwell, so to speak, in the head or intellect, who rarely allow themselves to be moved by feelings and the interior voice. To heed these two things is to follow the true guide of human beings' lives. In a conscious state of drowsiness the interior human being emerges and with its gaze it is able to penetrate the exterior world, which occurs neither in dreaming nor in sleep. In many respects, drowsiness is the clearest state of awareness because here the interior, spiritual human being lives unfettered and free from the body! Hence, in states of drowsiness the interior human being or the state of spiritual awareness emerges. These states occur only in moments in which the sleeping person can lose him- or herself in oneself or exit from oneself. Here, the spirit is completely free and can separate itself from the I and the body; it can go where it wills, much like a ray of light. Whereas psyche is primarily lodged in the brain, spirit has its seat in the well of the heart.[30]

The life of spirit can be experienced in states of mind in which one is between consciousness and sleep. In such states, one experiences the inner voice that is not purely the expression of body or psyche. Here, one experiences the free movement of the inner voice, and "the inner human being" (*innere Mensch*) emerges: the inner voice dominates and guides the human being. One of the more powerful aspects of Walther's phenomenology is her turn to other forms of consciousness in order to draw out aspects of our being that are not always visible within more traditional acts of consciousness, including representations, presentifications, memory, empathy, and imagination. The exploration of in-between states of consciousness provides her with the manifestation of unique content, which she identifies as belonging to the life of spirit. In many of her works, Walther mines unique states of mind to uncover knowledge about who and what we are. She explores telepathic, unconscious, pathological (e.g., schizophrenia), mystical, ecstatic, and paranormal states, to name the more important ones.

In the aforementioned interior region of spirit, one finds the highest I, which is distinct from the I-center. Walther announces another form of I experience than the orientational I of the I-center.[31] Here, we find a spiritual love, judging, and valuing that arise in the life of spirit. She is very clear, however, to note that, unlike Stein and Husserl, the aforementioned acts are not identical with acts of the intellect. The intellect and its capacity for reason can guide an individual, and its work can be seen in the life of higher animals,[32] but Walther ascribes to spirit a capacity distinct from intellect. Again, she turns to a unique mental state to make her case. She gives the example of a person who is tormented by an irresolvable problem. Reasoning offers multiple possible solutions, but it cannot arrive at a definitive one. It can bring no clarity to the problem or crisis. All remains dark and obscure, Walther says.[33] All of a sudden, from within one's interiority, one experiences an illumination—a solution to the problem—which comes spontaneously from nowhere. Walther also describes the solution as coming from elsewhere, from behind or above, for example. The I-center is displaced, but it is not the source of the solution, which is not of my own doing or origin. Walther does not deny that such I-based solutions are possible, but there are also situations, she says, in which one feels that something from the outside brings some kind of illumination and understanding: one feels as if a ray of light surrounds and lifts one out of distress, ultimately bringing ease, clarity, and comfort.[34] In spirit, one lives fully as oneself, in oneself as an individual: here one finds a spiritual light that burns within the human being.[35] Walther is very clear that the spiritual realm of the human being is not simply a personal space: it is also a world.[36] The individual spirit is part of a broader spiritual world, which need not be human and, therefore, need not be rooted in psyche and body. What could this mean? Citing philosophers like Avicenna and Averroes, Walther conceives of the realm of spirit as a kind of Agent Intellect.[37] In the life of spirit, one can plug into and be activated by a larger form of active intellect that supersedes human knowing, which many philosophers have described as the divine intellect.

Following Alexander Pfänder, her teacher at the University of Munich, Walther also describes the spiritual aspect of the human being as possessing spiritual will, feelings, love, and dispositions.[38] These aspects seem to be unique spiritual aspects that are not dependent on the guidance of human reason; rather, they are informed by the larger spiritual world described above. Spiritual willing is a capacity to will and brings about an action in and through one's own personal freedom. In the spiritual world, an individual person experiences a life of willing, judging, and valuing with other spirits, including the divine. There is communication between them, and one can unite with other spirits to experience intensely what the others live and experience. This is a much deeper experience than empathy, in which one understands what the other is experiencing but does not live it as the other lives it. In telepathic experience, by contrast, one can live what the other is living: the other appears in my consciousness and I live what the other is living. I do not simply understand it. In the spiritual world, a "spiritual we" form of sociality is possible. Walther notes that in this we, two I's are united and are contained in the we as "two points."[39] The spiritual realm described by Walther is deeply communal and shared: the I's do not stand parallel to one another; rather, they are engulfed by a spiritual love.

In her work on the social ontology of communities, Walther claims that the most intense form of human community is one of fusion on oneness,[40] in which individuals fuse as one individual in and through a certain intense experience of community, for example, the deep solidarity of a political community.[41] But, in this text, persons remain immersed in history and culture and may belong, for example, to a people, a state, or a union. In the *Phenomenology of Mysticism*, Walther expands her claim in the sense that the human social and political experience of fusion, always immersed in time and space, can also plug into deeper spiritual communities and world. In the earlier text, empathy is necessary to understand others, but in the spiritual world it seems direct fusion and the living of others' experiences as they experience them becomes possible. The spiritual realm is marked by a profound intimacy and bonding. One could certainly read the description of the spiritual realm in the *Phenomenology of Mysticism* as a deepening and an extension of Walther's analysis carried out in her earlier work on community. At the end of her treatment of spirit, Walther herself notes that there is no universal paradigm of what a human life should be: each individual must build their own life. Yet, human beings can share certain affinities and undertake communal projects. Human beings can "proceed together" in life.[42]

The Emergence of Interiority and Its Porous Unity

If we examine the results of Walther's phenomenological analysis summarized above, we note that interiority consists of various elements, including the I, self, and a fundamental essence, all of which work together to create a unified sense of personhood. The interlacing and working together of each of the constitutive elements help develop a specific understanding and sense of who and what we are as human beings. And this sense manifests inwardly, creating an interiority marked by a unique spiritual inner voice. Sense and sense-making help us experience and navigate this inner world. Collectively and individually, we bestow senses and values on what the foregoing elements allow us to experience. Though Walther devotes much analysis to the structures and aspects of human being that permit us to experience ourselves as persons, one must not underestimate the societal, historical, and cultural content of such experiences—the content that the structures of our personal being work with and are conditioned by. In her work on social communities, Walther is very clear that outer experiences, especially cultural, historical, and economic situations, affect our sense of ourselves and others. She notes, for example, that knowledge and social acts shape the external life of communities. Walther distinguished performative collective acts "in the name of" from personal acts. She gives the example of parliament in which a government may enact certain laws in the name of government or the king.[43]

Unlike her teachers Husserl and Stein, Walther maintains that the very unity of the elements constitutive of personhood are neither absolutely individual nor indissoluble. In fact, the defining experience of personal unity may be understood not only as individuating and unifying of parts to form a whole but also as fusional or collectivizing and rupturable. Given her own studies of, and interest in, a broader range of psychological experience, Walther rethinks the legacy of the Cartesian ego and its capacity to be the source of its own certainty and clarity. The Husserlian and Steinian view of a highly individuated, rational, and eternal ego or monadic structure of the person is tempered by Walther in the sense that though the I, self, and fundamental essence of personhood are unified and work together to create interiority, which Walther does not emphasize as being marked by a strong sense of ownness, the person can find itself in situations and encounters in which the personal sense of the whole, or unity, is broken or transcended. This is different than the *Ich-Spaltung* of Husserl, which tries to account for different I experiences, including the personal, transcendental, phenomenological, and the I of the natural attitude. Walther focuses on the possibility of the very unity of the ego.

Psychotic breaks, deep mental anguish, psychological crises, and certain pathologies can cause one to lose a sense of oneself or feel trapped in a very confined mental space, thereby causing suffering. In the case of feeling trapped, one loses a broader sense of the self or one's interiority as one feels pressured and confined. The I, self, and person of interior life may be diminished or disappear. Walther describes being on the train and feeling very depressed by the recent news of her father's declining health. She feels great anguish and is consumed by sadness. At a certain moment, her grief is lifted. Rodney Parker writes,

It was also during this period that Walther turned toward mysticism. In November of 1918, while on a train to Freiburg after visiting her dying father, she underwent an intense spiritual encounter. Walther claimed that she was touched by a presence that enveloped her in a sense of warmth and goodness, which she took to be an experience of the Divine. This event prompted her to pen *"Ein Beitrag zur (bewusstseinsmäßigen) inneren Konstitution des eigenen Grundwesens als Kernpunkt der Persönlichkeit (und Gottes)"* in early 1920. A version of this text was presented to Pfänder in honour of his fiftieth birthday, and served as the basis for her *Phänomenologie der Mystik* (1923). Shortly after her experience on the train, Walther stumbled upon a copy of Stefan George's *Der siebente Ring* while visiting Karl Löwith's apartment. She found the writings of the members of the George-Kreis compelling, and after returning to Munich she became romantically involved with Percy Gothein, a close associate of George.[44]

On one hand, Walther is consumed and weighed down by the illness of her father, and on the other hand Walther describes the feeling of being engulfed by another presence. If we bracket the content of the experience, we are left with a description of interiority that finds itself pressured and sad yet consoled by an outside source. Walther's understanding of interiority reveals that it can be severely limited but also porous; what enters can cause great psychological and spiritual diminishment but also intense relief and pleasure.

Walther views the person as permeable, able to telepathically receive and experience the life of another person, not as mere presentification of another's experience (as in empathy) but as the very life of the person. She describes how, after fighting with a friend, L., she returns to her apartment and begins to read her book. While reading, she feels herself being solicited by something from the "outside" and she cannot return to her book. Something is nagging at her. She lies down and closes her eyes in order to rest and regain her concentration. She then experiences her friend and his apartment; she feels his feelings and thoughts. Her own I has been set apart, and she lives the experience of her friend.[45] Walther notes that telepathic experiences, unlike empathy, not only displace the I but also show that others can live intimately within my interiority. Telepathic experiences do not seem to be I-dependent: the other comes to live in us, displacing our I, thereby challenging the centrality of the individuating I as the source of all phenomenological experience. Marina Pia Pellegrino notes,

> From the beginning, the experience of telepathy is saturated by this aura that stems from the transmitter. Walther returns to the image of the ancient lamp, the image to which she compared the human person. The I-center is similar to a wick that burns and floats upon a combustible liquid (*Flüssigkeit*), which in ancient times was oil and which can be said to be like an embedment or the subconscious. All is surrounded by a container (namely, the lamp), strictly understood, to which the body is compared. By drawing upon reported experiences of telepathy, Walther observes that we are each a different lamp with our own wicks that burn our own flames (our I-centers). However, the oil in the lamps seems to be able to flow from lamp to lamp, which means that each wick can be fed simultaneously by the oil of another person. The two lamps remain distinct. Often, the oils may not mix, and even in cases where the oils do mix, an individual wick may decide to withdraw from the oil of the other and burn one's own oil. Walther affirms, based on her studies, that one is able to preserve one's own freedom within the lived experience of telepathy insofar as that one is able to shake oneself off or even take one's own position vis-à-vis the lived experience of the other. Telepathic union, then, is achieved only in embedment and not in the I-center.[46]

Walther shows the porosity of the I in that others can telepathically enter our interiority, enabling us to live the interiority and life of another. Also, the I can be displaced such that we may experience a divinity that enters and brings consolation in times of anguish and distress. As an example, Walther describes a sudden spiritual light that gave her great strength to persist and endure her suffering while she was imprisoned by the Gestapo in 1941. The strength that came about through prayers offered by a friend shows how others can work through prayer for divine intercession.[47] But the interiority of a person is not only porous such that others can enter the realm of personal interiority, but it is also fusional and collective: it is not a purely individuated realm.

In her treatise on the social ontology of communities, Walther makes the case that the most intense form of sociality is community. Communities come in various forms, sizes, and intensities. Whether small (e.g., communities of friends and families) or large (e.g., political parties), what typifies them is a feeling of inner unity (*Vereinigung/Einigung*). In intense forms of community, the bond between members is so strong that they form a collective whole: all members become a unit. This means that individual members' egos are displaced and members experience, instead, the intense pleasure and warmth of fusion or collective union. A collective person emerges, who has a unique spirit and on whose behalf one can speak (*Einzelperson/Einzelpersönlichkeit*).[48] Walther notes that communities can bond internally in the sense that members unify with one another, but they also indirectly bond together by subscribing to an external object, ideal, wish, or project. Such indirect, externally motivated communities are unified through knowing.[49]

Though human beings are social by nature,[50] the inner experience of community can be so strong that it can create a collective personality or spirit that expresses the inner life of that community to the external world. A "we" comes to manifest itself that can carry out various social acts, for example it can carry out a collective act, make promises, or undertake a specific task. The collective life of a we that takes up and even displaces the life of an individual ego has a personality, spirit (*Geist*), and life. And this we of a community has an inner expression as well as an outer expression, both in terms of the bonding between members and what may drive them externally to form a union. Following the logic of Hegel, Walther fortifies her claims about the unique sociality of community by noting that it must be understood as having an *an-sich* and *für-sich*, an in-itself and for-itself.[51]

Interiority

Gerda Walther phenomenologically justifies the possibility of an interior realm, marked by constitutive elements of the I, self, and the fundamental, personal essence of a unified body, psyche, and spirit. The working together of these elements in their given unity gives meaningful content and contributes to the development of the inner life. But Walther's idea of interiority does not simply start and end with the individual person. It is not to be understood as a world of pure immanence; rather, the ego of the individual person may be displaced for various reasons such that a community or divine presence may come into the life of an individual. Interiority can also be social and communal: one can live and communicate with other individuals (in telepathy), with communities and social realities, and with the divine.[52] In each of these experiences the I is displaced for something else, suggesting a capacity of the I to allow itself to be grasped by other realities that are larger than itself. The social and religious phenomena Walther describes are truly communal and intimate; they bespeak a larger reality outside the realms of a determining, conscious ego. The fundamental way we live and experience these larger communal, social, and divine realities is in and through our interiority. Our inner experience of these realities, according to Walther, reveals that these larger social and religious phenomena really do form meaningful worlds.

Notes

1. Gerda Walther, *Ein Beitrag zur Ontologie der sozialen Gemeinschaften*, in *Jahrbuch für Philosophie und phänomenologische Forschung*, vol. 6, ed. Edmund Husserl (Halle: Niemeyer, 1923), 1–158.

2. Gerda Walther, *Phänomenologie der Mystik* (Freiburg im Breisgau: Walter Verlag, 1955).

3. Gerda Walther, Ana 317 B V.2, in *Munich Staatsbibilothek Archives*. See also, Gerda Walther, "Die Bedeutung der phänomenologischen Methode Edmund Husserls für die Parapsychologie," in *Psychophysikalische Zeitschrift* 1, no. 2, 22–29, and vol. 1, no. 3, 37–40.

4. Walther, *Phänomenologie der Mystik*, 100.

5. Walther, 39.

6. Walther, 39.

7. Walther, *Ein Beitrag zur Ontologie der sozialen Gemeinschaften*, 6–7, 14, 83.

8. Walther, *Phänomenologie der Mystik*, 45.

9. Walther, 22–23.

10. Walther, 21.

11. Walther, 100–3.

12. Walther, 102.

13. Walther, 100–1.

14. Walther, 104.

15. Walther, 107–8.

16. Walther, 107–9.

17. Walther, 108–9.

18. "*Einfühlung auch in das andere Geschlecht: Hier sei der Versuch der Erklärung meines Verständnisses derselben aus einem Analogieschluss von vornherein widersinnig.*" Edmund Husserl, *Zur Phänomenologie der Intersubjektivität (1905–1920)*, in *Husserliana*, vol. 13, ed. Iso Kern (Den Haag: Martinus Nijhoff, 1973), 75.

19. Max Scheler, *The Nature of Sympathy*, ed. Graham McAleer, trans. Peter Heath (Piscataway, NJ: Transaction Publishers, 2008), 109–11.

20. Walther, *Phänomenologie der Mystik*, 111–12.
21. Walther, 112.
22. Walther, 112. Translation mine.
23. Walther, 112.
24. Walther, 113.
25. Walther, 116.
26. Walther, 116.
27. Walther, 117.
28. Walther, *Ein Beitrag zur Ontologie der sozialen Gemeinschaften*, 86–87.
29. Walther, *Phänomenologie der Mystik*, 82–85.
30. Walther, 113–14. Translation mine.
31. Walther, 138.
32. Walther, 119.
33. Walther, 120.
34. Walther, 120.
35. Walther, 122.
36. Walther, 122.
37. Walther, 123.
38. Walther, 124.
39. Walther, 124.
40. Walther, *Ein Beitrag zur Ontologie der sozialen Gemeinschaften*, 99–100.
41. Walther, 97–98.
42. Walther, *Phänomenologie der Mystik*, 130.
43. Walther, *Ein Beitrag zur Ontologie der sozialen Gemeinschaften*, 105.
44. Rodney K. B. Parker, "Gerda Walther (1897–1977): A Sketch of a Life," in *Gerda Walther's Phenomenology of Sociality, Psychology and Religion*, ed. Antonio Calcagno (Dordrecht: Springer, 2018), 6.
45. Walther, *Phänomenologie der Mystik*, 64–66.
46. Marina Pia Pellegrino, "Gerda Walther: Searching for the Sense of Things, Following the Traces of Lived Experiences," in *Gerda Walther's Phenomenology of Sociality, Psychology and Religion*, ed. Antonio Calcagno (Dordrecht: Springer, 2018), 19.
47. Walther, *Phänomenologie der Mystik*, 125.
48. Walther, *Ein Beitrag zur Ontologie der sozialen Gemeinschaften*, 102–3.
49. Walther observes,

> Dies Wissen-um-einander braucht nun allerdings nicht immer notwendig direkt zu sein, es kann auch vermittelt sein. Die Art des Wissens der Mitglieder umeinander, die für eine Gemeinschaft erforderlich ist, dürfte von dem jeweilgen Wesen der betreffenden Gemeinschaft, vor allem auch von ihrer intentionalen Fundierung in der Einigung abhängig sein. Je mehr eine Einigung von Menschen durch die Einigung mit irgendwelchen Gegenstandlichkeiten (Zwecken, Zielen, Idealen usw.)

als solchen bedingt ist, desto weniger wird unter Umständen eine direkte, unvermittelte, leibhafte (originäre) wechselseitige Erfahrung und Gegebenheit voneinander der betreffenden Menschen vonnöten sein. So ist etwa eine Gemeinschaft von Gelehrten sehr wohl denkbar, bei der ihre Mitglieder nur durch wissenschaftliche Abhandlungen u. dgl. voneinander wissen, ohne sich persönlich zu kennen, während ein intimer Freundschaftsbund oder elne Ehe fast undenkbar ist, bei der die Mitglieder nur durch ihre Beziehung zu irgendwelchen Gegenständlichkeiten voneinander wüßten. (Walther, *Ein Beitrag zur Ontologie der sozialen Gemeinschaften*, 82)

50. Julia Mühl, "Human Beings as Social Beings: Gerda Walther's Anthropological Approach," in *Gerda Walther's Phenomenology of Sociality, Psychology and Religion*, ed. Antonio Calcagno (Dordrecht: Springer, 2018), 71–84.

51. Walther, *Ein Beitrag zur Ontologie der sozialen Gemeinschaften*, 82–83.

52. The work of Clementina Carbone shows how Walther's understanding of interiority and its capacity to seize self, other, and God parallels and contrasts with Edith Stein's projects. See Clementina Carbone, *Antropologia Duale: Comunità e mistica in Edith Stein e Gerda Walther* (Rome: Aracne, 2018).

Contributors

Angela Ales Bello is professor emeritus of history of contemporary philosophy at the Lateran University in Rome and past dean of the faculty of philosophy. She is the president of the Italian Center of Phenomenological Research (Rome), which is affiliated with the World Phenomenological Institute, Hanover, New Hampshire. She is also president of the International Society of Phenomenology of Religion, in Rome, Italy, and is the past director of the International Research Area dedicated to Edith Stein and Contemporary Philosophy at the Lateran University. She is a visiting professor in the faculty of psychology at the State University in São Paulo and of the Catholic University in Campinas, Brazil. Her scholarly research focuses on German phenomenology in relationship to other contemporary philosophical currents. Her recent books include *The Divine in Husserl and other Explorations* (2012) and *The Sense of Things: Towards a Phenomenological Realism* (2015). Her latest book is *Assonanze e dissonanze: Dal diario di Edith Stein* (2021). She is the coeditor of the Italian translation of Edith Stein's works.

Brian W. Becker is professor of neuropsychology and associate chair in the Division of Psychology and Applied Therapies at Lesley University in Cambridge, Massachusetts. He obtained his PhD in clinical psychology and MA in theology from Fuller Theological Seminary in Pasadena, California. He is coeditor-in-chief of the *Journal for Continental Philosophy of Religion* and an associate editor of the Routledge Psychology and the Other book series. He authored the book *Evil and Givenness: The Thanatonic Phenomenon* (2022) and has coedited several volumes including *Unconscious Incarnations: Psychoanalytic and Philosophical Perspectives on the Body* (2018).

Elodie Boublil is associate professor of philosophy at the University of Paris Est Créteil (UPEC, France). After completing her PhD at McGill University, she held a Marie Sklodowska-Curie fellowship at the Ecole Normale Supérieure de Paris (2015–2017, Archives Husserl-CNRS) and an Alexander von Humboldt Fellowship at the University of Cologne (2018–2020). During her research stay in Cologne, she specifically worked on Edith Stein, interiority, and phenomenological approaches of the heart. She specializes in phenomenology, ethics, and philosophy of health (vulnerability, care, empathy, phenomenological psychiatry) and has published the following: *Nietzsche & Phenomenology: Power, Life, Subjectivity* (2013; coedited with C. Daigle), *Individuation et vision du monde: Enquête sur l'héritage ontologique de la phénoménologie* (2014), and *Vulnérabilité et Empathie* (edited volume, 2018).

Antonio Calcagno is professor of philosophy at King's University College at Western University in London, Canada, and codirector of the Centre for Advanced Research in European Philosophy. He is also the author of *On Political Impasse: Power, Resistance and New Forms of Selfhood* (2022), *Lived Experience from the Inside Out: Social and Political Philosophy in Edith Stein* (2014), *Badiou and Derrida: Politics, Events and Their Time* (2007), *The Philosophy of Edith Stein* (2007), and *Giordano Bruno and the Logic of Coincidence* (1998). Along with Ronny Miron, he is the coeditor of *Hedwig Conrad-Martius and Edith Stein: Philosophical Encounters and Divides* (2022). He is a College member of the Royal Society of Canada.

Carla Canullo teaches philosophy of religion at the University of Macerata (Italy), where she also holds the chair of intercultural hermeneutics. Her research focuses on phenomenology, hermeneutics, and contemporary French philosophy. Her publications include *Coscienza e libertà: Itinerario tra Maine de Biran, Lavelle le Senne* (2001), *La phenomenological rovesciata. Percorsi tentati in Jean-Luc Marion, Michel Henry, Jean Louis Chrétien* (2004), *L'estasi della Speranza: Ai margini del pensiero di Jean Nabert* (2005), *Être mère: La vie surprise* (2017), *The Renewal of Hermeneutics: With Paul Ricoeur and Beyond* (2020) and *Renewing Hermeneutics: Thinking with Paul Ricœur (Renouveler l'herméneutique: Penser aver Paul Ricœur)* (2021) (both volumes are coedited with Johann Michel), and *Padecer la Immanencia: Diálogos con Michel Henry* (2022). On translation as a method of intercultural hermeneutics, Canullo wrote *Il chiasmo della traduzione: Metafora e verità* (2017).

Christina M. Gschwandtner teaches continental philosophy of religion at Fordham University. She is the author of *Reading Jean-Luc Marion: Exceeding Metaphysics* (2007), *Postmodern Apologetics? Arguments about God in Contemporary Philosophy* (2012), *Degrees of Givenness: On Saturation in Jean-Luc Marion* (2014), *Marion and Theology* (2016), *Welcoming Finitude: Toward a Phenomenology of Orthodox Liturgy* (2019), *Reading Religious Ritual with Ricœur: Between Fragility and Hope* (2021), and many articles and translations at the intersection of phenomenology and religion.

Emmanuel Housset is professor of history of contemporary philosophy and metaphysics at the University of Caen-Normandie. His research focuses on Husserl and the whole of phenomenology. He was awarded the 2021 French Academy's Grand Prize in Philosophy for his entire work. He recently published *The Gift of Hands: Phenomenology of Incorporation* (2019), *Personal Difference: An Essay on the Dramatic Identity of the Human Person* (2019), and *Husserl and the Idea of God* (2010).

Steve G. Lofts is professor of philosophy at King's University College at Western University and codirector of the Centre for Philosophy and Culture. He received his PhD from the Université catholique de Louvain, was a Humboldt Fellow in Heidelberg and Berlin, and was a Japan Foundation Fellow in Kyoto. His current research focuses on the Kyoto School of Japanese philosophy. He has translated Cassirer's *Logic of the Cultural Sciences, The Warburg Years* (2014), and the three volumes of *The Philosophy of Symbolic Forms* (2020).

Christian Lotz is professor of philosophy at Michigan State University (East Lansing). His main research area is post-Kantian European philosophy. Among his book publications are *The Art of Gerhard Richter: Hermeneutics, Images, Meaning* (2015), *The Capitalist Schema: Time, Money, and the Culture of Abstraction* (2014), *From Affectivity to Subjectivity: Revisiting Edmund Husserl's Phenomenology* (2008), and *Vom Leib zum Selbst: Kritische Analysen zu Husserl und Heidegger* (2005). His current research interests are in classical German phenomenology, critical theory, Marx, Continental aesthetics, and contemporary European political philosophy.

Ann V. Murphy is professor of philosophy at the University of New Mexico. She is the author of *Violence and the Philosophical Imaginary* (2012) and coeditor with Gail Weiss and Gayle Salamon of *50 Concepts for a Critical Phenomenology* (2020). Her current book project, *Ethics of Hunger*, explores a critical phenomenology of hunger and accounts of responsibility to and for others' hunger in twentieth century continental philosophy. She has longstanding research and teaching interests in nonviolence, theories of vulnerability, and phenomenology.

Hans Rainer Sepp, together with Karel Novotný, is director of the Central European Institute of Philosophy at Charles University in Prague. By asking about the mutability of life on the basis of knowledge in religion, art, and science, he develops an understanding of philosophy as *oikology*, which proves to be a metatheory in relation to philosophy and science. It is an area of research that is prior to other fields of philosophy such as logic, ethics and moral theory, or ontology and metaphysics. Oikology is grounded in a renewed philosophy of the human living body and its corporeality and, as *prima philosophia*, seeks to establish intercultural and interdisciplinary thinking. Recent monographs include *Philosophie der imaginären Dinge* (2017), *Phenomenology and Oikology* (in Chinese) (2019), and *Grundrisse der Oikologie* (2022).

Index

a-rationality of moral agency, 146
absolute nothingness (*zettaimu-no-basho*), 138–39
absolutely contradictory self-identity, 133
acceptance, divine, 82–84
acosmic interiority, 25. *See also* lived space, rethinking
Adorno, Theodor W., 47, 155
"Almost Always More Than Philosophy Proper," 164–65
analogia entis, 80–82
Analogieschluss, 201
animals. *See* beings, separation of
animation (*Inkarnation*), 60
Anselm of Bec, 77
Ansich, 39
anxiety, concept of, 184–88
appearing, discontinuity of, 23–26
Aquinas, Thomas, 80, 184
Aristotle, 17–18, 28, 130
atheism, 74, 82
Athenaeum, 43
Augustine of Hippo, 4–5, 77
Auseinandersetzung, 121–29, 131

Bachelard, Gaston, 120–21, 134
Being and Time (Heidegger), 42–49
Being and Time (Stein), 184
being-alongside-with (*Sein-bei*), 43

being-in (*Insein*), 42–49
being-in-the-world (*In-der-Welt-sein*), 42–49
being-toward-death, 185
being, analogy of (*analogia entis*), 80–82
beings, separation of, 55–56
  doubled interiority, 60–62
  implications, 62–69
  inner *Retroszendenz*, 60–62
  interiorization (*Innerung*), 56–59
  self-owning interiority (*selbsthafte Innerlichkeit*), 56–59
Benedicta, Teresa, 103
Bergson, Henri, 188–91
Bernasconi, Robert, 164–66
bestiality, 92
Black Paintings (c. 1819–1823), 85
bodies, human beings, 85–86, 97–102
  corporeal super-ego, 88–90
  heterocoporeality of sin, 93–94
  limbs of phenomenology, 86–88
  phenomenology of dividedness, 96–97
  senselessness of super-ego, 90–92
  thanatonic phenomenon, 94–96
body (*Leib*), 21–23
Bonhoeffer, Dietrich, 144, 152–55
Buddhism, 36–37
Butler, Judith, 168

Index

Cartesian Meditations (Hegel), 106
Cassirer, Ernst, 120–21, 121–29
Chrétien, Jean-Louis, 2–5, 109–10, 114
cogitatio, 106
cogito, 1–2, 119
communities
cognition, 127–28
    social ontology of, 208–9
compassion, 113–15
Confessions (Augustine), 94
Conrad-Martius, Hedwig, 39, 55–56. See also beings, separation of
conscience, 143–46, 155–56
    defining, 146–51
    and exception, 152–55
    and extraordinary situation, 151–52
consistent existence (*Bestand*), 136
contiguity, 28
continental philosophy, 2
continuous, concept, 18
conviction (*Überzeugung*), 150–51
corporeal feelings (*Leibgefuhle*), 58
corporeal in-dividual, positionality of, 46
Crespo, Mariano, 179
critical phenomenology, 159–60
    critique, 166–70
    defining, 162–66
    interiority and, 160–62
"Critical Phenomenology," essay, 163
critical turn, critical phenomenology, 162–66
critique, critical phenomenology, 166–70

Dasein, 3, 42 – 45, 105, 145, 184 – 87, 191
Daseinsanalytik, 43
Davis, Bret, 129, 134
death drive (*Todestrieb*), 90–92
der Fremdkörper. See foreign-body

Descartes, René, 29
desire, understanding, 75–76
dharmas, 136, 139
dialectic of outside, 120–21
Diet of Worms (Luther), 147
discourse (*Rede*), 43
discursive thinking, 120–21
distant interior, 105, 107, 110–12
dividedness, 96–97
divine, human beings
    acceptance of, 82–84
    analogia entis, 80–82
    defining religious experience, 73–76
    in human interiority, 76–80
    rejection of, 82–84
Dōgen, 36, 133–39
doubled interiority, 60–62

East Asia, 35, 49
ego, 179–81
Einführung in die Philosophie (Stein), 79
elements (*Elemente*), 131
elements (*Momente*), 124–25
emotions (*Gemutsbewegungen*), 58
empathy (*Einfühlung*), universal form of, 66
enowning (*Ereignis*), 45
entangled vines, language, 138
epoché, 4–5
Erlebnis, 75
Essence of Christianity, The (Feuerbach), 74–75
Ethics (Bonhoeffer), 145, 154
European Apollonianism, 45
events of exteriority, 26–28
exception, conscience, 152–55
existence (*Bestand*), 123
existence (*Dasein*), 145
Exkarnation, 59
extended-body (*le corps étendu*), 86
    limbs of phenomenology, 86–88

exterior, primal, 38–42
exteriority, 53–54
  being-in, 42–49
  inside-outside, 49–52
  primal exterior, 38–42
  primal interior, 35–38
externality (*Äußerlichkeit*), 59
extraordinary situation (*Grenzsituation*), 151–52

fatigue (*leibseelisch*), 58
feelings (*Empfindungen*), 57
Feuerbach, Ludwig, 74
Finite and Eternal Being (Stein), 176–77, 179–81
Fink, Eugen, 47
Five Lectures of Psychoanalysis (Freud), 90
for-itself, 1
foreign-body (*le corps aliéné*), 86
  limbs of phenomenology, 86–88
Freud, Sigmund, 90–92
Fukanzazengi, 135
functioning inside, 41–42
fundamental essence, interiority, 195–96
  phenomenology, 197–205
  porous unity, 205–9

Gay Science, The (Nietzsche), 105
Geist, 56–59
Gemüt, 57
genesis, interiority, 181–84
Genjokoan, 135–37
geometrism of thinking, 120–21
  ontological interpretation, 130–33
  philosophical confrontation (*Auseinandersetzung*), 129–30
God, 74–75, 81–82, 132
good life, quest for, 177–79
Goya, Francisco, 85
"Great Noon" (*der Grose Mittag*), 44–45

Guenther, Lisa, 159–60, 163, 166

H
Hegel, G. W. F., 104 – 5, 125, 132, 146–51
Heidegger, Martin, 3, 18, 26, 143–44
  emphasizing insertion, 42 – 45
Henry, Michael, 23–26, 36
Heraclitus, 50
higher animals, 61–62
Hitler, Adolf, killing, 154
Huber, Kurt, 144, 152–55
human interiority, divine in, 76–80
Humboldt, Wilhelm von, 44
Husserl, Edmund, 5, 18–23, 76, 175

I
"I," transcendental, 105–7
Ich-Spaltung (Husserl), 206
idealism, 38–42
Ideas II, 21, 189
identity, 94–96
identity-thinking, 125
impression (*Empfindniss*), 25
in-between, 122
in-carnation, 58–59
in-itself, 1
Incarnation (Henry), 23
individualization (*Vereinzelung*), 185
individuation. See joy
Inkarnation, 59
inner human being (*innere Mensch*), 204
inner life, joy, 181–84
inner *Retroszendenz*, 60–62
inner space, cultivating
  compassion, 113–15
  disappearance of interiority, 107–8
  distant interior, 105, 107, 110–12
  dwelling in hope, 115
  patience, 103–5
  patient interiority, 108–10

220 | Index

inner space, cultivating *(continued)*
  pure I, 207
  recollection, 112–13
  transcendental "I," 105–7
inside-outside, 49–52
inside, primal interior, 35–38
inside/outside binary, 17–18
intensification, 28
"intentional" and "intimate"
  (*l'intentionnel et l'intime*), 5
interconnection, interioirty, 119–20
  Auseinandersetzung, 121–29
  discursive thinking, 120–21
  function of language as symbolic
    form, 121–29
  meontological interpretation, 133–39
  philosophical confrontation
    (*Auseinandersetzung*), 129–30
interiority, 209–10
interior, primal, 35–38
interiority, 1–13
  attire of, 22
  Christian conception of, 103–4
  conscience, 143–57
  critical phenomenology, 159–74
  disappearance of, 107–8
  divine in human beings, 73–84
  and ego, 179–81
  exteriority-interiority relationship,
    35–54
  and foreign-body, 85–102
  fundamental essence, 195–212
  genesis, 181–84
  and inner space, 103–16
  interconnections of, 119–42
  joy, 175–94
  phenomenology of, 197–205
  and quest for good life, 177–79
  rehabilitation of, 159–74
  rethinking lived space, 17–33
  separating beings, 55–69
  spacious interiority, 26–28
  and spiral of space, 28–31

interiorization (*Innerung*), 56–59. *See also* inner space, cultivating interiorization
internality (*Innerlichkeit*), 59
Introduction to Philosophy (Stein), 80

Japanese language, 125
Jaspers-Review, 152
joy, 175–77
  and anxiety, 184–88
  constitution of the self, 188–91
  and ego, 179–81
  inner life of subject, 181–84
  quest for good life, 177–79

Kant, Immanuel, 19, 132
kinaesthesis, 21–22
Körper, 56–59
Kyōto School, 47

La Lueur du secret (Chrétien), 108
Lacan, Jacques, 89
langauge, function as symbolic form,
  121–29
language, 89
Lebensphilosophie, 181
Lectures on Moral Philosophy (Adorno),
  155–56
Lectures on the Human Person (Stein),
  186–87
Legion, 93–94
Leib, 56–59
Leibniz, 132
*Les Deux Sources de la Morale et de la
  Religion,* 190
Levinas, Emmanuel, 37, 48
Life of Power (Butler), 168
Life, self-revelation of, 24
lived space, rethinking
  discontinuity of appearing, 23–26
  inside/outside binary, 17–18
  phenomenology of space and time,
    18–23

spacious interiority, 26–28
spiral of space, 28–31
lived-body (*le corps vécu*), 86
limbs of phenomenology, 86–88
living present (*lebendige Gegenwart*), 178

material body (*Exkarnation*), 60
me-ontology, 129
meontic, term, 41
meontological interpretation, geometrism of thinking, 133–39
Merleau-Ponty, Maurice, 4
Mersenne, Marin, 29
metanoeite (conversion), 186
metaphysical thinking, 131
Metaphysische Gesprache, 56
middle, experience of, 44–45
modern moral subject, conception of, 147–48
mortal (*Sterblicher*), 45
Moses and Monotheism (Freud), 90
mystical joy, 188–91

negative relation, 146–51
New Testament, 93
Nietzsche, xxx, 1, 44–45, 49, 73, 106 – 7, 160, 175, 178
Nishida, Kitarō, 36, 47, 129, 133–39

O'Byrne, Anne, 167
On Phenomenology of Internal Time Consciousness (Husserl), 19
"On the Diversity of the Human Language Structure and its Influence on the Intellectual Development of Humankind," 44–45
ontological interpretation, geometrism of thinking, 130–33
Opuscules de piété (Bérulle), 109
original face, 135
originary-relationship (*Urverhaltnis*), 124

outside, primal exterior, 38–42
οὐσία, theory, 130

Parker, Rodney, 206–7
Parmenides, 130
pathos, 24–25
patience, 103–5
patient interiority, 108–10
Pellegrino, Marina Pia, 208
people's court (*Volksgerichtshof*), 153
personal core (*Persönlichkeitskern*), 77–81
Pfänder, Alexander, 204
phenomenological material, 25
phénoménologie de la vie, 36
phenomenology
 dividedness, 96–97
 heterocorporeality of sin, 93–94
 interiority and, 160–62
 of life, 23
 limbs of, 86–88
 of religion, 83
Phenomenology (Hegel), 148
Phenomenology of Mysticism (Walther), 205
Phenomenology of Perception (Merleau-Ponty), 161, 166
Phenomenology of Spirit, The (Hegel), 104–6
Phenomenology of the Perception (Merleau-Ponty), 4
phenomenon, word, 23
philosophical confrontation, geometrism of thinking, 129–30
Philosophy of Psychology and the Humanities, The (Stein), 187–88
plants. *See* beings, separation of
Plato, 175
Poetics of Space (Bachelard), 120
Potency and Act (Stein), 78–79
Potkay, Adam, 177
practice-awakening, 133

Problem of Empathy, The (Stein), 181
progressive universal poetry (*progressive Universalpoesie*), 43–44
Protestantism, 146–47
próton pseúdos, 39
psyche, 201–2
psyche, 2
Pure Experience, 47, 48
pure I, 107

Qingyuan Weixin, 135–37

radical outside, 45
real (*reell*), 46, 48, 51–52
realism, 38–42
recollection, 112–13
reell, 42
rejection, divine, 82–84
religious experience, 73–76
religious manifestations, 82–83
reoccuring question, 104
resistance, 146–51
Retroszendenz, inner, 60–62
Reuben, Apul, 85
Ricoeur, Paul, 1–2

Sache selbst, 30–31
Saint Teresa of Avila, 77
Salamon, Gayle, 162, 164
satori, 50
Saturn Devouring His Infant Son (1636), 85
Schadenfreude, 183–84
Scheler, Max, 38–39, 175
Schlegel, Friedrich, 43
Scholl, Hans, 144, 152–55
Scholl, Sophie, 144, 152–55
Scotus, Duns, 78
Seele, 56–59
self (*selbsthaft*), 57
self-attachment (*selbsthaft*), 58
self-manifestation, 24–25

self-owning interiority (*selbsthafte Innerlichkeit*), 56–59
self, constitution of, 188–91
sense (*Sinn*), 121, 124
sentiment, dimenion of, 5–6
shell (*Hulle*), 62
Shōbōgenzō (*Treasury of the True Dharma Eye*), 135–36
sichhaft, 56, 61
Simmel, 202
sin, heterocorporeality of, 93–94
soku-hi ("is and is not"), 137–39
Solitary Confinement: Social Death and its Afterlives (Guenther), 163
soul of the soul, 188
soul space (*Seelenbereich*), 58
soul, depth of (*eigenster Innenraum der Seele*), 58
space and time, phenomenology of, 18–23
space, spiral of, 28–31
spacious interiority, 26–28
spatial environment, 18–23
spatial turn in contemporary philosophy, 17
spatiality, 1–3, 94–96
  of acosmic interiority, 17–33
  phenomenology of space and time, 18–23
species. *See* beings, separation of
spiral, space, 28–31
spirit (*Geist*), 60–62, 202–3
spirit-soul (*Geistseele*), 60
spread-body (*le corps épandu*), 86
  limbs of phenomenology, 86–88
Stagirite, 17
state of mind (*Befindlichkeit*), 43
status termini, 79–80
Stein, Edith, 5, 76, 81, 104, 115, 175, 181–84, 188–91
Story of Joy, The (Potkay), 177

Straus, Erwin, 5–6
Studies in Hysteria (Freud), 90
subject *versus* event (*Ereignis*), 45–46
śūnyatā, 138
super-ego
  corporeal, 88–90
  senselessness of, 90–92

temporal environment, 18–23
temporality, 94–96
thanatonic phenomenon, 94–96
theoría, 36
Thing and Space (Husserl), 19–21
things (*Sachen*), 123
thinking, discursive, 120–21
thought (*cogitio discursive*), 123
totum, 48
Transcendental Aesthetic, 18
transcendental poetry
  (*Transzendentalpoesie*), 43
twofold nature of appearance, 23–28

unconscious, considering, 88–90
understanding (*Verstehen*), 43

unity, interiority, 205–9
universal poetry, 43

van der Leeuw, 83
Visible and the Invisible (Merleau-Ponty), 4
vital force (*Lebenskraft*), 179, 181–82, 188

Walther, Gerda, 195–96. *See also* fundamental essence, interiority
Weisse Rose, 144
Wesen, 55, 65, 126
"What Makes Critical Phenomenology Critical?," 162
world as such, questioning state of, 40

Zarathustra (Nietzsche), 44–45
zazen, 36
Zazen, 134–35
Zen Buddhism, 36, 47, 49, 50, 120, 130, 133–39
zu den Sachen selbst! ("to the things themselves!"), 22